The League of Nations

FROM 1929 TO 1946

George Gill

Associate Professor of History Emeritus
Fordham Univerity

Series Editor, George J. Lankevich

Avery Publishing Group
Garden City Park, New York

Cover design: William Gonzalez
Series editor: George Lankevich
In-house editor: Elaine Will Sparber
Typesetter: Bonnie Freid and Kay Rangos
Printer: Paragon Press, Honesdale, PA

The photographs on pages 5, 81, 113, 114, 124, and 142 are used courtesy of Popperfoto, Overstone, Northampton, England.
The photograph on page 2 is used courtesy of U.S. Library of Congress.
The photographs on pages 4, 6, 7, 10, 11, 13, 27, 33, 38, 43, 44, 50, 54, 58, 60, 64, 71, 72, 78, 86, 98, 99, 111, 112, 113, 116, 118, 120, 122, 123, 125, 126 (top), 126 (bottom), 127, 128, 129, 130, 132, 134, 135, 136, 137, 138, 139, 140, 141, 143, 145, 146, 148, 149 (top), 149 (bottom), 153, 154, 155, 157, 158, and 159 are used courtesy of U.S. National Archives.

Library of Congress Cataloging-in-Publication Data

Gill, George J.
    The League of Nations, 1929–1946 / George J. Gill.
      p.   cm. — (Partners for peace ; v. 2)
    Includes bibliographical references and index.
    ISBN 0-89529-637-3
    1. League of Nations—History.   2. International cooperation—
History.   3. World politics—1933–1945.   I. Title.   II. Series.
JX1975.G46 1996
341.22—dc20   94-7634
                                                 CIP

Printed in the United States of America

10 9 8 7 6 5 4 3 2 1

Contents

To my parents and brother.

Acknowledgments

My hope is that this volume reflects the scholarly example of Dr. A. Paul Levack, my professor, mentor, colleague, and friend of many years. Whatever academic merit the work has is due to that long association, for which I am deeply grateful.

The editor of the series, Dr. George Lankevich, suggested revisions that substantially improved content and style. His encouragement and patience are greatly appreciated. I was also fortunate in having Elaine Will Sparber as editor of the manuscript. She not only corrected errors and omissions but suggested changes and clarifications in the text that made her assistance invaluable. The remaining lapses are my responsibility.

I am also indebted to the late Anne M. Murphy, director of Fordham University Libraries; Mary F. Riley and the staff of the reference department of Duane Library, especially Joseph A. LoSchiavo, who arranged interlibrary loans; Marie R. Barnes, government documents collection; and Edmund P. Maloney, circulation librarian. Their responses to my requests were always models of professional and personal service.

Lastly, my wife, Winifred, and Christine, Winifred, George, Catherine, James, and Eileen provided help when it was most needed.

Foreword

Philosophers and theologians from the dawn of recorded history have been drawn to the great, perhaps unresolvable question—what is a human being? Among their many answers are a speck in primal chaos, a "reasoning animal," a creature in the image of God, a social being, a creator of art, a born hunter, and, in the words of Mark Twain, "the Only Animal that blushes. Or needs to!" Whatever answer one postulates is complicated by the undeniable tendency toward violence that seems a constant part of our nature. Whether humans are "apes or angels," warfare has been a constant companion of *homo sapiens*, and by some calculations, less than 5 percent of human history has been lived in times of peace. Yet equally a part of human nature is hope, the idealistic belief that we can somehow rise above baser instincts and achieve a better reality through cooperative effort. That dream has never lost its attraction for questing peoples even as war and its attendant evils have reached epidemic proportions. This series of volumes attempts to assess the progress of humanity toward that higher goal amidst the many horrors that have occurred during the twentieth century.

On a few occasions in the history of the globe, peace and cooperation became more than a temporary reality. During the two centuries of the *Pax Romana*, the Mediterranean Basin was freed from the scourge of war, although legions constantly battled on Rome's frontiers. Periods of great stability and ordered development were ofttimes achieved by Chinese dynasties such as the Ming, and the peace of feudal Japan was real, though imposed by the swords of the samurai. Safety was a reality for the elite members of Meso-american and African cultures, but we now understand that that condition was enjoyed by a relative few and only at the cost of much suffering at the base of the social pyramid. We may argue whether these eras represent positive advance, or merely mark the effective suppression of dissent, but they were important just the same. And in nineteenth-century Europe, after the long period of Napoleonic Wars, a conference of nations at Vienna did establish a "concert" whose melody was stability, peace, and order. For perhaps the first time, several nations attempted mutually to cooperate in a shared structure of peace, but the construct violently collapsed after less than a century. Always and everywhere, traditional enemies of peace such as poverty, imperial expansion, virulent nationalism, competitive trade, and simple fear of "the other" proved able to overwhelm the better human instincts. All too often, people avoided the "better angels" of their nature, and the world remained a battleground.

Partners for Peace: International Cooperation Towards Peace in the Twentieth Century is a series of volumes that examines how humanity's hope for a finer and more cooperative globe has fared in the twentieth century. The volumes chronicle the institutions, events, personalities, crises, and resolutions that have made the ageless dream of our species seem somewhat more attainable. Nations in the twentieth century have indeed taken a series of small steps toward the trust that must precede any attempt at universal peace. Powerful forces such as national sovereignty and ethnic chauvinism conspire to keep people at odds, but as wider recognition of our common interdependence has evolved, the sense of a world community has been created. In retrospect, one lesson taught by the twentieth century is that no single nation or empire is so great and powerful that it can deal unilaterally with the intractable problems of humankind. Whether the issue be war, famine, disease, trade, scientific cooperation, or ecological crisis, the nations of the world have gradually become aware that the ancient enemies of humanity can best be confronted through cosmopolitan effort. And each small advance against the traditional enemies of progress creates a more stable world community that can dare to dream of a better future.

This series traces human progress by considering national cooperation through international institutions. The first two volumes examine the checkered history of the League of Nations, and subsequent ones discuss the United Nations and the leadership provided to the world community by its successive secretaries-general. *Partners for Peace* recognizes that national insistence on sovereign autonomy made both the League and the UN vulnerable, for governments are rarely capable of putting the larger interests of humankind above their own. Yet for much of this century, the quest for cooperation beyond national boundaries has clearly inspired some world leaders. That hope has been a dominant theme of the century, even when it has been denounced as outmoded, intrusive, or foolish. In each volume of this series, a leading scholar will provide a synthetic overview of the period under consideration, along with a chronology of the vital events that have made the history of our century so turbulent. This material is hardly intended to resolve all questions, but rather is intended to provide an entry point to the history of the particular era. Substantial bibliographies are also provided so that readers can continue to study the events that created our contemporary world.

No reader will reject the assertion that politics in 1900 was dominated by societies that matured in the North Atlantic area of the globe. Impelled into modernity by revolutionary changes in literacy and mechanization, these "advanced" societies had successfully taken control of much of the Earth. These nations were envied for their capitalistic productivity, feared for their imperial ambitions, and emulated as models of human attainment by less developed societies. Yet even these nations had not overcome a tendency to savage themselves in war, and so they nurtured the hope that greater security for them all might be achieved if they could agree on rules of international conduct. Thus the nineteenth century ended with more than ritualistic discussions of such ideals as anti-imperialism, Anglo-American union, European disarmament, and schemes whereby nations would become morally accountable for their actions. Nor did it seem that these humanistic dreams were without substance. Advocates of world cooperation could point to accomplishments such as the Hague Peace Conferences of 1899 and 1907, the establishment of a Nobel Prize for Peace, agreement on a Permanent Court of Arbitration for international disputes, and a growing belief that civilized people would be able to avert future wars, at least among themselves. As the Victorian Age came to an end, hopeful people in advanced lands believed that war was too awful to contemplate. They placed their faith in human rationality and contemplated a happy new century.

We now know that these hopes were in vain. In the summer of 1914, the conflict that would ultimately be called World War I erupted in the Balkan area of Europe and rapidly engulfed the globe. Before it ended, about 20 million people died and the facile belief in the wisdom of advanced societies would be discarded. But the dream of cooperative effort did not die. Indeed, it was held more strongly than ever by many national leaders, who called for an association of nations to work for world peace.

The League of Nations began its career during the 1920s as an organization committed to advancing both world peace and international cooperation. The first volume of the *Partners for Peace: International Cooperation in the Twentieth Century* series details its rather creditable achievements, even though as a young institution the League did suffer some growing pains. Perhaps the highlight of that decade's optimism was the signing of a treaty that aimed at nothing less than the outlawing of war as an instrument of national policy. Sixty-two nations were to accept a peace pact that endorsed this proposal, a proposal that required them to donate neither men nor money towards a goal that had eluded humanity for all of history.

Today, we cynically understand that the Kellogg-Briand Pact was impossibly utopian, and we find it difficult to comprehend the world's joy when President Herbert Hoover proclaimed the treaty to be in effect on July 24, 1929. On that day, citizens of many nations dared to hope that the most ancient dream of humanity would be at last fulfilled. Yet only a decade later, the world entered the most devastating conflict in its history. One of its casualties was to be the League itself.

In this second volume of the series, Professor George Gill chronicles the League's downward spiral from the high hopes of 1929 through the terrible 1930s. Covering a period from the start of the Great Depression to the last formal meeting of the League Assembly, Professor Gill shows how President Woodrow Wilson's dream of a world peace organization crumbled under pressure from extreme nationalists in Japan, Italy, and Germany. The 1930s were a time of economic dislocation, but outlandish national ambitions and the fragility of the international cooperative spirit were far more critical to the League's demise. In 1933, Joseph Avenol replaced Sir Eric Drummond as secretary-general, but he did little to alter the organization's downward trajectory and, indeed, may have quickened the fall. By 1939, the hollowness at the core of the League of Nations was cruelly exposed, and war would engulf a globe that yearned for peace.

In Professor Gill's well-written volume, we see the League pummeled by body blows from the world's dictators. China is ravaged by Japan. Germany deserts the organization and repudiates the Versailles Treaty.

Ethiopia falls to Italy's savage invasion. Faced with a diplomacy of oppression and instances of ruthless aggression, the League became a caricature of the hopes that had brought it into existence. Wilsonian ideals collapsed when the men who served them lacked the strength to enforce international standards of behavior.

As war came, only the most dedicated internationalist could believe that the world organization launched with such hope only two decades earlier would survive the conflict. A shell of the institution remained, but the dream of the men who drew up the League Covenant had become a nightmare. Professor Gill's volume performs the signal service of reminding us of the complexities of a still-controversial period, while pointing out a few largely forgotten triumphs. The League did expire, but the dream of international cooperation managed to survive.

George Lankevich
Series Editor

Preface

It is more enjoyable to read about success than about failure, but historians remind us that we must also study the mistakes of the past if we are to avoid repeating them. In the initial volume of this series on international cooperation in our century, *The League of Nations: 1919–1929*, Gary B. Ostrower described the aspiration of the League's founders to prevent the tragedy of another conflict after the horror of the world war they had experienced. Advocates of the new organization believed that the collective power of the member states would either deter a potential aggressor or impose effective sanctions on it for breaking the peace.

During the formative years of the 1920s, under the first secretary-general, Sir Eric Drummond, the League enjoyed considerable success, not only in political affairs but also in social, economic, and cultural activities. Supporters of the world body anticipated that even greater achievements would mark its work in the 1930s, especially in the quest for world peace through disarmament, in the promotion of international trade and economic cooperation, and in the enrichment of living conditions for the people of all nations.

Unfortunately, most of these expectations went unfulfilled. Beginning in 1929, at the start of the Great Depression, the history of the League reads like a litany of misfortune. Both the World Economic Conference and the World Disarmament Conference failed. The League's social and economic agencies struggled against opposition from some national governments and sometimes from the Council itself. Collective security did not deter aggression by Japan against Manchuria in 1931, nor by Italy against Ethiopia in 1935, nor by Germany against Poland in 1939.

By the end of the second decade, many advocates of the League were attributing its decline to the inept leadership of Secretary-General Joseph Avenol, who had taken office in July 1933. This judgment was developed in James Barros's study of Avenol's tenure, *Betrayal From Within*, and the present volume reflects that critical assessment. However, readers should consider the following questions while making their own evaluations of Avenol's conduct: How much responsibility should the secretary-general bear for what was also a failure of the League's members, especially Great Britain and France, to whom the smaller states looked for leadership? Were Avenol's concessions to Japan, Germany, and Italy substantially different from the British and French appeasement of Adolph Hitler and Benito Mussolini? Was the principle of collective security an ideal to which statesmen raised in the tradition of the balance-of-power and alliance systems were unwilling to entrust the fates of their nations?

This book provides a chronological narrative, beginning with the celebration of the tenth anniversary of the Assembly and concluding with the failure of the League to prevent the outbreak of World War II. Among the victims of the war was the League itself. The acting secretary-general, Sean Lester, labored to preserve the League during the war years, and its faithful advocates hoped it would rise from the ashes, but the victorious Allies chose to replace the League with a new world body, the United Nations. However, many of the specialized agencies and services of the League were retained by its successor. And the principle of collective security, also adopted by the United Nations, was invoked in the recent crises arising from Iraq's invasion of Kuwait, the conflagration in Bosnia, and the effort in Somalia. Hopefully, the United Nations' actions have provided another positive chapter in the history of that organization, but its responses also represent a continuing trust in the vision of the founding fathers of the League of Nations.

The photo below shows the ceremonial setting of the cornerstone for the Palace of Nations on September 7, 1929.

The League and World Affairs | *1*

What is surprising today to those who examine the decline of the League of Nations during the 1930s is the atmosphere of optimism and confidence that surrounded the organization as representatives of fifty-three nations gathered in Geneva for the tenth session of the Assembly in September 1929. Peace advocates were encouraged by the new agreements on reparations and the Rhineland between Germany and the former Allied powers that promised to provide further healing of the wounds from World War I, called the Great War. Compulsory arbitration agreements, the Kellogg-Briand Pact to outlaw war, and naval limitation treaties seemed to assure the success of the forthcoming League disarmament conference. Programs to expand international trade were also underway, when the sudden collapse of the American stock market in the fall of 1929 plunged the world into a catastrophic depression. The failure of the League conference in London in 1933 to restore economic stability weakened the world organization's prestige, but more damaging blows to its authority came in the political arena. Japan resigned from the League rather than submit to censure for its aggression in Manchuria, and Germany withdrew after a bitter disagreement with France at the disarmament conference. Taking office in 1933, Secretary-General Joseph Avenol faced a much different world and League of Nations than his predecessor, Sir Eric Drummond, had known in 1929.

Twilight of the "Golden Days"

Marking the tenth anniversary of the Assembly, South African General Jan Smuts, a founding father of the League, described the world body as "one of the great miracles of history" by which "mankind has . . . in the short space of ten years jumped from the old order to the new. . . . One epoch closes in the history of the world and another opens." A former deputy secretary-general remembered the decade as "golden days," and the *Contemporary Review* led many journals in predicting a new period of political and judicial growth.

These sentiments were echoed in the opening addresses of the session, which was highlighted by the attendance of nine prime ministers and twenty ministers of foreign affairs. From nonmember states came similar praise, like that of senior American statesman Elihu Root, who extolled the League for "rendering the best service in the cause of peace known to the history of civilization." Arthur Sweetser, an American serving in the Secretariat,

Sir Eric Drummond skillfully led the League as its first secretary-general from the organization's inception in 1919 until July 1, 1933.

recalled the impressive accomplishments of the League under the leadership of Sir Eric Drummond, whose outstanding diplomatic and administrative skills had been guiding the organization since its inception in 1919. During its first ten years, the League had resolved eighteen political controversies, repatriated 400,000 prisoners of war, resettled 4,000,000 refugees, allocated $400 million in reconstruction loans, and undertaken health, cultural, and social programs. "Its cardinal results," Sweetser concluded, "have been to introduce first, an insurance against war and second, a method of peaceful progress."

League prospects for preserving peace, at least in terms of the relations between Germany and the Allied powers of World War I, were greatly encouraged by the success of the recent Hague Conference on reparations. The Young Plan, named after its American designer, financier Owen D. Young, had decreased the principal owed by Germany to $9 billion, a significant reduction from the original $32 billion established by the London Conference in 1921. Delegates believed the new agreement would erase the bitter memories of the reparations disputes of previous years. The Allies also agreed to evacuate the last of their troops from the Rhineland by June 1930, five years before the date established by the Treaty of Versailles. And British Prime Minister James Ramsay MacDonald announced that his nation would accept the compulsory arbitration of disputes, a step in which it was joined by the other members of the Commonwealth, France, Italy, and several additional nations. Arthur Henderson, the British foreign secretary, believed that acceptance of the obligatory reference of conflicts to the Permanent Court of Arbitration at The Hague would safeguard world peace.

But most challenging to the imagination was the invitation by France's Foreign Minister Aristide Briand for the League to consider the vision of a United States of Europe. Twenty-seven European members of the world body agreed in September 1929 to study the concept of a federal union that Briand believed would enable Europe to remain the "mistress of her own destiny." He envisaged "the most important link" to be an economic agreement, but he anticipated political and social pacts as well. Gustav Stresemann, the German foreign minister who had helped Briand rebuild Franco-German relations through the Locarno Pact of 1925, joined him in the appeal to end "conditions in Europe today which seem to belong to the Middle Ages."

Ironically, the shock and despair of the Great Depression were only a month away as delegates listened sympathetically to invitations to reduce tariffs and remove other barriers to international trade. High on the League's agenda were steps to implement recommendations that had been made by some thirty nations at the World Economic Conference of 1927. Raymond G. Fosdick, an American who had served briefly as under secretary-general, believed the conference had provided the imperative to seek "economic disarmament as well as military disarmament" and to realize that "prosperity is not something that can be enjoyed in small compartments." Eduard Beneš, foreign minister of Czechoslovakia, predicted an economic reorganization of Europe under League auspices and anticipated that economic cooperation would encourage political harmony. League supporters were also encouraged by the response of U.S. Secretary of State Frank B. Kellogg to Briand's vision of a pact to outlaw war. Signed in Paris on August 27, 1928, the Kellogg-Briand agreement had caught the imagination of peace advocates throughout the world, and nearly every nation had endorsed it. Petitions had been signed by 2,000,000 Americans favoring its acceptance, and Kellogg received the Nobel Peace Prize for 1929. Although Briand had intended the pact to be a bilateral treaty binding the United States to France, Kellogg had turned it into an international agreement to the chagrin of the French minister. Whether the agreement had any real value is debatable; Senator Carter Glass of Virginia believed it was not "worth a postage stamp in bringing about peace," and MacDonald viewed it as "still a castle in the air," although he thought the League could "build up [the] foundation to support the castle. . . ." In any event, in 1929, the world wanted the concept to be true, and Glass conceded that "it would be psychologically bad to defeat it." The pact also softened the attitudes toward the League held by most American editors.

The United States additionally was expected to continue its participation in naval disarmament negotiations that had been started at the Washington Conference on the Limitation of Armaments in 1921–1922 and resumed in Geneva in 1927. Although conducted outside the League, these efforts paralleled the world body's steps toward general disarmament, and the Assembly welcomed MacDonald's announcement that new naval talks were imminent. In fact, invitations were extended on October 7, 1929, for a conference in London in January 1930. This revived hope for a successful World Disarmament Conference, which had been under discussion since the early 1920s. The League had appointed a Preparatory Commission for the World Disarmament Conference in 1925, with representatives invited from nonmember nations, including the Soviet Union and the United States, but technical issues and political differences between the French and German delegates had hampered progress. It was not until 1930 that the Preparatory Commission submitted a final draft convention to the Council, and the opening of the World Disarmament Conference was finally scheduled for February 2, 1932. Thus, as the League moved toward the celebration of its tenth anniversary in 1930, there existed many reasons for confidence in its future development and tangible proof of its contributions to international stability. However, a more cautious appraiser could discern several serious challenges on the horizon.

In the autumn of 1929, while League members discussed new trade policies to stimulate economic growth, the collapse of the American stock market signalled the beginning of a worldwide depression, which would devastate the 1930s. Although the Great Depression's impact was not felt immediately in Europe, Americans' reductions of their extensive foreign investments presaged the difficulties ahead. One of the first victims of the fiscal crisis was the movement toward tariff reduction and free trade. The United States already had erected protective walls in the 1920s with the Fordney-McCumber Act, but the Hawley-Smoot legislation, passed in June 1930, was the most protectionist legislation in that nation's history. An American critic condemned it as "the blind, desperate effort of a great country to hang on to the top of the ladder by kicking at every other country." The example was not lost on Europe. Despite warnings from the League's economic advisers, each nation sought to ensure its own well-being behind high tariffs. By the summer of 1932, even Great Britain had abandoned the free-trade policy it had maintained since the mid-nineteenth century and, at the Imperial Economic Conference in Ottawa, adopted preferential rates to bolster the sagging economy of the Common-wealth.

As the crisis became acute in the spring of 1933, the League sponsored a world conference on monetary and economic policy. Representatives from sixty-four nations gathered in London on June 12 to seek common solutions to the depression. The appeal for economic cooperation was complicated by political developments involving Germany and the Far East, but it was the United States that disrupted the meeting. The primary objective of the European "gold bloc" nations—to restore the international gold standard—clashed with President Franklin D. Roosevelt's abandonment of the gold standard and his commitment to inflate the American economy through a broad program of New Deal legislation. When the delegates moved toward a currency stabilization formula based on the gold standard, Roosevelt cabled the American mission that it would be "a catastrophe amounting to a world tragedy" if the conference let that become the priority. In what came to be known as the bombshell message, he attacked the "old fetishes of the so-called international bankers" that had to give way to new ideas on planning national currencies. U.S. Secretary of State Cordell Hull hoped to promote tariff reciprocity in London, but he found little encouragement among the victims of the "bombshell." France's President Albert Lebrun exclaimed, "To speak of tariff adjustments while moneys are variable is pure Utopia!" Within five weeks, the delegates abandoned the effort, and as one League official lamented, "economic nationalism was in the saddle." The collapse of the London conference alarmed those who realized that economic nationalism could inflame political nationalism, which was an explosive combination that had already brought war to Asia.

Japan and the Manchurian Crisis

The impact of the Great Depression was especially severe on Japan, which depended on overseas markets. As the empire's trade with the United States and other nations plummeted, Japanese leaders who had advocated expansion on the Asian mainland found new support. Their attention now focused on Manchuria, where, as a result of a victory over Russia in 1905, they controlled the South Manchurian Railway and guarded it with troops.

Manchuria's population was predominantly Chinese and ruled by a Chinese governor, but its rich natural resources attracted immigration and investments by Japanese. This antagonized the Chinese. At the same time, Japan was concerned that the emergence of a strong centralized government in China would challenge or eliminate Japanese imperial interests in Manchuria. The combination of these forces, fused with the extreme nationalism of the Japanese military, finally created the Mukden incident of September 18, 1931. Alleging Chinese responsibility for an explosion that

U.S. Secretary of State Henry Stimson at first rejected Secretary-General Drummond's September 1931 invitations to support a Commission of Inquiry to look into the Manchurian crisis and to send an American to sit with the Council while it discussed the controversy. He later sent representatives to participate in both. On February 16, 1932, the Council adopted the Stimson Non-Recognition Doctrine.

destroyed a section of track on the South Manchurian Railway, Japanese troops attacked Chinese forces and began a major offensive that would eventually sweep through Manchuria.

Responding to China's appeal for League assistance, the Council, on September 22, requested an end to the fighting and appointed a Committee of Five, which considered an on-site investigation. Hoping to enlist American support, Secretary-General Drummond forwarded a copy of the Council's proceedings to U.S. Secretary of State Henry Stimson. Stimson's Far Eastern specialists, however, advised him that the civilian authorities in Tokyo had not instigated the attack and that the United States should act with restraint in order to give these authorities time to regain control over the military. Since he was also wary of League efforts to "dump [the] Manchurian baby" on Washington's doorstep, he disappointed Drummond by rejecting the invitations to support a Commission of Inquiry and to have an American representative sit with the Council. "I fear," he informed Hugh R. Wilson, United States minister at Berne, "that American membership will be used by the League as a threat to Japan and this would not in my opinion, produce the results anticipated by the League but would do exactly the reverse and furthermore, would destroy future American usefulness as a mediator should the League not succeed."

The British government was equally reluctant to challenge its former ally, especially in Manchuria, where English economic interests were minimal compared to those in China and Hong Kong. British, French, and other Western subjects affected by the wave of antiforeign demonstrations and riots in China sparked by Sun Yat-sen and his followers during the

The Council discusses the Manchurian crisis in November 1931 in the French Foreign Office in Paris, the site of the League's creation twelve years earlier. Representatives of thirteen nations are present, including (from left to right at the left-hand table) Vittorio Scialoja of Italy, Aristide Briand of France, Sir Eric Drummond, and Sir John Simon of Great Britain. Seated behind Briand is Lord Cecil (Robert Cecil) of Great Britain.

Kenkichi Yoshizawa, the Japanese delegate to the League, assured fellow delegates on September 30, 1931, that Japan has "no territorial designs" on Manchuria. But on October 24, he vetoed a Council resolution calling for the withdrawal of Japanese forces by November 16.

1920s expressed their understanding of Japan's "chastizing" of the unstable Chinese in Manchuria. The Japanese delegate to the League, Kenkichi Yoshizawa, relieved the Council's concerns with assurances that the matter could be settled by talks between his country and China. Using a phrase that would become tragically familiar to victims of aggression, he assured his colleagues that Japan had "no territorial designs" on Manchuria. The Council, on September 30, finally adopted a mild resolution that called for both parties to resume normal relations. The resolution noted both Japan's pledge to withdraw its troops and China's guarantee of the safety of Japanese nationals and property outside the railway zone. Drummond concurred with the Council's action; he realized that economic sanctions against Japan would lack support, and he hesitated at risking a confrontation with Tokyo.

The Japanese army, however, ignored the League's resolution and, on October 7, opened a new phase of operations by attacking Chinchow, where many Chinese military and civilian authorities were concentrated. Alarmed by the deteriorating situation, Stimson now changed his position and requested that an American representative be allowed to attend the next Council session. Despite Japanese objections, Drummond supported Stimson's request, and Prentiss B. Gilbert, the American consul in Geneva, was permitted to sit in. Although his instructions confined his participation to discussions concerning the Kellogg-Briand Pact, Gilbert's presence at the Council table on October 16, 1931, was considered "one of the most dramatic moments of inter-war diplomacy" and was enthusiastically received by League supporters in the United States. But there was also vehement opposition by American isolationists, and American editorial opinion reflected this polarization. The *Literary Digest* cited several papers that praised the League for containing the conflict and even urged the United States to join the world body in a boycott against Japan. Other journals—including the Philadelphia *Record*, Washington *Post*, and Hartford *Courant*—considered Gilbert's appointment a threat to relations with Japan and insisted that the League was already bankrupt as an international force. Faced with the choice of bolstering the League or silencing the domestic critics (whose numbers may have been exaggerated), U.S. President Herbert Hoover first reduced Gilbert's role to that of silent spectator at several meetings and then withdrew him completely from the Council despite pleas from Drummond.

On October 24, Yoshizawa vetoed a Council resolution calling for the withdrawal of Japanese forces by November 16. After some diplomatic maneuvering in which Drummond was deeply involved, China and Japan agreed, on November 20, to the appointment of a Commission of Inquiry. Although this meant a further delay in League action, the Council accepted this solution rather than challenge Japan. The secretary-general knew that the British Foreign Office would not support the use of sanctions and that there were strong pro-Japanese sentiments among the French. He also knew that neither Germany nor Italy was prepared to act and that the United States would not intervene. The *Contemporary Review* added the warning that the threat of economic sanctions could drive Japan out of the League.

In January 1932, the Council appointed a five-member commission chaired by England's Lord Lytton (Victor Lytton) and including General Henri Claudel of France, Count Luigi Aldrovandi-Marescotti of Italy, Dr. Heinrich Schnee of Germany, and Major General Frank R. McCoy of the United States. Leaving on February 3, the group travelled by way of the United States and Japan, with stops in China, before reaching Manchuria in April. Taking this time-consuming itinerary rather than the European route appeared to be a deliberate delay, which some League officials judged "embarrassing and even discreditable." And by the time the commission finally began its investigation, other events had become more newsworthy.

Despite the Commission of Inquiry, the Japanese continued their military operations and captured Chinchow to assure their control of Manchuria. Stung by this flagrant violation of the pledge given to him on November 24 that Chinchow would not be attacked, Stimson now issued a highly publicized note on January 7, 1932, informing the Chinese and Japanese governments that the United States would not recognize any change in Manchuria that was achieved in violation of the Kellogg-Briand Pact. Although he had not solicited prior British or French support for his action, the secretary of state was disappointed by the failure of the British Foreign Office to endorse his position and by the silence of France and other nations. Conversely, there was exasperation in European quarters with the diplomatic platitudes and moral lectures that Washington offered in place of effective sanctions. Japan realized the European powers were no threat and correctly judged that the United States would not press its opposition beyond verbal protests. By mid-February 1932, the Japanese had completed their military conquest and defiantly announced the creation of the independent state of Manchukuo.

When the Japanese army ended its operations, the Japanese navy suddenly attacked Shanghai. Fleet commander Admiral Koichi Shiozawa justified his action by calling it a response to Chinese harassment of resident Japanese nationals. Unlike Manchuria, however, Shanghai's International Settlement was the center of substantial Western business interests in China, and there was greater sensitivity to Shiozawa's attack. Moreover, the heavy loss of life caused by Japan's bombing of the Chinese district of Chapei aroused condemnation in a world still unused to the indiscriminate employment of air power against nonmilitary targets. China requested Council action against Japan, and Drummond created a committee composed of foreign officials in Shanghai to furnish information about the incident. To offset the critical international reaction, Japan asked for neutral mediation, and when Great Britain and the United States responded favorably, Drummond deferred League action to their initiative. British Foreign Secretary Sir John Simon believed that the military weakness of Great Britain in the Far East and the vulnerability of its economic interests in Asia dictated a peaceful resolution of the crisis. Stimson initially supported Simon, but after Japan rejected the Anglo-American mediation proposal and continued its buildup in Shanghai, the American secretary of state encouraged Drummond to mount a more vigorous League effort. On February 16, the Council adopted the Stimson Non-

British Foreign Secretary Sir John Simon originally believed that the military weakness of Great Britain in the Far East and the vulnerability of its economic interests in Asia dictated a peaceful resolution of the Manchurian crisis.

Recognition Doctrine, which paralleled Stimson's January announcement. The secretary of state then sent, on February 23, a public letter to Senator William E. Borah, chairman of the Senate Committee on Foreign Relations, warning that violation of the territorial and administrative integrity of China guaranteed by the Nine Power Treaty could release the United States from the naval and Pacific fortification limitations also established by the Washington Conference. The letter would, he hoped, "encourage China, enlighten the American public, exhort the League, stir up the British and warn Japan." The Assembly backed Stimson by passing a nonrecognition resolution on March 11, a step that Simon declared was "squarely in line with America." Eight days earlier, with the foreign pressure mounting, Japan had agreed to a cease-fire, which led to a formal armistice on May 5. But by then, Chapei had been devastated and over 6,000 Chinese troops and 2,500 Japanese had been killed or wounded.

League action on Manchuria was postponed pending the submission of the Lytton Commission report, which was given to the Assembly in September 1932. The long document acknowledged Chinese failures in the administration of Manchuria but denied that they justified the Japanese occupation. The commission concluded that Manchukuo's existence, which Japan had brazenly recognized before the League had reviewed the report, was the result of Japan's imperialism rather than of the will of the native Chinese. After four months of delaying tactics by the Japanese delegation and then protracted debate, the substance of the report was adopted by the Assembly on February 24, 1933. The Japanese delegate, Yosuke Matsuoka, in a dramatic gesture, walked out of the meeting, and on March 27, Japan submitted its notice of withdrawal from the League.

Contemporary observers considered the Manchurian crisis to be the League's "first great defeat," a judgment that history has confirmed. In the April 1932 issue of *Foreign Affairs*, A. Lawrence Lowell concluded that if the League did not enforce sanctions, its prospects for deterring war in the future would be seriously compromised. Beneš prepared a companion piece for *Foreign Affairs* in which he criticized the League's protracted response and failure to impose the sanctions justified by Japan's aggression. Tyler Dennett, an American diplomatic historian, praised the Lytton Report but—significantly—entitled his next article, in the April 1933 issue of *Current History*, "Japan Defies the World."

Whatever the merits of the Lytton Report, the fact remained that the Japanese had refused to be forced out of their Manchurian coup by the League. Dennett undoubtedly expressed the sentiments of the vast majority of his countrymen when he wrote, "I didn't raise my boys to be soldiers to displace Japan." But this was an American response, and the failure of the League to act in either the economic or military sphere was far more troubling. In his history of the Far Eastern conflict, *The Limits of Foreign Policy*, Christopher Thorne questioned the causal role that some statesmen and historians have attributed to the crisis and the subsequent breakdown of the international order in the 1930s, but there seems no doubt that the Covenant powers, especially Great Britain and France, proved weak and hesitant when put to the test. The crushing depression, domestic political crises, vivid memories of the carnage of World War I, and the geographic remoteness of Manchuria all served to justify inaction. But the consequences to the League were lost commitment and confidence even before it had to face the greater challenges that soon would be provided by Germany and Italy. For many League supporters, however, the discouragement arising from the Manchurian crisis was offset by the faith in the long-awaited World Disarmament Conference, which convened in Geneva on February 2, 1932, with fifty-nine nations represented.

The World Disarmament Conference

The hopes of millions of people were reflected in the parade through the Old Town of Geneva, with the white armbands of the marchers proclaiming *pax* ("peace") and massive petitions inundating the stage of the conference hall. A prominent American educator, Nicholas Murray Butler, captured the hope and fear of the moment: "It is not too much to say that the fate of the world for the next generation will be at stake. . . . . Should it fail no man would dare predict the future or its results."

Once the public demonstrations were over, however, the long-standing obstacle of national interest impeded progress. Years of work by the Preparatory Commission were virtually ignored when the draft proposal that it had produced was debated. Among other weaknesses, the document failed to address directly one of the most serious problems that faced the conference. German representatives to the Preparatory Commission had repeatedly insisted that their country's disarmament provided a legal and moral obligation for the other major powers to disarm. They cited the preamble of Part V of the Treaty of Versailles, which stated that Germany's disarmament was intended "to render possible the initiation of a general limitation of the armaments of all nations." They also recalled the assurances of French officials that the military clauses were "the first steps toward the general reduction of armaments . . . which it will be one of the first duties of the League of Nations to promote." German delegates, therefore, sought an international arms-reduction agreement that would apply equally to all powers and, in effect, replace the unilateral limitation imposed by Versailles.

The French, however, continued to emphasize national security as their priority and opposed any concessions to Germany. Faced with American isolationism and British reluctance to make a commitment to mutual military assistance, the French government submitted a new plan to the conference. The French plan called for control by the League of all major offensive weapons—land, sea, and air—except in the emergency of self-defense against an unexpected aggression. France also proposed the creation of an international force under Council authority and for broader sanctions to include responses to violations of the disarmament agreements. Behind this proposal was the apparent hope to prevent any relaxation of the Versailles terms. These terms had prohibited conscription and had reduced the German army to 100,000 officers and men serving long enlistment tours to prevent the training of successive classes of reserves. Restrictions on Germany's military industry and armaments development

German Chancellor Heinrich
Bruening negotiated for military
equality for his country at the World
Disarmament Conference, which
finally convened in Geneva on
February 2, 1932. On June 2, 1932,
President Paul von Hindenburg
replaced Bruening with Franz von
Papen, who turned to the Nazis for
support rather than offer
concessions at the conference.

were intended to reduce the offensive capability of the army and to convert it into essentially a constabulary force. Abolition of the German air force and limitations on the sizes and categories of naval vessels were further requirements of the Versailles treaty.

The long-standing sensitivity of German nationalists to these restrictions had heightened in the late 1920s; the Nazis had made revision of what they called the Versailles diktat one of their principal appeals. Thus, by 1932, to protect itself politically, the incumbent government of Chancellor Heinrich Bruening demanded an agreement that would recognize German equality. Bruening insisted that this did not necessitate the rearming of his country, since if other nations reduced their military establishments to the sizes allowed Germany, the Weimar Republic would be satisfied. There was, however, no concession to Germany in the French plan, and the suspicion in some League quarters was that the French did not expect their plan to be adopted. France's real intent, some believed, was to obstruct the revision of Versailles.

In the midst of these deliberations, the German delegation was distracted by national elections. Bruening's vulnerability had been evident in the pattern of Reichstag elections since 1928. At that time, Hitler's party had elected only 12 members to the lower house, with 810,000 votes. Two years later, however, on September 14, 1930, nearly 6,500,000 voters elected 107 Nazis, raising the party from the smallest to the second largest in the Reichstag. This surprising success encouraged Hitler to enter the presidential campaign in 1932. Running against the elderly incumbent, Field Marshal Paul von Hindenburg, and two other major candidates representing the nationalists and the communists, Hitler received over 11,000,000 votes. He trailed Hindenburg by over 7,000,000, but since the field marshal had not received an absolute majority, a second election was necessary. On April 10, Hindenburg won the run-off with over 19,000,000 votes, but Hitler received nearly 13,500,000.

Following the reelection of Hindenburg, Bruening resumed the negotiations on disarmament. He asked for a reduction of the enlistment term from twelve to six years and for an increase in the size of the army to 200,000 men, in addition to other changes in the Versailles restraints. The symbolic point for renewed German nationalism, however, was that this new agreement would replace the albatross of Versailles. But despite British, Italian, and American support for Bruening, the French were unwilling to make these concessions. One explanation for France's intransigence was later traced to its Berlin embassy, which was secretly informed by Lieutenant General Kurt von Schleicher that Bruening would be removed from office if his overture failed. His successor might be easier to deal with, the French assumed. Schleicher was correct in his prediction of Bruening's loss of favor with Hindenburg—which was actually due to factors other than the disarmament negotiations—but, unfortunately for the French, Bruening's successor sought support from the Nazis rather than offering concessions in the disarmament talks. Chancellor Franz von Papen did not moderate the attacks against the Versailles treaty, and the conference remained deadlocked.

U.S. President Hoover tried to break the impasse in June 1932 by proposing the abolition of offensive weapons and the reduction by one-third of

Incumbent German President Paul von Hindenburg (second from right) was declared the winner of the run-off election on April 10, 1932, but Adolph Hitler came in a strong second. Hindenburg garnered 53 percent of the vote, with Hitler collecting 36.8 percent and Ernst Thaelmann, 10.2 percent.

all others. Under the American plan, bomber aircraft, mobile heavy artillery, and tanks would be prohibited. Capital ships would be reduced by one-third, and limitations would also be placed on other categories of vessels. Army strength would be reduced by one-third, with the objective of setting forces at levels required only for defense and constabulary purposes. Although immediate public reaction was enthusiastic and the smaller nations praised the plan, there was less interest among the delegations of the major powers. France was obsessed with the issue of security, while Great Britain objected to the abolition of armored forces and bombers. The Japanese, busily incorporating Manchuria's wealth, found the entire program unacceptable.

After the failure of the American proposal, the World Disarmament Conference moved rapidly toward adjournment. Noting that no progress had been made concerning equality for Germany, the German delegation announced its withdrawal from the proceedings until such equity was granted. The shock of the German action prompted movement among the Great Powers when the conference reconvened in September 1932. After bitter exchanges with the German representatives, the French delegates proposed short enlistment terms for all Continental conscript armies, which satisfied one of Berlin's requests. The British government announced its support for equal rights for Germany, and both British Prime Minister James Ramsay MacDonald and Foreign Secretary John Simon worked closely with the interested powers to reach an agreement. On December 11, representatives of France, Germany, Great Britain, and the United States adopted a formula that acknowledged Germany's "equality of rights in a system that would provide security for all nations." That claim, of course, also recognized France's principal concern. The settlement was an obvious attempt to run with the hares and hounds, but on that note, the conference adjourned until January 31, 1933.

In the intervening weeks, the tragedy of the Weimar Republic entered its final stages. Papen had been replaced as chancellor by Schleicher on December 2, but Schleicher later complained that during the fifty-seven days he had held office, he had been betrayed fifty-seven times daily. Out of the maze of conspiracies that marked the end of the Weimar Republic finally came Hitler and the Nazis. As thousands of Hitler's followers massed outside the presidential palace chanting *"Heil Hitler! Deutschland erwache!"* ("Hail Hitler! Germany awake!'), Hindenburg offered "the Bohemian corporal" the chancellorship on January 30, 1933.

Hitler's appointment had an immediate impact on the League's last major attempt to build a disarmed world. At the reconvened conference, France was determined to protect its security against a German leader who had made revision of Versailles a party pledge. Hitler initially pursued a carrot-and-stick policy by combining assurances of his desire for disarmament with a warning that Germany would withdraw from both negotiations and the League if concessions were not made. France remained unmoved and insisted on a plan that would defer arms reductions for four years while barring any change in the existing military status of any nation. When it became apparent that there was general support for the French position among League members, Hitler ordered the German delegation to leave the conference and simultaneously announced Germany's resignation from the world body. (For a further discussion of Germany's resignation, see "Hitler Resigns From the League," on page 14.)

The somber mood of the delegates in Geneva in the spring of 1933 contrasted sharply with the optimism of the tenth anniversary celebration in 1929. The Great Depression had strangled economic life, and the collapse of the World Economic Conference had disheartened those who had hoped that international cooperation would lead to recovery. Japan's aggression in Manchuria, culminating in its resignation from the League, had marked a major breech in the Covenant and had created a dangerous precedent for other nations that might be tempted to use force to secure objectives.

The impending withdrawal of Germany from the world body, amid heightened French distrust of Hitler, signalled the end of the "Spirit of Locarno" that French and German statesmen had fostered with the treaties of 1925. The likely collapse of the World Disarmament Conference disillusioned those who had been crusading since the end of the Great War for the reduction of military forces. In these inauspicious circumstances, with the extraordinary challenges they presented, Joseph Avenol succeeded Sir Eric Drummond as secretary-general on July 1, 1933.

Joseph Avenol succeeded Sir Eric Drummond as secretary of the League of Nations on July 1, 1933.

Hitler Resigns From the League

The reconvening of the World Disarmament Conference on January 31, 1933, followed by one day Hitler's appointment as chancellor of Germany. The racial policies, territorial ambitions, and revisions of the Treaty of Versailles that Germany's new leader had advocated in *Mein Kampf* provided a grim warning to the defenders of international peace and cooperation among nations. Initially, however, it was Hitler who restrained the German Foreign Office and the Ministry of Defense with respect to League disarmament proposals. The Foreign Office had wished to force the issue of equality immediately and compel the Geneva conference to either reduce the military strength of the other nations to that of Germany or permit German rearmament. Hitler shared this objective but did not want the collapse of the negotiations to saddle Berlin with responsibility for their failure. He recognized the hostility with which many foreign leaders viewed his rise to power and the need to avoid conflict while Germany was militarily unprepared.

France was especially alarmed by Hitler's appointment and tried to retreat from the formula of "equality of rights in a system which would provide security for all nations," agreed upon in December 1932. French apprehension increased as the Nazis dominated the German elections of March 1933, winning 288 seats to combine with their nationalist allies' 52 seats for a majority in the Reichstag. An elated Hitler proclaimed, "The Nazi Revolution is on its way!" The French government pressed London for new mutual guarantees before yielding equality, but the British refused specific commitments. For several weeks, the French and German delegations engaged in acrimonious discussions and obstructive tactics before Great Britain finally made an attempt to salvage the talks. On March 16, Prime Minister James Ramsay MacDonald chided the delegates for having "done jolly little" in thirteen months. It was time, he said, to recognize that "either Germany is given justice and freedom or Europe will risk destruction." He said he trusted that changes would come "not at the point of the bayonet, but at the point of reason." He called for parity of troop strength among France, Germany, Italy, and Poland at 200,000, with Russia allowed 500,000. France would be permitted an additional 200,000 colonial troops, and Italy, 50,000. In addition, artillery and tanks would be restricted by caliber and weight, respectively; chemical and bacteriological weapons would be banned; and each major power would be limited to 500 military aircraft.

To the consternation of the delegates who anticipated a spirited attempt to win support for his plan, MacDonald immediately left for Rome to meet with Mussolini. The Duce was convinced that the key to political and economic stability was the "collaboration of the four great Western Powers" and therefore proposed a four-power pact in which France, Germany, Great Britain, and Italy would support treaty revision and pledge equality to Germany if the Disarmament Conference failed to do so. They would also pursue common policies concerning political, economic, and colonial questions. The French found the equality clause objectionable and excised it from the final draft of the pact, but the plan also antagonized the smaller nations attending the Disarmament Conference as another humiliating example of major-power negotiations that ignored them. League officials realized that Mussolini's insistence on leadership by the stronger nations threatened the constitutional principles under which the Assembly and Council functioned, and they opposed the creation of what a French minister derided as a "directory of Great Powers laying down the law to the smaller nations. . . ."

Although the MacDonald plan contained significant concessions, including a stipulation about it being a replacement for the disarmament provisions of Versailles, the German delegation insisted on several amendments that raised speculation over whether Berlin *wanted* the conference to fail so that Hitler would be free to proclaim rearmament unilaterally. Foreign criticism was intensified by reports of Nazi brutality, persecution of Jews, and militant orations reminiscent of former Chancellor Otto von Bismarck's "blood and iron." Hitler, in discussions with his Cabinet on May 12, seemed prepared to challenge Geneva by threatening withdrawal from the League, but four days later, he shifted his tactics. On May 16, U.S. President Franklin D. Roosevelt appealed for support of the British plan and insisted that "if any strong nation refuses to join with genuine sincerity in these concerted efforts for political and economic peace . . . the civilized world will know where the responsibility for failure lies." In one of his most impressive and successful speeches, Hitler cleverly exploited Roosevelt's message and portrayed himself as an ardent champion of disarmament and Germany as the victim of the injustices of the Treaty of Versailles. He said he deplored war as "unlimited madness [that would] cause the collapse of the present social and political order." To avoid such a catastrophe, he assured the world, "Germany would also be perfectly ready to disband her entire military establishment and destroy the small amount of arms remaining to her, if the neighboring countries will do the same thing. . . . Germany has only one desire, to be able to preserve her independence and defend her frontiers." Members of the Reichstag interrupted Hitler repeatedly with prolonged applause, and the reception abroad was quite favorable among those who felt that they had heard the voice of reason that they had wanted to hear. The same as the London *Times,* many were convinced that Hitler had made an "irrefutable" case for equality. However, there had been a warning in the speech that had generally been overlooked in the initial euphoria. Hitler had insisted on equality of treatment and had coupled the demand with the threat of withdrawing not only from the Disarmament Conference but also from the League.

Despite these positive and negative incentives, the delegates failed to reach an agreement by June, and the conference again adjourned. The example of Manchuria convinced some that it was folly to disarm when aggression went unpunished by the League. France and Russia explored the revival of their prewar alliance against Germany, and Great Britain insisted on retention of a strategic bombing capability. Other delegates simply became preoccupied with preparations for the London Economic Conference, which was to open on June 12. During the summer, Arthur Henderson, president of the Disarmament Conference, reviewed the negotiations with officials in London, Paris, Prague, and Rome; in Berlin, he had the unpleasant task of advising Foreign Minister Konstantin von Neurath that France wanted the MacDonald plan modified. During an initial four-year period, no armaments would be produced for land warfare and no reductions imposed on existing forces. If these conditions were verified as fulfilled, the arms levels set in the British program would then be executed in the following four years. There was no possibility, however, that Hitler would submit to a probationary period that preserved the status quo. In memoranda to the United States and Great Britain, Germany again argued for equality, but the British and American delegations supported France, as did the Italian government. Hitler initially encouraged continued negotiations despite opposition from his diplomatic and military advisers, but when he learned that there were no prospects of concessions, he stunned the delegates in Geneva by suddenly announcing, on October 14, Germany's withdrawal from the conference and from the League. In an emotional broadcast to the German people, he spoke of the long years of patient compliance with the Treaty of Versailles, whose disarmament terms the Allied powers had failed to honor. This situation constituted "an unjust and humiliating discrimination against the German nation," and his government would not tolerate the status of "outlawed and second-class" country. The chancellor called for a referendum, and on November 12, some 95 percent of the electorate responded with a decision that "shall be recorded in the history of our people as a day of salvation."

Foreign reaction was mixed, but most experts considered the failure of the Disarmament Conference and the loss of Germany, coupled with the resignation of Japan, to be serious blows to the world body. Secretary-General Joseph Avenol, appointed on July 1, 1933, conceded that "the very large majority of countries in the world who still believe in the League appear to be losing confidence in its ability to deal effectively with the major problems of the day." Contemporary observers tended to blame the French paranoia for the failure of the conference, but neither Great Britain nor the United States provided the guarantee of security that France required. Some British and French observers judged Hitler's action to be premeditated and indicative of the belligerent intentions of the Nazi government. In a memorandum circulated to the British Cabinet, Major General A. C. Temperley warned of "a mad dog abroad once more" that had to be confined or destroyed.

Hitler was concerned about the possibility of retaliation and ordered defense planning, but no punitive action against Germany was ever considered. Although the French and British intelligence services were aware of Germany's secret rearming during the 1920s, they hesitated to use this violation of Versailles as a basis for sanctions. The chancellor continued to confuse foreign analysts with periodic references to his desire to renew disarmament talks. "I shall be," he assured a French interviewer, "only too glad to enter into negotiations with anyone who wants to talk to me." He was also able to defuse some criticism of Nazi policy by suggesting that Germany might return to the League. An American historian, Allan Nevins, described this as Hitler's "dual foreign policy"—defiant gestures coupled with conciliatory speeches. Unfortunately, Secretary-General Avenol proved to be most vulnerable to such tactics.

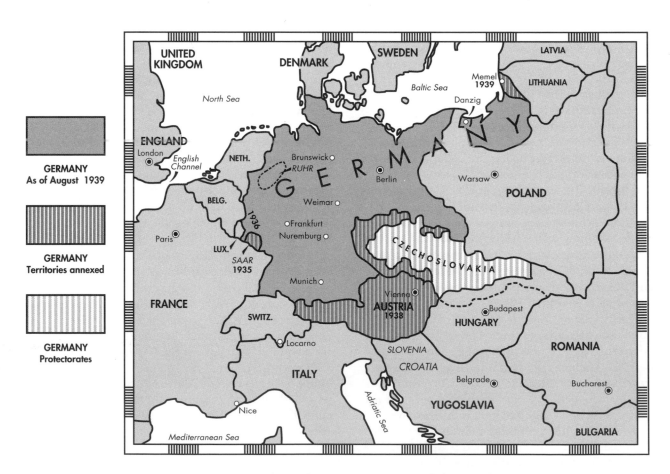

After withdrawing from the World Disarmament Conference and from the League of Nations in the fall of 1933, Germany embarked on a program of territorial expansion, especially on its eastern border. The above map shows the growth of Germany as of August 1939.

The League in Transition | 2

At a reception on the eve of Joseph Avenol's inauguration as secretary-general, Sir Eric Drummond assured officials and guests that the League would be "safe in the best of hands." During the next two years, Avenol's leadership qualities would be tested as he tried to reconcile Japan and Germany with the League, oversee Russia's admission to the world body, and negotiate an end to the war between Bolivia and Paraguay. Not all observers would continue to share Drummond's confidence in Avenol's ability and policy. The new secretary-general's deference to Hitler during the Saar plebiscite, the Danzig controversy, and the disarmament negotiations antagonized those advocating resistance to Nazi Germany. And Avenol's cautious administration of the League's aid program for China alienated delegates who wished to strengthen the Nanking government against Japan.

The Soviet Union's application for admission to the League aroused opposition from anticommunist delegates, with whom Avenol was not unsympathetic, but the new secretary-general concluded that the USSR's participation would probably strengthen the world body and supported its entry. In Latin America, the war between Bolivia and Paraguay taxed the perseverance of Avenol and the delegates as they tried for several years to resolve the conflict. It was generally acknowledged that Avenol's succession came at a critical time in the League's brief history, and his background was examined with more than the usual interest.

Avenol's Appointment as Secretary-General

In January 1932, Sir Eric Drummond, who had been serving as secretary-general since the League's inception in 1919, announced his decision to resign. He cited family considerations but also noted that he had served beyond the ten years he believed was the maximum period of time one could sustain constructive leadership.

With respect to a successor to Drummond, the obvious choice appeared to be Deputy Secretary-General Joseph Avenol. However, Drummond questioned the wisdom of that selection because of the growing dissatisfaction of the smaller nations with the control exercised by the major powers in the Council and the Secretariat. Drummond preferred to see the new secretary-general chosen from one of the smaller states, and his own choice was Willen Jan Marie van Eysinga, a Dutch jurist serving on the Permanent Court of International Justice (PCIJ, World Court). Eysinga,

17

however, was also a candidate for president of the PCIJ and declined consideration for the League office. Among the other smaller-nation candidates were Eduard Beneš of Czechoslovakia, Salvador de Madariaga of Spain, and Nicolas Titulescu of Rumania. But there was concern that a secretary-general recruited from a lesser power could be influenced by France or Great Britain. In addition, Drummond anticipated opposition from Berlin or Rome to a French successor, since public opinion in Germany reportedly described Avenol's appointment as "most undesirable" and Rome wanted greater Italian representation in the Secretariat. When both governments subsequently endorsed Avenol, and the new secretary-general appointed a German as under secretary-general and an Italian as deputy secretary-general, it appeared to many that a bargain had been struck. Avenol was the unanimous choice of the Council, and on December 9, 1932, he was officially elected by the Assembly, receiving forty-two of forty-four secret votes (one vote was negative and one, blank). His appointment became effective on July 1, 1933.

The new secretary-general had been raised in the small town of Melle, in the province of Poitou, where he had been born on June 7, 1879. His father had been a member of the Papal Zouaves, the small garrison that defended the Papal States, a career that had reinforced the religious and conservative training the younger Avenol received from the Marianite Brothers at the Collégè de la Rochelle. After the Collégè, Avenol attended the University of Poitiers and the University of Paris, where he studied political science and law. In 1905, he joined the staff of the general inspector of finances in the French Treasury after achieving the highest grade in the qualifying examination. He served with distinction and rose to the post of inspector general. During World War I, he went to London as the finance delegate of the French Embassy and served on the Inter-Allied Commission for Reconstruction and the Permanent Committee of the Inter-Allied Supreme Economic Council.

French President Raymond Poincaré suggested that Avenol seek the office of deputy secretary-general of the League of Nations. Antonio Salandra, Italy's delegate to the Council, challenged Avenol's appointment and urged the selection of an Italian colleague serving as under secretary-general. This provoked a heated debate between those supporting promotion by seniority from within the League and those defending Secretary-General Drummond's prerogative to select his own candidate, although it was understood that Avenol's selection would fulfill France's expectation that a French national would hold the post of deputy secretary-general. Finally confirmed in 1923, Avenol assumed the responsibility for economic reconstruction in several nations, including Austria, Hungary, Bulgaria, Greece, and Estonia.

In his critical study of Avenol (*Betrayal From Within*), James Barros portrayed a political conservative whose sympathies were more monarchist than republican and who was captivated by the British traditions of government and society, which were similar to the customs that France somehow had lost during the Revolution. Avenol's associates in the Secretariat placed him in the "ultraconservative French cast," with aristocratic preferences and a disdain for democratic principles and public opinion. Of necessity, Avenol had concealed these convictions during his employment by the Third

Republic, but his monarchist preferences surfaced after France's defeat in 1940. At that time, he supported the succession of the Count of Paris, whom monarchists recognized as the legitimate heir to the French throne. In the tradition of "Throne and Altar," Avenol sometimes invoked his Catholic faith to defend his political judgments and actions. These qualities, according to Barros, made it impossible for Avenol to have the broad-mindedness and flexibility that leadership of the League required in the crisis-laden 1930s.

Prior to Avenol's election, assessments made of him in the British Foreign Office warned of his subjectivity and his deference to French officials regarding League policy. Evaluations by some of his League colleagues were not flattering, and among the adjectives used were *vain, secretive, lazy, bureaucratic, weak, cynical, unprincipled, chameleon-like, cold,* and *politically uninformed.* Although some of these comments may have reflected the common price paid by all those in authority, Avenol himself described his conception of the power of the Secretariat in negative terms. He did not believe that the secretary-general should initiate policy but rather should act as a mediator between the opposing factions that might arise in the various organs of the League. He believed the secretary-general should function essentially as an executive and administrator, although he might indirectly affect policy formation. There was nothing in Avenol's commentary to suggest that he himself would try to exert vigorous personal leadership or would try to expand the powers of the office of the secretary-general. And his emphasis on the role of the secretary-general as a conciliator must have been strengthened by the problems he inherited from Drummond. From among them, Germany's relationship with the League occupied his immediate attention.

Avenol and Germany

In his farewell remarks to the Secretariat staff on June 30, 1933, retiring Secretary-General Sir Eric Drummond conceded that there was "a certain feeling of pessimism as to the future of the League." He said that the political horizon was "a little black," but he expressed confidence that the League was in "an unassailable international position." Only three and a half months later, on October 14, the "unassailable international position" was breeched by Germany's resignation from the League.

Avenol did not share the hostility and apprehension that many of his countrymen felt toward Germany. Instead, he hoped to encourage Hitler's reconsideration of membership in the world body. His policies toward the Saar plebiscite, Polish-German relations in Danzig, and disarmament negotiations were designed to facilitate that re-entry. He reminded League members that Germany's resignation would not be formally effective for two years.

With respect to the Saar plebiscite, scheduled for 1935, Avenol was determined to conduct a model election in which the will of the people would be freely expressed; he expected the impartiality of the League-supervised vote to impress Hitler. The League had assumed responsibility for this rich coal-producing region after World War I, when the United States and Great Britain had opposed France's attempt to secure it as compensation for the wartime destruction of its own mines. The final agreement provided for a Saar Basin Governing Commission, appointed by the League, to oversee the area for fifteen years, after which the Saarlanders could vote to continue association with the world body, be integrated into France, or return to German rule. There were German complaints in the early 1920s about the Council's appointment of a Frenchman, Victor Rault, as chairman of the Governing Commission. Rault tended to be heavy-handed in dealing with other members of the commission and was accused of allowing his French background to influence his policy decisions against the German population, especially during the Ruhr crisis of 1923–1924. The Council approved open hearings on these charges in July 1923, which not only provided an opportunity for both sides to explain their position but also demonstrated the determination of the Council to ensure just treatment for its wards. There were no major incidents afterward, and by the late 1920s, the inhabitants seemed satisfied with the commission's rule.

However, the fact remained that some 750,000 Germans were without an effective voice in their own government and looked forward to 1935, when they could decide the future of the Saar. The rise of Hitler complicated the situation for many Saarlanders, who were repelled first by the record of Nazi brutality and then by Hitler's decision to end Germany's relationship with the League. Earlier estimates that 90 percent of Saarlanders favored rejoining the Weimar Republic pressured Hitler to equal or surpass that prediction. Rather than risk a loss of face, the chancellor tried to bypass the plebiscite by proposing, in the fall of 1933, that France agree to the restoration of the Saar without a vote. This would, he assured France, remove the only territorial issue dividing the two nations. When the French government rejected the offer, the Nazis intensified their campaign of intimidation of the local people and demonstrations along the frontier. Some League officials became concerned that the provocations would jeopardize the freedom of the vote, but in June 1934, Germany and France agreed to prevent all interference by their nationals in the plebiscite. During the summer, Hitler intensified his appeals to the Saarlanders, pledging economic support to the workers. By autumn, however, there were reports of an impending Nazi coup, and the new chairman of the Governing Commission, Geoffrey Knox, informed the Council that his thirty-six-man police force was inadequate to ensure a peaceful plebiscite. To avoid exacerbating the situation, France withdrew—under German protest—an earlier commitment to provide troops to support the commission. However, the British Cabinet agreed to supply 1,500 soldiers as part of an international force that would include 1,300 Italian, 250 Swedish, and 250 Dutch contingents. The Saar force was the first and only one the League ever used, and despite some protests from the Nazis, the unit accomplished its mission without incident. Avenol apparently had some reservations about the military force, but his concern over the German reaction proved unnecessary. When the votes were counted, 90 percent of the electorate supported immediate reunion with Germany, less than 50,000 desired to remain with the League, and only 2,214 wished to unite with France. On March 1, 1935, Hitler welcomed his "beloved compatriots in the Saar" to reunion with the Fatherland after "fifteen years of oppression." There was no acknowledgment of the League's scrupulous fulfillment of the terms of the Treaty of

Versailles, but its officials could take justifiable pride in the peaceful conclusion of a difficult responsibility.

Avenol displayed similar concern regarding Danzig, the former German Baltic port that had been made a Free City and placed "under the guarantee of the League of Nations" by the Treaty of Versailles as part of the settlements restoring an independent Poland after World War I. Leaders of the restored Polish state desired Danzig's incorporation, but the port was enjoying political autonomy even though it was subject to Polish customs jurisdiction and was intended to serve the economic needs of Poland. In 1920, the Council had appointed a High Commissioner to Danzig, whose primary function had become mediation between the Free City's Germans and Poles. During the 1920s, both parties had complained frequently, and by the early 1930s, German economic interests had been disturbed by the rising competition from a new Baltic port created by Poland at Gdynia. Dismissed as an unrealistic project in the previous decade, Gdynia had become a viable facility commanding half as much trade as Danzig. At the same time, the political situation in Danzig had become more tense because the city's rising Nazi Party was advocating reunion with Germany. The Polish minority responded with new appeals for annexation by Warsaw, and the inevitable street disorders followed. The Polish government wanted its troops called in to maintain order, but High Commissioner Count Manfred Gravina brought the matter to the League Council, which secured a mutual pledge of cooperation from the parties in 1931.

Poland then attempted to restrict the selection of the next High Commissioner to a candidate from one of the lesser powers. Avenol opposed this as an obvious effort to install someone whom Warsaw hoped it could influence. The local Nazi Party also tested the League when it gained a majority in Danzig's Volkstag (Senate) and began to flout some of the liberal provisions of the constitution that the League was obliged to uphold. The new High Commissioner, Helmar Rosting, asked the Council in November 1933 to review the Nazi actions, but Avenol decided to delay a confrontation and dismissed as unnecessary Rosting's petition for a special meeting of the Council. In 1934, Arthur Greiser, a Nazi, became president of the Volkstag and decided to emulate the Saar electoral victory. In February 1935, the Volkstag was dissolved and new elections were scheduled. If the Nazis secured a two-thirds majority, they would be able to amend the constitution at will. In a familiar pattern, the opposition leaders were threatened, sometimes arrested, and denied access to radio and press facilities. From Berlin came prominent members of the Nazi hierarchy to emphasize Hitler's interest in the outcome. The results fell far short of expectations, as the Nazis gained only 57 percent of the vote and failed to win the two-thirds necessary to control constitutional revision. Frustrated, the Nazis resorted to violence, and the next High Commissioner, Sean Lester, was besieged by appeals from Polish victims. Lester presented their petitions to the Council at a time when the League still had some leverage in dealing with the situation, since neither Germany nor Poland wished to see the organization withdraw from its role in Danzig. Hitler was not yet ready to resort to war, and Poland was not prepared to challenge Hitler by trying to incorporate the city. In the summer of 1936, however, the Council had to endure a bitter and insulting speech from Greiser, who appeared before it to answer charges of continued Nazi abuses in Danzig. Following instructions received from Berlin, he assailed the League's interference in the lives of the German population of Danzig and attacked Lester personally for his defense of the minorities. He demanded that either a new High Commissioner be appointed without authority in domestic political affairs or the office of High Commissioner be abolished with its functions assumed by the president of the Volkstag. Greiser concluded his speech with a Nazi salute, which drew ridicule from the press gallery. He then paused before the press correspondents, but instead of repeating the Nazi salute, thumbed his nose and stuck out his tongue at them. The childish but defiant gesture was symbolic of what would follow in Danzig. Yet instead of responding to the blatant challenge, Avenol and the Council began an unseemly retreat by asking the Polish government to assume the responsibility for constitutional freedoms in Danzig. Protection of its own nationals was of concern to Warsaw, but it hesitated to defend other victims of Nazi attack at a time when it was trying to reduce the areas of tension with Germany following their signing of a nonaggression pact in 1934.

Further evidence of Avenol's cultivation of Germany was found in his efforts to secure its return to the disarmament talks, the success of which, he believed, depended on German participation. He also saw the negotiations as a channel for contacts between Germany and the League that could lead to reunion. Tactically, he considered it unwise to reconvene the general conference until preliminary conversations produced understandings among the principal powers. Therefore, in November 1933, he proposed the "unthinkable" to France, namely, that it accept the "controlled rearmament of Germany," a ploy immediately rejected by the French delegate to the League, Joseph Paul-Boncour. Undeterred, the secretary-general then visited Rome to win support for his approach and to encourage Italy's sense of responsibility for the progress of the Disarmament Conference. He must have been embarrassed by Mussolini's public reference to the League as "an absurdity" following the resignation of Japan and Germany but was probably relieved when the Duce told reporters that "one must not abandon the bedside of a sick man." Mussolini's diagnosis was that the League's illness stemmed from the principle of unanimity and the role of the minor nations in the decisions of the world body. The only hope for recovery for the World Disarmament Conference, he said, was negotiations among the "Big Four," as he had advocated earlier in the year. Avenol conceded that the size of the Council made it unwieldy when dealing with "delicate political European problems" and suggested the possibility of establishing a smaller European committee within the Council to handle regional issues. But France opposed Mussolini's suggestions, and Paul-Boncour insisted that his government would not "permit the least injury, directly or indirectly, to the League." From Berlin came the cry for change: "It is now up to the League to meet the demands of our time or sink into empty nothingness." British Foreign Secretary Sir John Simon observed that since Italy's proposals had not been formally presented to the League, no action was necessary, and Avenol accepted that advice. In an article in *The New York Times* on December 31, 1933, the secretary-general blamed "selfish nationalism" for the current League crisis and departed from his usual deference to the major powers. He traced the disarmament impasse

to the issue of equality, a European issue that had been allowed to dominate the conference and push the primary objective—the reduction of
arms—into the background. Equality was "dealt with almost entirely by the
great powers," Avenol said in his article, but their failure to resolve it led to
Germany's withdrawal from the world body. Responding to Mussolini's criticism that the League postulated an equality among states, Avenol explained
that the Covenant "accepts the existence of great powers and gives them as
permanent members of the Council adequate opportunities of exercising
the authority in world affairs which belongs to great people."

The major powers, however, did not fulfill Avenol's hopes for a meeting
on Italian soil, and when the German budget for fiscal year 1934–1935 was
released in March 1934, its 90-percent increase in military expenditures
convinced the French government that no further basis for negotiations
existed. Although bitterly disappointed by this development, the secretary-
general remained creative. Hugh R. Wilson, the United States delegate to
the Disarmament Conference, reported Avenol's concern that the fate of
the League was being linked to the fate of the conference and that it would
be better if the world body could be "disembarrassed" of it. The secretary-
general suggested that the conference be abandoned and replaced by a
Council committee composed of the Great Powers, which would resume
contact with Germany when the opportunity arose. British leaders were
independently moving toward a similar proposal for a small committee of
European nations, and even some members of the French government
proved receptive to the idea. Arthur Henderson, president of the World
Disarmament Conference, had interpreted Avenol's earlier initiatives as
evidence of a lack of confidence, and despite assurances of support from
the secretary-general, their relations became strained. Henderson now
opposed dissolution of the conference and criticized those who wanted to
"cut [our] losses and go home" at a time when military budgets were increasing and the international situation was becoming more threatening.
Successful in his appeal to the Council and the delegates, Henderson presided over the reconvened conference in May 1934 only to see it become quickly stalemated after bitter exchanges between French and British delegates.
Sir John Simon insisted that Germany's demand for a "measure of rearmament" should be conceded, but Louis Barthou sensed in Hitler's Third
Reich a reawakened "spirit of war, the spirit which has been called the
Prussian spirit," and said he would not tolerate letting Germany "impose
her will" on the conference. For Paris, security was paramount and no concessions to Germany were acceptable; for London, agreement with Germany
was paramount and no new security obligations were acceptable. France's
allies among the smaller European powers joined its call for security, while
the United States supported the British. Henderson, who had made the
conference the last task of his long political career, blamed its "desperate"
situation on the intransigence of Barthou and the French government. The
conference "holds the lives of the young men of the world in its hands,"
Henderson anguished, "and public opinion despairs of its deliberations."

Over all of the delegates hung the realization of failure, and on June 11,
the conference adjourned. It would not meet again. The fervor and optimism of 1932 were gone, and the lengthy petitions were forgotten. The
armbands inscribed with *pax* had yielded to ones inscribed with the

swastika, a portent of things to come. Avenol's attempt to court Hitler's favor through his handling of the Saar, Danzig, and disarmament issues thus had proved fruitless. However, it did not discourage the secretary-general from a parallel effort to restore Japanese membership in the world body. Unfortunately, his attempt to avoid conflict between League policy and Tokyo's interests in the Far East came at the expense of China.

Avenol, China, and Japan

Although China had been a member of the world body from its inception, China's political instability and periodic violent antiforeign outbursts tended to alienate the Western powers and infuriate Japan. In the mid-1920s, Dr. Ludwik Rajchman, chairman at the time of the League's Health Organization, had visited China and recommended a program of technical assistance. Deeply sympathetic to the Kuomintang government, he had believed that aid provided by the League would assist China's evolution into a stable modern state. He had therefore also signed a contract with the Chinese government and had become—in addition to a director for the League—a trusted and influential adviser to Chiang Kai-shek, T. V. Soong, and other nationalist leaders.

In 1928, a representative of the Nanking government sat for the first time in the League Assembly; but that same year, China failed to receive the necessary two-thirds vote to retain its position on the Council. The loss of face was aggravated by the embarrassment of unpaid dues. There was no connection between the debt and the defeat for the Council seat, but the then secretary-general, Sir Eric Drummond, sensed a growing alienation in Nanking and feared that China might resign. In late 1928, Drummond sent Deputy Secretary-General Avenol to soothe Kuomintang feelings and to explore China's access to the League's technical programs. During this Far East assignment, Avenol also visited Japan and concluded that Tokyo had "only one foreign policy: China." He believed that Japan underestimated the nationalism developing in China that would challenge all foreign presence and that the League's cooperation with China could be "a factor of the first importance for the peoples bordering on the Pacific." Avenol was well received in China, as were the officials who followed him in later years.

In July 1933, Secretary-General Avenol informed the United States of the creation of the Special Committee on Technical Collaboration with China, which would oversee the several areas of League activity in China, ranging from agriculture to telephone and telegraph service. Avenol invited American participation in the committee, and the State Department took the matter under consideration. However, Nelson Johnson, the American minister in China, warned that Rajchman's association with the plan would arouse Japanese opposition and "doom [the] effort." As Johnson anticipated, Tokyo did object to the League's continuing aid to China and to possible American participation in the programs. When Stanley K. Hornbeck, chief of the Far Eastern Division of the State Department, denied that the assistance had a political character, the counselor of the Japanese Embassy in Washington insisted it would still have "an inevitable political effect." The counselor said that his government wanted the League and the United States to avoid these "ill-advised and ill-timed" efforts on behalf of China.

In the following months, Japan continued its pressure on the secretary-general to terminate League operations in China. Meeting with Prentiss Gilbert, the American consul in Geneva, Avenol mentioned the allegations of political activity by Rajchman and the need to investigate the situation. If Rajchman had "engaged himself politically," Avenol said, he would be "repudiated." The secretary-general was determined to avoid involvement in the political affairs of China and risk offending Tokyo. The press, however, publicized "the Rajchman Question" and warned that his censure by Avenol "could only be interpreted as a final abnegation by the League of its entire position [in the] Sino-Japanese matter." The situation eased somewhat when the Japanese delegate to the League informed the secretary-general that his government would not present formal charges against Rajchman. Avenol then told Rajchman that it was not feasible for him to both serve in China under contract to the nationalist government and hold an office in the League. Forced to choose between them, Rajchman decided to retain the post of chairman of the Health Organization and remain in Geneva.

Diplomatic quarters linked Avenol's action to Tokyo's pressure, and Gilbert concurred that "political influences were definitely at work." The American consul found the secretary-general anxious "to denude this League endeavor [technical assistance] . . . of any political connotations which might be offensive to Japan or embarrassing to any important government, notably perhaps the British." When asked if he would name a replacement for Rajchman, Avenol referred to the unique role the chairman had played in China and implied that it was unlikely the question of a successor would arise. He reduced other aspects of the aid program in deference to Tokyo's wishes, and acting as if the Manchurian crisis had never occurred, he blandly informed the press, "I have decided to do nothing that could prejudice the relations between Japan and the League."

Chiang Kai-shek's supporters were also distressed by the secretary-general's attitude toward China. Avenol disparaged China's military response during the Manchurian crisis, they said. He also pointed out undiplomatically that the nationalist leaders had called on the League to maintain the policy of nonrecognition even as they themselves engaged in trade negotiations with the puppet Manchukuo regime, which amounted to de facto recognition. Avenol questioned whether League members should be committed indefinitely to a nonrecognition resolution under these conditions, and he obviously saw in its abandonment a key to renewed contact with Japan. When China requested in October 1934 the creation of a Council seat for Asia, he opposed the step and informed the British Foreign Office that he thought reduced visibility of China in the League might be helpful in restoring relations with Japan.

The importance of closer cooperation between Geneva and Nanking had been impressed upon Avenol during his visit to China in 1928, but after the Manchurian crisis, he had chosen to sacrifice China's interests to regain Japan's association with the League. He had deferred to Tokyo's objections to the technical aid programs that the League had been providing for

China, and he had maneuvered Rajchman out of the advisory position with the nationalist government. The secretary-general had belittled China's military resistance during the Manchurian crisis, and he had encouraged revocation of the nonrecognition formula. Japan, the same as Germany, had ignored Avenol's overtures. However, one unexpected effect of Japan's unchecked aggression in the Far East, coupled with Hitler's anticommunist policy in Germany, was the USSR's re-examination of its relationship with the League.

Avenol and the USSR

The initial hostility of Lenin and the Bolsheviks toward the League stemmed from the support that France, Great Britain, Japan, and the United States had provided to the anticommunist factions during the Russian civil war. Since these nations were also associated with the founding of the League, the world body became in Russian minds a "Holy Alliance of the bourgeoise for the suppression of the proletarian revolution." Lenin ridiculed it as a "thieves' kitchen," and the Russian newspaper *Isvestia* portrayed it as "the arena in which a motley crowd of capitalist wolves are trying to tear each other's throats." However, Russia's need for foreign capital to rebuild its devastated economy compelled Lenin to set aside the Bolshevik goal of world revolution and seek detente with his capitalist enemies.

A Russian delegation attended the general economic conference in Genoa in April 1922 but also used the occasion to negotiate the Rapallo Treaty with Germany. This agreement outraged British and French leaders, who attacked the "unholy alliance" of Russia and Germany as "an open defiance and studied insult to the Entente powers." Tentative Soviet steps toward the League stopped, and in October 1924, Commissar of Foreign Affairs Georgi Chicherin warned his superiors that membership in the organization would mean Russia's domination by its former allies.

Isolation from the League continued until Joseph Stalin introduced the first Five Year Plan in October 1928. Since the ambitious goals of massive industrialization and collectivization of agriculture required foreign aid and a period of international stability, Stalin authorized rapprochement with the West. This included cooperation with the League, and Soviet representatives began to participate in meetings of the Preparatory Commission to the World Disarmament Conference, the World Disarmament Conference, and the Federal Union of Europe.

The USSR's interest in the League was also stimulated by Japan's conquest of Manchuria, which aroused Soviet concern for the security of its maritime provinces in the Far East. When Tokyo rejected a Soviet bid for a nonaggression pact, Stalin turned to Geneva. Hitler's rise to power reinforced this decision, as the Nazi threat to communism began to erode the Russo-German connections that had developed during the 1920s. Hitler's explicit statements in *Mein Kampf* that he would seek *lebensraum* ("living space") to the east from "Russia and her subject border states" could not be ignored. The dual menace of Japan and Germany forced the USSR to consider the advantage of having League support if it were to again become a potential victim of aggression by its former enemies. In an interview with Walter Duranty of *The New York Times* in December 1933, Stalin offered a cautious commitment: "If the League is only the tiniest bump . . . somewhat to slow down the drive toward war and help peace, then we are not against the League."

With disarmament hopes foundering and Great Britain reluctant to shoulder new security guarantees, France looked east for an ally against Germany, just as it had in the 1890s. Miriam S. Farley, a contributor to *Current History*, accurately surmised, in July 1934, the French intent to lay the groundwork for an alliance with the USSR through the League. She cautioned, however, that if bilateral rather than international responsibilities were to be emphasized, the League "was gaining a liability rather than an asset." In the November issue of the same journal, Allan Nevins offered the more positive evaluation that Soviet participation gave the League support in two of the great danger spots of the world—Eastern Europe and eastern Asia.

France's Foreign Minister Louis Barthou undertook the delicate task of smoothing the path for an invitation from the Assembly for the Soviet Union. Unfortunately, an invitation from that body had to be unanimous, and three states—Switzerland, the Netherlands, and Portugal—opposed the admission of a communist nation. To bypass this obstacle, the Soviet government was asked if it would accept an invitation from a large number of member states rather than from the Assembly. Moscow said it would. In the ensuing debate, Giuseppe Motta, the Swiss delegate, warned that the League was "attempting to wed water and fire," but Barthou successfully preached the gospel of utility. France's advocacy of the USSR's entry apparently softened Avenol's anticommunist convictions, and he did not resist Soviet membership. On September 18, 1934, the Assembly voted to admit the USSR by a vote of thirty-nine in favor, three opposed, and seven abstained. The subsequent vote to provide the Soviet Union with a permanent seat on the Council found forty in favor and none opposed, with ten abstained. When Commissar of Foreign Affairs Maxim Litvinov delivered the first speech for the newly confirmed member, he used one passage that illustrated Moscow's motivation: "Now war must appear to all as the threatening danger of tomorrow. . . . Now the organization of peace . . . must be set against the extremely active organizing of war. . . . Now everyone knows that the exponents of the idea of war, the open promulgators of the refashioning of the map of Europe and Asia by the sword, are not to be intimidated by paper obstacles. Members of the League of Nations knew this by experience. We are now confronted with the task of averting war by more effective means."

The admission of the USSR closed a long postwar chapter of Soviet hostility toward the League, and Litvinov became a familiar participant in Council discussions, especially those concerned with disarmament and collective security. Soviet entry also encouraged delegates such as Salvador de Madariaga of Spain to hope the United States might reconsider its relationship with the organization. Avenol anticipated that the conflicts in Latin America, particularly the war between Bolivia and Paraguay, would produce closer ties between Washington and the League as they pursued the common goal of peace in the Western Hemisphere.

Commissar of Foreign Affairs Maxim Litvinov delivered the first speech to the League of Nations for the Soviet Union, which was not only admitted as a member on September 18, 1934, but was also given a permanent seat. Litvinov went on to become a familiar participant in Council discussions, especially those concerned with disarmament and collective security.

Avenol and Latin America

The long-simmering dispute between Bolivia and Paraguay over their undefined mutual borderland had erupted into an undeclared war in December
1928. It was a clash stimulated in part by reports that the Gran Chaco area
north of the Pilcomayo River was rich in oil deposits. At the time of the incident, the International Conference of American States on Conciliation and
Arbitration had been meeting in Washington, and its members proposed
to Bolivia and Paraguay the establishment of a Commission of Inquiry and
Conciliation to resolve the dispute. Since both nations were also members
of the League, the Council too had expressed concern in restoring peace.
But on December 19, 1928, La Paz and Asunción informed then Secretary-
General Drummond that they had chosen the Pan American group.

Organized in March 1929, the five-nation body—composed of Colombia,
Cuba, Mexico, the United States, and Uruguay—began a long and tedious
effort to find a formula for peace. Shifting military fortunes generally dictated how the two belligerents responded to the proposals made by the
group, which came to be known as the Washington Commission of Neutrals.
Although both nations were impoverished and could scarcely provide for
their needs in peacetime, they found suppliers among the major powers
who were willing to extend loans and furnish military equipment to them.
In addition, the Bolivian forces were trained by Hans Kundt and Ernst
Roehm, both from Germany. (Roehm later commanded the Nazi Brown
Shirts and was executed in June 1934 during Hitler's terrible Night of the
Long Knives.) And one of the most successful commanders of the
Paraguayan army was Major General José Félix Estigarribia, a graduate of
St. Cyr who brought France's military traditions to his command. Europeans,
preoccupied with problems closer to home, easily dismissed this war as an
insignificant clash of minor nations, but the human toll was dispropor-
tionately high. Modern weaponry increased the combat losses, while field
diseases and the terrain contributed their own attrition. All in all, 52,000
Bolivians and 36,000 Paraguayans died in the conflict.

Sensitive to League intervention in Western Hemispheric affairs, the
United States wanted the Chaco dispute to be settled by the Washington
Commission, and the secretary-general initially deferred to the American
wish. However, as the war escalated in 1932, Council members demanded
League action, and Drummond explained to Secretary of State Henry
Stimson that he could not ignore the Chaco conflict while intervening in
the Manchurian crisis. Hugh Wilson, the American minister to Switzerland,
observed that "a number of the small states have been feeling their oats and
insisting on a rigid application of the terms of the Covenant, having been
frightened by what they consider the laxity of the great states in dealing
with the Manchurian problem." As Wilson anticipated, the Council appointed a Committee of Three, which recommended an on-site study of the dispute, but agreed to delay sending a Commission of Inquiry pending the
results of renewed mediation by the Washington Commission. When both
belligerents rejected the Washington Commission's proposals, however, the
commission disbanded in June 1933. The preceding month, Paraguay had
formally declared war, and Bolivia now appealed to the League, which dis-

patched its own Commission of Inquiry in October. Unfortunately, the efforts of the Commission of Inquiry also proved fruitless, as it reported to the Council in May 1934, though it attributed part of its failure to the continued flow of military supplies—including aircraft, armored vehicles, and automatic weapons—to the belligerents from foreign sources. The British delegation therefore initiated a new call for an arms embargo and for the states neighboring the belligerents to seal their borders. Argentina, Denmark, Italy, and Spain issued strong statements of support, and the United States prohibited the sale of arms and munitions. By the end of May 1934, twenty-eight nations had given either full or conditional agreement to the embargo. Bolivia protested the action as unjust because it lacked a munitions industry while Paraguay possessed at least a token establishment, but the Assembly formally endorsed the suspension of the arms trade with both parties. By November 1934, the Subcommittee of Conciliation, created by the Assembly's Chaco Committee of Twenty-Two, prepared a treaty providing for a cease-fire, demobilization, and neutral supervision of the disputed area. When Bolivia accepted the proposal and Paraguay did not, the League lifted its arms embargo against La Paz. Charging that it was being treated unfairly, Paraguay resigned from the League on February 23, 1935. But what mediation had failed to accomplish, mutual exhaustion did, and by the late spring of 1935, both belligerents were ready to end the war. Avenol had intended that the League would be the agency of peacemaking, but the challenge of a rearming Germany abruptly diverted the attention of France, Great Britain, and Italy from South America to Europe. So in May 1935, the League entrusted the settlement of the Chaco dispute to the Buenos Aires Mediatory Conference (Argentina, Brazil, Chile, Peru, the United States, and Uruguay). This last participant in the dispute completed a cycle of Pan American mediation that had begun in 1928.

Although a formal peace treaty lay in the future, international jurists cited the important precedent established in the Chaco conflict. For the first time, nations cooperated in imposing sanctions against states that had failed to comply with the League's efforts to restore peace. Manley O. Hudson, a member of the Permanent Court of Arbitration, concluded that to achieve joint action, it is necessary to have an organization such as the League. Unfortunately, Avenol's attempts to enlist direct American commitment to League action in the war had failed. Although the United States had served on the Pan American mediation groups and had supported the arms embargo, Secretary of State Cordell Hull had refused to accept any role that could be construed as active cooperation with the world body. (For a further discussion of the League's involvement in the conflict between Bolivia and Paraguay, see "The League and the Chaco Dispute," on page 31.) Isolationist sentiment was still dominating American policy, a stance that was further confirmed in January 1935, when the Senate defeated United States membership in the Permanent Court of International Justice. The Roosevelt administration had strongly supported joining the PCIJ but could not overcome domestic resistance.

The first years of Avenol's tenure thus ended on an uneven note. He had assisted in the restoration of peace between Bolivia and Paraguay, although honors had to be shared with the Buenos Aires Mediatory Conference. The United States had cooperated with him in the Latin American peace initiatives, but Washington had continued to resist any substantive commitment to the League. Russia's admission had brought a vigorous advocate of collective security to the world body, although Moscow's motives were suspect among the anticommunist members. Avenol's conspicuous failure had been the continuing refusal of Japan and Germany to reconsider League membership.

During an interview in September 1934, the secretary-general acknowledged the difficulties that he and the League faced in the changing international situation. Avenol conceded that previous "hopes of a new world order perhaps ran too high." The world body had "lost in popularity and prestige," he said, but he warned that the alternative was "complete anarchy." The League "is not, nor will it ever be, a panacea for all ills. There is no such thing," he advised. But he did offer a note of hope: "Loyalty to its [the Covenant's] principles and a will to observe them are more likely to prove a steadying influence through all the problems which face the world today and which will always be facing it, than any other proposition I can conceive." Whether the members of the League would defend the principles of the Covenant would be tested when Mussolini embarked upon empire building in Africa.

The League
and the Chaco Dispute

From the founding of the League of Nations, the United States had sought to restrict the organization's activity in the Western Hemisphere, while the Covenant's recognition of the Monroe Doctrine frustrated those Latin American nations hoping to use the world body as a counterweight to the Yankee colossus. Participation in the League by the Latin American states was uneven. Among the larger powers, Chile was an active member, but Argentina withdrew in 1920 when the first Assembly did not act on an amendment proposed by its foreign minister; it did not return until September 1933. Brazil resigned after failing to receive a permanent seat on the Council, an honor extended to Germany at the time of its entry in 1926. Preoccupied with the aftermath of its revolution, Mexico did not become a member until 1931. Costa Rica left the League in 1925, citing the heavy financial obligations of membership, which Guatemala, Honduras, and Nicaragua also found too onerous. Public interest in Latin America generally was dominated by the volatile politics that swept governments in and out of office. During 1930–1931, there were ten successful revolutions in the twenty Latin American republics, and "international affairs" frequently meant the rivalry among Argentina, Brazil, and Chile.

When its conflict with Paraguay over the Gran Chaco broke out in December 1928, Bolivia returned to the Assembly for the first time in six years. But neither Bolivia nor Paraguay showed any disposition to submit their problem to the League despite the Council's reminders to them of their obligations under the Covenant. Instead, they turned to a Commission of Inquiry and Conciliation created by the International Conference of American States on Conciliation and Arbitration. This five-member body—composed of Colombia, Cuba, Mexico, the United States, and Uruguay—

met in Washington in March 1929 and began extended negotiations to arrange a permanent settlement of the long-standing territorial controversy. However, the Washington Commission of Neutrals, as it came to be called, found itself repeatedly frustrated by the aroused nationalism of the two belligerents, both of whom wanted military victory, not mediation. Although neither nation had a strong economy, each found little difficulty in obtaining military supplies abroad, and by 1932, the war was intensifying. The escalation prompted the two nations to register charges against each other with Secretary-General Sir Eric Drummond, but neither requested League action.

The League itself was not inclined to intervene. On August 3, 1932, Acting Secretary-General Albert Freiherr Dufour-Féronce confided to Prentiss Gilbert, the United States consul to Geneva, that the world body hoped to leave the matter in the hands of the Washington Commission. The following month, Drummond advised Hugh Wilson, the United States minister to Switzerland, that he had "every desire" to cooperate with the commission, but he feared that inactivity in the Chaco dispute would adversely affect the League's resolution of the Manchurian issue. He was searching for some way "to avoid the reproach of indifference and at the same time strengthen your [the League's] position in the matter. . . ." He believed that he could "readily persuade" the Council to advise both parties of their responsibilities as League members and then recommend that they resolve their conflict through the Washington Commission. U.S. Secretary of State Henry Stimson thought this would "help very materially," and when Drummond requested access to confidential information to avoid "making a slip," Stimson authorized Wilson to brief him on the United States' evaluation of the belligerents, the plans of the commission, and the status of the negotiations.

The cooperation between Drummond and Stimson was welcome news to Francis White, U.S. assistant secretary of state for Latin American affairs, who was serving as chairman of the Washington Commission and was trying to maintain the commission's jurisdiction over the conflict. White also was facing attempts by Argentina alone and by a coalition of Argentina, Brazil, Chile, and Peru to enter the mediation ranks. Relations between Buenos Aires and Washington had deteriorated in 1928, when the U.S. Department of Agriculture had banned the importation of Argentinian meat, grapes, and alfalfa. In retaliation, Argentina had led the Latin American denunciation of the Monroe Doctrine and of the United States' military intervention in Nicaragua at the Sixth Pan American Conference that year. White learned, however, that previous controversies between Argentina and Bolivia, and the current support Buenos Aires was providing to Paraguay nullified these initiatives. When Bolivia launched a major offensive in June 1932, White drafted a declaration advising the belligerents that the American nations would not recognize any territorial changes resulting from force. He thus succeeded in applying the Stimson Non-Recognition Doctrine of the Manchurian crisis to the Chaco dispute when nineteen American states endorsed the declaration on August 3, 1932.

Unfortunately, the declaration made no impression on the belligerents, and several members of the Council called for independent action by the League. In reporting this initiative, Gilbert recalled that in the course of the Manchurian incident, the smaller states had tended to assert themselves "more strongly in the matter of League policy," which meant "a more insistent and perhaps idealistic regard for the prestige of the League. . . ." Stimson was disturbed by the prospect of Council intervention and predicted that if it acted, it would "most assuredly get a severe rebuff." Stimson prevailed, but Paraguay rejected the latest proposal of the Washington Commission and then withdrew from the talks. Exhausted by the years of tedious negotiations and seeing no prospect for success, White recommended dissolution of the Washington Commission. In a joint memorandum to President Franklin D. Roosevelt, Acting Secretary of State William Phillips endorsed White's analysis of the sit-

uation and concluded that it was time to "leave it [the Chaco dispute] to the League and the South Americans." The failure of the Washington Commission was an obvious blow to the prestige of the United States, and American acknowledgement of the League's new role was not enthusiastic.

The termination of the Washington Commission overlapped a new phase of the conflict. On May 10, Paraguay formally declared war, and Bolivia appealed to the League, which appointed a Commission of Inquiry, composed of France, Great Britain, Italy, Mexico, and Spain. Once again, military fortune dictated the response to the peace initiative, as Paraguay celebrated a major victory and rejected the Council's plan. On March 4, 1934, the Paraguayan government refused a revised proposal, and Bolivia gave it only conditional approval. Rebuffed by both parties, the Commission of Inquiry then reported on May 11, 1934, that neither nation would accept arbitration. Among the reasons for its failure, the commission cited the continuous flow of military supplies from foreign sources to the combatants. This turned the Council's attention to the earlier proposals of Éamon de Valéra in 1932 and of France and Great Britain in 1933 for an arms embargo. Anthony Eden renewed the call for the suspension of military trade with the belligerents, and on May 18, the Council approved the step. Within a month, thirty-five nations were participating in the prohibition of the export and transit of weapons and munitions to Bolivia and Paraguay.

The United States was among the initial supporters of the embargo, and Secretary-General Joseph Avenol tried to draw Washington into closer cooperation with the League, although on different terms than those permitted by his predecessor. Meeting with Gilbert on September 1, 1934, Avenol criticized Drummond's deference to the Washington Commission, an act that he judged "somewhat questionable" in terms of the League's responsibility when faced with a war between member states. He hoped, however, to enlist the United States in the search for peace, and on November 24, the newly formed Advisory Committee on the Chaco War invited Cordell Hull, who had replaced Stimson as secretary of state in March 1933, to join in its work. But Hull declined the offer, explaining that the United States "is not willing to take part on any committee which is constituted to sit in Geneva and which is responsive solely to the necessities of the

League organization. . . ." Then, while Avenol was courting the United States, the Assembly approved a new peace formula, but flushed with success on the battlefield, Paraguay refused it. Bolivia, however, accepted the plan, and the League Advisory Committee recommended lifting the embargo against La Paz and continuing it against Paraguay. Rather than submit, Paraguay followed the examples of Japan and Germany by announcing its resignation from the League on February 23, 1935.

An unexpected complication arose with Hitler's announcement of German rearmament in March 1935, which shocked French and British leaders, who then sought League condemnation of the chancellor's violation of the Treaty of Versailles. Gilbert believed that to secure the support of Argentina, Chile, and Mexico in the Council for the censure of Germany, France and Great Britain would have to offer those Latin American nations "a free hand in the League's disposition of the Chaco matter." During a special session on April 15–17, the Council adopted the resolution against the German Army Law desired by France and Great Britain, and the following month, a Council subcommittee approved mediation by Argentina and Chile in the Chaco dispute. The Assembly confirmed this step and transferred the responsibility from the League to the Buenos Aires Mediatory Conference (Argentina and Chile joined by Brazil, Peru, the United States, and Uruguay), an arrangement that compromised Avenol's desire to have the Chaco peace achieved under manifest League auspices. By this time, however, the military and economic exhaustion of the belligerents was reinforcing the ingenuity of the diplomats, and on June 12, 1935, Bolivia and Paraguay signed the protocols that ended the Chaco dispute. When peace came, Hull could find satisfaction in the composition of the conference recruited from the Americas, and Argentina took pride in the leadership exercised by its foreign minister, Carlos Saavedra Lamas. Saavedra Lamas had made it clear that he had no intention of sharing the role of peacemaker with the League when he rejected the Secretariat's request to have an observer at the conference.

In his *Politics of the Chaco Peace Conference, 1935–1939*, Leslie B. Rout, Jr., concluded that in abdicating its primary legal responsibility to end the war, the League had "abrogated a good deal of its remaining moral influence." However, contemporary international jurists such as Manley O. Hudson believed the organization established an important precedent in imposing the arms embargo on Bolivia and Paraguay, and that the maintenance of the embargo against Paraguay "was a striking vindication of the support which can be mobilized for the collective system of pacific settlement." What remained to be seen was whether the League would impose sanctions as readily on a major power as it had on two smaller nations. Mussolini would provide the test when he ordered the Italian army to invade Ethiopia.

A Bolivian convoy crosses the barren terrain of the Gran Chaco.

The Italo-Ethiopian Crisis | 3

Mussolini asserted at one time that his ambition was "to make a mark on history with my will, like a lion with his claws." He traced his mark on history in part through colonial expansion in Africa, but the unfortunate African natives were also marked by the claws of the lion. During his earlier political career as a socialist, Mussolini had denounced imperialism, but after embracing fascism, he supported colonial expansion as a fundamental aspect of the new doctrine.

The harsh fascist suppression of native resistance in Italian Somaliland during the mid-1920s set the pattern for the brutal campaign that took place in Libya from 1929 to 1932. The Italian military destroyed villages, confined civilians to concentration camps, gave no quarter to captured insurgents, and hanged leaders. Mussolini proclaimed to the Black Shirts, "Words are very fine things, but rifles, machine guns, warships, airplanes and cannon are still finer things." Although some Italians criticized the pacification methods as immoral, the fascist press extolled what Foreign Minister Dino Grandi described as Italy's "mission to civilize the black continent." Ample precedent existed, therefore, when Mussolini decided to broaden the stroke of his mark on history by annexing Ethiopia. A series of Italian encroachments along the undefined frontier between Somaliland and Ethiopia culminated in an incident at the Wal Wal oasis that afforded the pretext for war.

The Wal Wal Incident

On December 5, 1934, over one hundred Ethiopians and about thirty native troops under Italian command were killed in a clash at the Wal Wal oasis. The incident was hardly a cause for war, but General Emilio de Bono later revealed that he and Mussolini had discussed plans for war against Ethiopia as early as 1933. Wal Wal simply provided the opportunity to execute them. Italy's conquest of Ethiopia would add the latter's resources of coal, oil, gold, and platinum to Mussolini's otherwise "worthless collection of deserts" in North Africa and the relatively poor colonies of Eritrea and Somaliland that comprised his "empire." In addition, an attack on Haile Selassie's nation would afford an opportunity to "wipe out the shame" of the Battle of Adowa, in which Ethiopians had massacred an Italian army in 1896. The annexation would also enable Mussolini to take another step in the restoration of the glory of the Roman Empire, which he had promised his followers.

Ironically, Italy had played a major role in Ethiopia's admission to the League of Nations in 1923 and had signed a treaty of friendship, conciliation, and arbitration with the kingdom in 1928. When Ethiopia invoked this treaty to resolve the Wal Wal crisis, Rome rejected its own conciliation and arbitration machinery. On January 3, 1935, Selassie asked the League to intervene under Article 11, which authorized the world body to "take any action that may be deemed wise and effectual to safeguard the peace of nations." During the next several days, Avenol consulted frequently with Massimo Pilotti, an Italian who was a deputy secretary-general of the League. Rome thus enjoyed the advantage of having its interests safeguarded by a member of the Secretariat who was not only one of its own but also in Avenol's confidence. The secretary-general kept Pilotti informed of his communications and meetings with the Ethiopian delegate, Bajirond Teclé-Hawariate, and Pilotti forwarded this intelligence to Mussolini.

To settle the crisis, Avenol suggested a procedure by which Italy could avoid public debate in the Council through the use of a League *rapporteur* ("reporter") in bilateral negotiations, but Rome rejected this approach because it implied League jurisdiction in the incident. Ethiopia, on the other hand, asked in mid-January to have the question placed on the Council agenda and expressed the emperor's willingness to accept any solution that the League might offer. Avenol suggested that Council debate could be delayed if the participants carried on bilateral negotiations. Since this served Italy's desire to avoid a public hearing, Rome agreed, on January 19, to arbitration under the treaty of 1928, and the Council postponed consideration of the subject until its next session, scheduled for May.

During the ensuing weeks, Avenol was also in close contact with Pierre Laval, the French foreign minister, and Anthony Eden, a British representative to the League. Eden believed that the Council should take an active part in the affair but reluctantly agreed to the formula of bilateral talks between Ethiopia and Italy. Laval was more conciliatory toward Italy in accord with his general policy of cultivating closer relations between the two countries. Indeed, in the first week of January, Laval and Mussolini had conferred in Rome, and correspondents reported that in addition to their delineating the border between Libya and French West Africa, the French minister had given Italy a "blank check" regarding Italian policy toward Ethiopia. Laval assured the French senate that he had made no concessions, but Mussolini's interpretation became clear when, instead of carrying out the arbitration agreement, he authorized a military buildup in Somaliland and Eritrea. Transportation and communication facilities were expanded, native contingents were mobilized, and Italian divisions arrived with mechanized equipment and aircraft. Faced with this ominous situation, the Ethiopian government, on March 17, invoked Article 15, which empowered the secretary-general to investigate "any dispute likely to lead to a rupture." League action was deferred, however, as the Council turned its attention to a sudden and fateful European crisis.

German Rearmament and the Stresa Conference

On March 15, 1935, Hitler announced the reintroduction of compulsory military service and a projected expansion of the German army from ten to thirty-six divisions. Only the previous week, he had revealed the existence of a German air force. Since both of these steps were open violations of the Treaty of Versailles, France called for an extraordinary session of the Council and, together with Great Britain, turned to Italy for support. Fresh in their minds was Mussolini's decisive response in July 1934, when Hitler had first attempted to annex Austria. Although the Nazis had brutally murdered Chancellor Engelbert Dollfuss, the coup had failed because Austrian authorities had reacted quickly and Mussolini had rushed four divisions to the Austrian frontier. At the time of his assassination, the chancellor's wife and children had been guests of the Mussolini family in Riccione. When Mussolini extended condolences to the chancellor's widow, he had publicly assured her that "the independence of Austria has been and will be defended by Italy." Avenol now strongly supported the prospect of Anglo-French-Italian cooperation to meet a new Nazi challenge.

Mussolini exploited the situation and invited British and French leaders to a meeting in Stresa. Although the Ethiopian question was excluded from the formal agenda, there were informal discussions of the subject. Responding to British concerns over reports of impending Italian military action, Giovanni Guarnaschelli, head of the African Department of the Italian Foreign Ministry, admitted that "the possibility of an offensive could not entirely be dismissed." Warned that the British government would oppose such a step, he pointed out that neither British official policy nor public opinion had prevented Japan's seizure of Manchuria. Mussolini later claimed that he had amended the wording of the final Stresa communiqué to insure himself a free hand in Africa. Although an early draft had pledged the three nations to oppose "any unilateral repudiation of treaties which may endanger the peace," the Duce maintained that he rewrote the phrase to read "peace of Europe" and that the British and French had accepted his revision and understood its implications. Some historians have accepted Mussolini's account, but the Stresa Conference records indicate that the words "of Europe" were already in the text and that Sir John Simon, the British foreign secretary, was not prepared to give Italy a "free hand." The practical consequence, however, was that Mussolini believed he had received the "green light," a conviction reinforced by the official silence on Ethiopia at Stresa and its exclusion by Italian request from the agenda of the Council session in April.

On April 17, the members of the Council adopted a resolution condemning German rearmament as a violation of Versailles. Hitler was unimpressed. He denied the right of the delegates to judge Germany, and his Foreign Office accused the delegates of destroying "all bridges between Geneva and Berlin." On May 21, the Fuehrer delivered another "peace speech" in which he committed himself to the Locarno Pact, the independence of Austria, continued demilitarization of the Rhineland, and disarmament. To Great Britain, he proposed that Germany be allowed to build to 35 percent of British Fleet strength, a direct violation of the Treaty of

Italian dictator Benito Mussolini took advantage of concerns over Hitler to invite British and French leaders to a meeting in Stresa on April 11–14, 1935. Although the possible Italian invasion of Ethiopia was officially excluded from the formal agenda, Mussolini manipulated the wording of the final Stresa communiqué to insure himself a free hand in Africa.

Versailles. England accepted the terms in June 1935 without consulting France or Italy, who reacted bitterly to this latest proof of the "perfidy of Albion."

As the regular Council meeting of May 20 approached, Italy announced the appointment of its members to a joint Italo-Ethiopian conciliation commission, a step that it had delayed in the past. At the same time, Mussolini told the fascist senate that there would be no suspension of the military preparations. Angered by British criticism, the Duce proclaimed to the Black Shirts leaving for Africa, "We will imitate to the letter those who presume to be our schoolmasters! They have shown that when it is necessary to create or defend an Empire, they did not take into consideration the opinions of the world." Staffing the conciliation commission permitted Italy to postpone Council debate until the end of July, and while August 25 was technically to be the final date for completing the talks, Avenol reminded the Italian delegates that the report had to be accepted unanimously. If the Italian members rejected the report, the matter would be back where it had started. In addition to serving Italy's diplomatic interests, the delays also helped it militarily. The rainy summer months were unsuitable for operations but adequate for transporting additional supplies to Africa in preparation for an autumn campaign.

In June, a change of government in Great Britain brought Stanley Baldwin to the post of prime minister; Sir Samuel Hoare replaced Simon at the Foreign Office, and Anthony Eden was appointed to the newly created position of minister for League of Nations affairs. The same month, a British poll asked voters to express their opinions on several questions, including England's membership in the League. The National Declaration—or Peace Ballot, as it was commonly called—found that the vast majority of the nearly 12,000,000 respondents favored the world body. About 10,000,000 supported the use of economic sanctions, with 635,000 opposed; and 6,784,000 favored the use of military sanctions, with 2,351,000 against. The Baldwin government might have drawn encouragement from this expression of British public support for the League and for the employment of sanctions, but it chose instead to seek an agreement with Mussolini over Ethiopia. The secretary-general encouraged this approach, since it complemented his own policy.

Anglo-French Efforts to Appease Italy

Writing to the new British minister for League affairs, Avenol forwarded the assurances he had received from General Prasco Visconti that Italy did not intend to attack Ethiopia. The secretary-general said he thought that Italy had not anticipated the international attention and sympathy for Ethiopia. He revealed his anti-Ethiopian bias when he compared Italy's situation to that of Japan's with China, in which the Chinese enjoyed considerable worldwide sympathy. Both Ethiopia and China had become symbols of the innocent victim, which Avenol contended was not the political reality. Avenol believed that Italy had failed to adequately publicize its legitimate grievances against Ethiopia, and he would shortly encourage Rome to undertake this public-relations effort. The secretary-general speculated on the possible consequences of a rupture in the Stresa Front that could drive Mussolini into Hitler's arms. Austria would probably be an early victim, with subsequent losses in central and southeastern Europe. Avenol believed that the official silence of France and Great Britain both at the Stresa Conference and at the special Council session in April had fostered Mussolini's belief that they would not oppose his Ethiopian policy. In an extraordinary reversal of the participants' roles, Avenol cast Mussolini as the misled leader being forced to go to war because the League and its major powers could not find a way to sacrifice the aggressive Ethiopia at the Council table.

In fact, the British government was trying to find a way to accommodate Mussolini while resolving its own policy dilemma. Support for Ethiopia meant alienating Italy, which would help Germany; but allowing the Duce a free hand would undermine Great Britain's position in the League. In both cases, the world body would suffer—Italy would resign if it was opposed, yet if it remained unopposed, collective security would be bankrupt. The British Foreign Office recommended a territorial compromise as a possible solution. In exchange for Ethiopia's cession of part of the Ogaden area to Italy, Great Britain would let Ethiopia use the port of Zeila in British Somaliland. But Avenol's portrait of an anxious Mussolini seeking an honorable exit from the crisis was not the Duce that Eden encountered on June 24. The Italian leader rejected the British offer and presented his own terms, which involved the surrender of all territory not inhabited by Ethiopia and creation of an Italian protectorate over the rest of the country. Mussolini warned that if he went to war, the name of Ethiopia would be removed from the map. In addition, he deliberately slighted Eden by failing to attend an official luncheon in his honor. Informed of Italy's demands, Laval was willing to grant the protectorate status, but Eden refused to even consider it, since he believed the Duce saw all concessions as signs of weakness.

While the British were making their overture, Avenol suggested to the Marchese Alberto Theodoli, president of the League's Permanent Mandates Commission, a new tactic that would enable Italy to counter the widespread sympathy for Ethiopia. He recommended that Rome accuse Selassie's government of long-standing violations of the treaty of 1928 and portray Ethiopia as incapable of fulfilling the responsibilities of a civilized nation. The scenario he anticipated had France and Great Britain, freed from the pressure of public opinion, exerting their influence in Addis Ababa to force concessions for Italy. The secretary-general apparently was prepared to accept Italian control of all of Ethiopia, and he visited London on July 10 to review the situation with Hoare and the British Cabinet. Anxious to keep the matter off the agenda of the Council meeting scheduled for July 25, Avenol asked the British foreign secretary to persuade the Ethiopian government to withdraw it. *The New York Times* reported that Hoare was sympathetic to Avenol but committed to League action. After the secretary-general met with Dino Grandi, Italy's ambassador to the Court of St. James, rumors circulated that Grandi proposed the cession of Ethiopian territory and recognition of Italy's economic control over the African nation. When the ambassador denied authorship, *The New York Times*, on July 12, traced the plan to Avenol, whose desperate purpose was to avoid confrontation between the League and Italy. Paradoxically, in a radio address to the British people on the following day, the secretary-general praised the League as the only existing model for "safe and saner ways" to resolve international problems and expressed confidence that Great Britain would not "turn aside when obstacles arise. . . . Remember," he counseled his audience, "this generation is shaping the world's destinies for a long time to come."

While publicly enlisting British support for League principles, Avenol privately sought concessions that betrayed its Covenant. He encouraged Great Britain and France to open negotiations with Italy under the Anglo-French-Italian Pact of 1906, which defined their spheres of influence in Ethiopia. The secretary-general had in mind recognition of Italy's predominance in Ethiopia, with British interests in Lake Tsana and French rights in the Djibuti–Addis Ababa railroad preserved. The League would restructure the political administration of Ethiopia to conform with Italy's new authority. Like Czechoslovakia later, Ethiopia was to be excluded from the deliberations that would determine its fate, while the potential aggressor participated in them. When negotiations began on August 16, France and Great Britain offered concessions, but Mussolini dismissed them as inadequate. The Paris conference ended in failure three days later. The Duce's telegram to General De Bono on August 21 summed it up: "Conference came to no conclusion; Geneva will do the same. Make an end."

League Sanctions Against Italy

Following the collapse of the tripartite talks, Hoare advised Sir George Clerk, ambassador to Paris, that the British Cabinet and public wanted both the League Covenant upheld and war avoided. Most people did not recognize the contradiction involved in these two objectives; the general feeling seemed to be that once collective action was announced, Italy would bow to the League. Hoare thought this was a simplistic judgment, given the many variables involved in applying even economic sanctions. However, he would "play out the League hand in September" because, if economic sanctions were in fact impracticable, the League must discover that for itself. Under no circumstances, he said, must anyone be able to blame Great Britain for discouraging their employment. He instructed Clerk to counter Laval's tendency to seek closer ties with Italy. Clerk reported that French public opinion was strongly opposed to applying sanctions and that Laval would have difficulty in overcoming this pressure. He also observed that the quid pro quo sought by Laval was a British guarantee to assist France against Germany in return for French support against Italy. No British government, Clerk believed, could issue that "blank cheque."

The conciliation commission's long-awaited report, submitted to the Council on September 3, found that neither party was responsible for the Wal Wal incident. This might have opened a way to resolve the crisis, but instead, Italy now introduced the indictment of Ethiopia that Avenol had suggested earlier. A lengthy memorandum detailed Ethiopian transgressions from 1906 to 1935, including civil and criminal offenses against Italian nationals; diplomatic, political, and economic incidents injurious to Italian interests; and Ethiopia's general unworthiness to be recognized as a civilized state entitled to membership in the League. Western observers were appalled that the only defense of Ethiopia came from Litvinov:

> Nothing in the Covenant of the League entitles us to discriminate between members of the League as to their internal regime, the colour of their skin, their racial distinctions or the stage of their civilization, nor accordingly to deprive some of them of privileges which they enjoy in virtue of their membership of the League.

The Council's response was the formation of a five-member committee (France, Great Britain, Poland, Spain, and Turkey) to study the deteriorating situation.

The world generally recognized that the League was facing a major test, and by the end of August, several nations—Czechoslovakia, Denmark, Finland, Norway, Rumania, Sweden, and Yugoslavia—had pledged their support for cooperative action. When the Assembly convened on September 11, it heard the British foreign secretary pledge "unswerving fidelity" and affirm his nation's acceptance of the obligations of League membership, "particularly for steady and collective resistance to all acts of unprovoked aggression." This stirring endorsement of the League had an enormous effect on the faltering states, but there was still uncertainty concerning France. The British ambassador to Paris advised Hoare that Laval understood the sentiment of the British public regarding Ethiopia, but the French premier asked whether the English people would be as prepared to support sanctions in a future European crisis as they were in the African case. Laval was deeply concerned that sanctions would lead to a war with Italy. He would not support a naval blockade and preferred to see Great Britain and France restrict themselves to a moral condemnation and an embargo on military supplies. Hoare was aware, as a careful reading of his address reveals, that the British government might have to face Italy alone, and he emphasized the common responsibility of League members: "If the burden is to be borne, it must be borne collectively. If risks for peace are to be run, they must be run by all. The security of the many cannot be ensured solely by the efforts of a few, however powerful they may be."

Laval's Council speech of September 13 thus was of particular concern to the British Foreign Office. Laval took care to acknowledge Italian cooperation in the Franco-Italian agreement reached in January and in the Stresa accords of April. He emphasized his desire to preserve this amity and asserted that France had "spared no effort at conciliation" in the present crisis. But Laval assured the world body that France's policy "rests entirely on the League. . . . Any attack on the League would be an attack on our security." While many in the audience were relieved by the address, not all British observers were convinced that "the French will ever play the game." In a caustic analysis of the consequences of relying on France, Sir Robert Vansittart, the permanent under-secretary to the British Foreign Office, warned of the "danger of Anglo-Italian war brought about not only by lack of French cooperation but disloyalty and treachery in its dirtiest and blackest form."

Avenol's major fear was that the speeches of Hoare and Laval would distract the Committee of Five from its search for a compromise and encourage its members to condemn Italy. He counseled the Italian delegation to

Fresh Italian troops arrive in Ethiopia after the start of the invasion on October 3, 1935.

emphasize Ethiopia's social and cultural weaknesses rather than political issues that might generate further support for Selassie. On September 18, the committee submitted a plan that was based in part on earlier suggestions of the secretary-general, but Mussolini again brushed aside the offer. His decision for war had already been made, and before the Council could take further action, Italy invaded Ethiopia on October 3. Four days later, fourteen members of the Council declared Italy in violation of the Covenant, and on October 10, fifty states of the Assembly concurred, with only Albania, Austria, and Hungary in opposition. Uruguay and Ecuador expressed reservations, and Switzerland invoked its neutrality.

The League now moved to consider sanctions but soon found itself divided by the traditional demands of national self-interest. The sanctions committee recommended a prohibition on military supplies and all loans and credits to Italy; restriction of the sale of goods and raw materials to Italy; and limits on the purchase of Italian products by other countries. Resistance came immediately from nations whose economies would be adversely affected and from others who feared that a rigorous sanctions program would provoke Italy to war. "To military sanctions," Mussolini had warned, "we shall reply with military measures."

Laval's determination to avoid hostilities inspired a peace plan, endorsed by Hoare, that was a capitulation to Mussolini's wishes. In response, outraged publics in France and England drove Laval and Hoare from office, and the integrity of the League was badly shaken. The obvious failure of the sanctions committee to approve an oil embargo was a major blow to Ethiopia, whose military situation was continuing to deteriorate. Then the Italian forces, to their superiority in conventional arms, added chemical warfare. Both belligerents already had filed charges with the League concerning the use of dumdum bullets, torture of prisoners, attacks on hospitals, and mutilation of the dead. Ethiopia now submitted evidence of the use

The Italo-Ethiopian crisis drove both French Foreign Minister Pierre Laval (left) and British Foreign Secretary Sir Samuel Hoare from office after outraged publics learned of their attempts to sacrifice Ethiopia to appease Italy. Hoare resigned on December 19, 1935, and Laval resigned on January 22, 1936.

of mustard gas against its soldiers and civilians. Italy had been a signatory to a 1928 convention barring chemical warfare as uncivilized; but Italian aircraft were equipped to spray mustard gas, and Mussolini authorized its use. (The use of gas later assisted fascist victories in the northern theater during February 1936.) British and French concern regarding Italy's violation of the chemical-warfare convention was eclipsed, however, by Hitler's sudden announcement on March 7 that German troops were taking possession of the Rhineland, an action that had been barred by the Treaty of Versailles.

The Rhineland Crisis

The signing of the Franco-Russian mutual assistance pact in May 1935 revived the specter of war on both the western and eastern fronts that had haunted the German general staff before World War I. The demilitarized Rhineland—an undefended invasion corridor on both banks of the Rhine River—added to that fear, but it had been accepted by Germany in the Locarno Pact of 1925. Ten years after the signing of the pact, Hitler publicly pledged to observe the existing status of the area, even as he ordered his army to prepare to enter it. When the French Chamber of Deputies ratified the Soviet pact in February 1936, Hitler carried out the occupation. The German command feared possible French resistance and authorized its units to retreat if they were challenged, but no opposition developed. The French and Belgian governments initially pressed for League sanctions—including military force—but the British government strongly opposed the step. To the dismay of Foreign Minister Pierre-Étienne Flandin, General Maurice Gamelin insisted that France was not prepared for war. The British seemed to regard the episode as merely a matter of the Germans returning to their own backyard, and Eden succeeded in restricting the League debate to a British proposal that would just mildly censure Germany. Given the failure of France and Great Britain to act, the other members hesitated to do more than formally note Germany's violation of the Treaty of Versailles and of the Locarno Pact.

The Rhineland coup undercut further League initiatives against Italy and exposed fundamental differences between the British and French. Paris pushed for the resumption of bilateral talks between Italy and Ethiopia, while London favored at least some League action. Avenol, as would be expected, supported the French and attributed England's difficulties in the African crisis to its attempt to base policy upon principle. By the end of March, Eden had weakened and participated in a joint Anglo-French-Belgian meeting with Grandi to explore new negotiations between the warring states. By then, however, Mussolini had no need for negotiations. The Battle of Lake Ashougi (March 31–April 3) gave Italian forces control of the northern front, and by the end of April, the southern theater was also in their hands. On April 20, the Council admitted that political talks were fruitless, and two weeks later, Selassie sailed from Jibuti aboard the H.M.S. *Enterprise*. Selassie hoped his departure would end "the most unjust and the most inhuman war of modern time" and prevent "the extermination of the Ethiopian people." On May 9, from the balcony of the Palazzo Venezia, Mussolini proclaimed "the African victory," which gave Italy "her empire at last." He informed the League of his claim the next day.

Avenol cautioned the Italian delegate to the League that the Council might not accept this declaration of sovereignty over Ethiopia, but Mussolini warned that if Italy was not sustained in its victory, he would withdraw the delegation from Geneva. When the Ethiopian representative appeared before the Council on May 11, the Italian delegate walked out, and shortly afterward, Avenol announced with regret that the entire mission was returning to Rome. In the following weeks, Mussolini made it clear that Italy's continued membership in the League was contingent on the ending of sanctions. Avenol reminded him that the British government had to contend with public opinion at home and that both England and France were vulnerable to criticism by the smaller powers that had followed their leadership in originally imposing sanctions. Selassie was continuing his resistance in exile, but Avenol tried to discourage the emperor's appearance before the Assembly, which he feared would further antagonize Mussolini. For Italy's use before the Assembly, the secretary-general drafted a note charging Selassie with the failure of the prewar conciliation efforts and with abandoning Ethiopia. Italian Foreign Minister Galeazzo Ciano followed Avenol's advice closely and appealed for the end of sanctions. The secretary-general encouraged French officials to remove sanctions and was pleased to hear Neville Chamberlain, chancellor of the Exchequer, describe their continuation as "the very midsummer of madness."

In a memorandum dated June 11, 1936, and prepared for the British Cabinet, Eden reviewed the arguments for and against ending sanctions. He acknowledged the adverse effect that yielding to Mussolini would have on the future of the League but weighed it against the reality of the Italian conquest of Ethiopia. The Cabinet concurred with his recommendation that Great Britain support the lifting of sanctions, an announcement that produced a bitter debate in the House of Commons the following day. Cries of "Shame!" and "Resign!" and "Sabotage!" interrupted the foreign secretary, and Opposition leader Clement Attlee charged that the government's action "destroyed the League of Nations." Former British Prime Minister David Lloyd George shared what he believed to be the humiliation of millions of Englishmen to see "the white feather embroidered across the Union

Jack!" Home Secretary Sir John Simon spoke for those who had no desire to see England drawn into the African conflict: "I declare myself unwilling to see a single ship sunk, even in a successful battle, in the cause of Ethiopia." And the citation for Eden's honorary degree at Oxford commended "his aim . . . to lead the nations to a paradise of peace." The government ended up surviving the attack, and Eden's policy was quickly adopted by France.

At the League itself, the voices of support for continuing sanctions were few but prophetic. The South African delegate, Charles Theodore te Water, termed it a "surrender of the high trust and ideals of world peace" that would "shatter for generations all international confidence and all hope of realizing world peace." Despite Avenol's opposition, Selassie persisted in his efforts to address the Assembly and succeeded on June 30. As he began, several Italian newsmen in the press gallery jeered him, and police had to eject them. Outwardly unperturbed by the interruption, the emperor portrayed his nation as a victim that had been pledged support by the League only to be abandoned because a "certain government" (France was not identified by name) was determined to retain the assistance of Italy for its European needs. The issue of aggression was not confined to Ethiopia, he insisted, but also touched "the very existence of the League"; he exhorted the delegates to consider that "God and history will remember your judgment."

Eden confessed the painfulness of the occasion but maintained that the "facts should be faced squarely." Only military sanctions by the League could reverse the tragedy, and the members would not vote that action. Eden did not believe that the League's defeat in this case meant the end of the organization's ability to preserve peace and joined the French premier, Léon Blum, in pledging support to "rebuild the authority of the League." The Assembly consoled itself with similar expressions and with thoughts of success the "next time." It then voted on July 4 to remove sanctions, with forty-four in favor, four abstaining, and Ethiopia casting the single negative vote. Once again, Mussolini appeared on the balcony of the Palazzo Venezia to announce the League surrender: "A white flag has been hoisted in the ranks of world sanctionism." (For a further discussion of the League's handling of the Italo-Ethiopian war, see "League Sanctions and Italy," on page 47.) Having yielded on sanctions, the next question for the League was whether to accept complete defeat and recognize Italian sovereignty over Ethiopia.

The League and Ethiopia

As the September meeting of the Assembly approached, Italy warned that it would boycott the session and possibly resign from the League if the Assembly allowed the Ethiopian delegation to participate. Avenol preferred sacrificing Ethiopia to losing Italy, and he devised a plan that he thought would satisfy Mussolini and also be acceptable to most League members. When the Ethiopian representatives arrived, the Assembly's committee on credentials would question the validity of their documents and prevent them from being seated. Without consulting other League officials, the secretary-general discussed this procedure with Ciano, who agreed that his delegation

League Sanctions and Italy

The decision of the Assembly in October 1935 to impose economic sanctions on Italy was a welcome surprise to the many statesmen who had been disappointed by the League's unsuccessful efforts to prevent the war with Ethiopia. It also helped to revive public confidence in the principle of collective security. The Assembly immediately established a coordination committee of fifty states, which in turn created a smaller group—the Committee of Eighteen—to handle much of the planning. On October 11, the coordination committee banned the shipment of military supplies to Italy, and three days later, it denied Italy loans and credits. However, the prohibition of imports from Italy divided the members, since Switzerland, Yugoslavia, and Rumania felt that they would be more seriously affected by this than would other states. A compromise reached on October 19 required each nation to try to substitute imports from member states for those formerly taken from Italy and to penalize noncooperating members by reducing imports from them. With respect to cutting off goods and raw materials vital to the Italian war effort, the League realized that Italy could secure many of these items from non-member nations. On October 19, the committee developed a list of commodities under the primary control of the sanctionists that included transport animals, rubber, bauxite, tin, aluminum, iron ore and scrap iron, manganese, and other metals. A second list, adopted on November 6, covered goods available from non-League sources, such as petroleum, iron and steel, coal, and coke.

The United States was among the nonmembers whose policies could significantly affect the sanctions effort. The Ethiopian crisis had developed while American peace groups were demanding neutrality legislation to prevent involvement in another war. In April 1935, college students across the nation had observed a one-hour strike against war, and on the anniversary of the United States' entry into the Great War, 50,000 veterans had marched for peace in a Washington demonstration. Spurred by these peace movements, along with the Senate's own Nye committee investigation of the munitions trade, Congress enacted a neutrality law on August 31, 1935, that prohibited the sale of arms and munitions to belligerents. President Roosevelt and Secretary of State Hull sought executive discretion in applying the embargo to exempt an obvious victim of aggression, but Congress refused to grant the president that power. The American arms embargo therefore became applicable equally to Ethiopia and to Italy. State Department officials disagreed over the timing of the embargo's imposition, but all were committed to reinforcing the League's actions. Roosevelt also asked that American merchants observe a "moral embargo" that would limit trade with Italy to at least prewar levels. When statistics indicated that shipments of important raw materials were increasing, Hull publicly denounced the trade as contrary to administration policy. The president's advisers warned him not to expose himself to domestic isolationist attack, but Roosevelt did not want to weaken the League and spoke of "walking a tight rope."

Neither Germany nor Japan would formally cooperate with the sanctions program, although Berlin promised to restrict its export trade to its normal volume, a step dictated in part by Germany's need for a number of these products in its own rearmament. An American historian, Allan Nevins, cautioned the readers of the journal *Current History* that Italian stockpiling prior to the war would weaken the immediate impact of the embargo; he anticipated greater damage to Italy's economy from curtailment of its export trade.

Aggressive sanctionists argued that closing the Suez Canal was a logical step in the escalation of pressure against Italy, since it would deny Mussolini's military forces the necessary supplies and reinforcements to prosecute the war. Since August 1935, the British Admiralty had built up its Mediterranean Fleet and transferred its base of operations from Malta to Alexandria, where it could easily control the canal. A cruiser squadron was deployed off Aden to block the southern approach to the Red Sea, while the battle cruisers *Hood* and *Renown* led a Home Fleet detachment to Gibraltar. In September, the press reported an "unprecedented array" of naval power in the Mediterranean, and British commanders expressed confidence that they could sever the Italian lifeline to Eritrea and Somaliland if war followed sanctions. Yet the order to close the Suez never came. Even as Hoare delivered his widely acclaimed address to the League on September 11, he and Laval privately agreed that there would be no military sanctions against Italy. "No wise man," Hoare advised the House of Commons, "will wish to throw a spark into this inflammable material by threats that cannot be collectively carried out or, if they were carried out, would turn the Abyssinian into a European war." Thus, the Royal Navy would wave the flag of deterrence, but it would fight only if attacked. Hoare's determination to avoid war also found some support in the Admiralty when the French government procrastinated in guaranteeing its support in the event of a Mediterranean war. In an unfortunately prophetic note, the Admiralty warned that if the navy were embattled in the Mediterranean, Japan might use the opportunity to move in the Far East. Although confident of victory over Italy, the Navy realistically anticipated the loss of ships and crews that could not be easily replaced to counter another threat. In this vein, the Admiralty noted that while the German navy was small, it posed dangers in the North Sea and in the English Channel if the Home Fleet was substantially reduced for other duty. With an unpredictable Hitler in command of the *Kreigsmarine*, the signal from the British navy to the Foreign Office was for peace in the Mediterranean.

Even the limited sanctions that were imposed weakened the Italian economy. Although the fascist media accused the League of trying to starve the Italian people into submission, in reality more food was available in Italy, since its exports were also reduced by the sanctions. Nonetheless, the fascists successfully exploited the image of "the mother of civilization" under attack by the world body on behalf of "a horde of barbarian Negroes." Initial indifference or opposition to the war eventually yielded to popular support, and even some antifascist exiles professed their patriotism by returning to Italy. More difficult for Mussolini to explain to his people was the slow progress of the war. By mid-November, General Pietro Badoglio replaced Emilio de Bono as commander-in-chief and high commissioner for Eritrea and Somaliland, but victory still eluded the Italian army as 1936 dawned.

While League members, in the fall of 1935, were studying the potential impact of an oil embargo, Mussolini substantially increased his purchases from the United States, the USSR, and Rumania. To exert pressure on Laval, he ordered troop movements along the French frontier and encouraged rumors of an air offensive against France if war came. The saber rattling had its expected effect when Laval asked for postponement of the League meeting scheduled for November 29, during which the oil embargo was to be discussed. Hoare, en route to a vacation in Switzerland, stopped in Paris on December 7–8 to see Laval, who expressed alarm over the possibility of a war with Italy arising from an expansion of sanctions. The two ministers agreed on a new plan to end the Ethiopian conflict, but they did not submit it to either the League or their respective governments for approval. Under the plan, Ethiopia would surrender to Italy some 60,000 square miles of territory along the Eritrean and Somaliland frontiers. In exchange, the Selassie government would receive 3,000 square miles of Eritrea to provide access to the sea. If Italy refused to make this compensation, access would be carved from either British or French Somaliland. The southern half of Ethiopia, about 160,000 square miles, would remain under nominal Ethiopian sovereignty, but administrative control and economic development would be vested in Italy.

The plan was leaked by the French press on December 9, even before the belligerents received it. Dismay and disillusionment swept the League states and their supporters, who found the betrayal of Ethiopia morally repugnant. Defending his action before the House of Commons on December 19, Hoare revealed that from the beginning of the crisis, he had feared that "we might lead Abyssinia on to think that the League could do more than it can do, that in the end we should find a terrible moment of disillusionment in which it might be that Abyssinia would be destroyed altogether as an independent state." Up to this point, he said, League members had cooperated in the imposition of economic sanctions, but an oil embargo would open "a new chapter in the war," requiring "real and effective" action for collective defense. "We alone," he maintained, "have taken these military precautions. There is the British Fleet in the Mediterranean, there are British reinforcements in Egypt, in Malta, and Aden. Not a ship, not a machine, not a man has been moved by any other member State." However, despite Hoare's protestations that his conscience was clear, the Opposition insisted that the plan be "immediately repudiated." The political outcry on both sides of the English Channel drove Hoare from office in December and Laval, the following month. Secretary-General Avenol seemed to be more offended by the circumvention of the League than by the terms of the proposal, which he pronounced to be fair. The British ambassador to Paris reported that the French people would not support a war with Italy. "The basic fact," wrote Clerk, "was that no Frenchman was ready to go to war save in defense of his country, and that any French Government that called upon them to do so would have been thrown out there and then." Intelligence reports tended to support Laval's apprehension that Mussolini would act out of desperation if oil sanctions were applied. Clerk defended Hoare's decision to accept Laval's plan, but the succession of Anthony Eden as foreign secretary, with his record as a League advocate and sanctionist, awakened hopes for more forceful British leadership in the world body.

Although Avenol formally expressed his pleasure with Eden's appointment, the secretary-general was having second thoughts about further sanctions. In February 1936, a League committee concluded that the denial of oil supplies would cripple the Italian military within three to three and a half months, even if normal supplies from the United States continued. Avenol apparently used the uncertainty of American cooperation to discourage League action when, in March, the sanctions committee entertained a proposal to embargo oil. France's new foreign minister, Pierre-Étienne Flandin, shared Laval's fear of war with Italy, and oil sanctions were again deferred. Germany's sudden reoccupation of the Rhineland on March 7 caught the French and British unprepared and revived their concern over enlisting Italian aid against Hitler. By June 1936, Eden led the retreat from sanctions, and France quickly followed.

Contemporary critics blamed France and Great Britain for the sanctions debacle, as would a later generation of historians, who wrote of "the mockery of sanctions." Some historians believed the Ethiopian crisis to be "the last nail in the coffin of the League," as Arthur W. Rovine phrased it. In his address to the Assembly on July 1, 1936, when he conceded the failure of the League effort against Italy, Eden compared the ideal of collective security with the reality. "Clearly the ideal system of collective security," he stated, "is one in which all nations are prepared to go to all lengths—military lengths—to deal with any aggressor." Eden's predecessor had been convinced that collective support for military sanctions "never existed" in Geneva. "I emphasize," Hoare had told the House of Commons, "the word 'collective' as it is the essence and soul of the League. Only by this essence can the League live—not by ringing bells or blowing whistles for policemen from outside." Yet in practice, neither France nor Great Britain contemplated military sanctions against Italy. Ethiopia did not touch their vital interests, as did Hitler's Germany. Faced with the options of either alienating Italy or cultivating it, national rather than international interests received priority.

A final passage from Eden's speech perhaps connects the dilemma of the world of the League of Nations with that of the world of the United Nations:

If such an ideal [collective security] cannot be at present attained—and I agree with M. Blum that a heavily armed world greatly increases the difficulty of the attainment—it is surely our duty to amend not necessarily our rule of law, but the methods by which it is to be enforced, so that these may correspond to the actions which nations are in fact ready and willing to take.

Such was the path of weakness taken by the League and its prime defenders.

Persistence paid off for exiled
Ethiopian emperor Haile Selassie
on June 30, 1936, when he was
finally allowed to address the
Assembly. "God and history will
remember your judgment," he told
the delegates, who had refused
to vote for military sanctions
against Italy and then removed
all sanctions on July 4.

would return once the Ethiopians had been barred. At that time and thereafter, Avenol insisted that he undertook the visit to Ciano on his own initiative, but Prentiss Gilbert, the American consul, informed the U.S. State
Department that the secretary-general had probably acted after consulting
with the British and French governments. Many delegates criticized Avenol's
trip to Rome as humiliating to the League, and rumors circulated concerning his concessions to Ciano. To respond to the complaints, Avenol met with
the Council and reviewed the matter as he had presented it to Ciano. He
insisted that the final decision rested with the credentials committee, and
when the Council did not dissent, he interpreted silence for consent.

The mood and reaction of the Assembly were more complex. Many members were shocked by Avenol's callousness toward Selassie; the sacrifice of
Selassie's kingdom was not lost on the smaller states, who saw themselves
as potential Ethiopias. They realized that the legal decision to be made by
the credentials committee carried serious political consequences and were
disturbed that Jules Basdevant, the legal adviser at the French Foreign
Ministry, was designated to help Avenol formulate the guidelines. Could a
sovereign who had fled his country and no longer had a real association
with it still select the individuals who would represent the country's interests and obligations at the League? The question of Ethiopia's continued
existence as a state was not under consideration. The committee on cre-

dentials ordinarily was staffed by representatives of smaller nations, but given the gravity of this question, the major powers also participated. Specifically, the committee consisted of Czechoslovakia, France, Great Britain, Greece, the Netherlands, New Zealand, Peru, Russia, and Turkey. In its report, delivered on September 23, the committee acknowledged concern about the validity of the Ethiopian credentials, but it invoked a procedural rule of the Assembly that allowed a delegation with disputed credentials to continue to sit until the issue was resolved. Without a dissenting vote, the committee then recommended that the Ethiopian representatives be seated, and the Assembly overwhelmingly concurred.

Selassie thanked his supporters, but everyone realized it was a hollow victory. The emperor had lost his nation, and the League had failed the test of collective security. Laval's preoccupation with Germany had compromised his support of Geneva, and Hoare was Janus-like, displaying a public face of resistance to Italy and a private face of appeasement.

Italy, in addition, did not escape a blow to its pride. Avenol's assurance that the Assembly would reject Ethiopia only increased Italian resentment over the League's equivocation. Published reports had Ciano and his colleagues waiting with packed bags for their triumphal summons to Geneva, and Ciano did not take the rebuff graciously. Avenol's plan and Italy's conditions for active membership were common knowledge in diplomatic and public quarters, so any change at all involved a loss of face for Mussolini. Although Mussolini did not officially withdraw from the League until December 1937, no Italian representative ever again attended a meeting of the Council or Assembly.

Italy's abstention and eventual withdrawal were personal defeats for Avenol, who had cooperated with the Italian officials throughout the African crisis, delayed League action, and drafted plans providing for Ethiopian concessions to Italy. When war came, he did not openly contest the use of sanctions, but the Secretariat realized that he did not really support them either. His peace initiatives sought to reward the aggressor and abandon the victim, making a mockery of the Covenant's commitment to "open, just and honourable relations between nations." To the end, he pursued the fantasy of an imperially satisfied Mussolini cooperating with the League in preserving the status quo in Europe, a policy that also served his native France. Even that delusion ended when Mussolini appeared on another balcony, this one in Milan's Piazza del Duomo, on November 1, 1936, and announced the Rome-Berlin Axis. Spurning Avenol's courtship, the Duce urged France and Great Britain to also abandon the League and "the lies that still constitute relics of the great shipwreck of Wilsonian idealism." There was a special irony, therefore, in Oxford's award of an honorary degree to the secretary-general later in the month when the sponsor claimed that "no one has done more to enable the League of Nations to do what it had up to the present." In private receptions at Cambridge and Oxford universities, Avenol blandly ignored the destruction of Ethiopia as he praised the League for "giving each country a voice intended to protect it from having its rights, its possessions and its very existence voted away." This self-delusion also affected France and Great Britain, who failed to learn from Avenol's appeasement of Italy how dangerous and tragic that policy could be.

Moorish reinforcements for Franco's rebel army landing in Spain, September 1936.

The Spanish Civil War | *4*

Although disappointed by Mussolini's boycott of the League and by Hitler's refusal to reconsider membership, Avenol persisted in trying to link Rome and Berlin with Geneva. Unfortunately, another obstacle to his hopes appeared with the outbreak of civil war in Spain in July 1936. The conflict climaxed years of bitter political turmoil that had begun after the collapse of the monarchy and the exile of King Alfonso XIII in April 1931. The same as England's Glorious Revolution of 1688, the fall of the Spanish monarch had been bloodless, but the domestic policies initiated by the new Republic had aroused violent opposition. The new government had committed itself to agrarian reform, secularization of education, and reduction of the army's officer corps, programs that had alienated the landed aristocracy, the Roman Catholic Church, and the military.

Dissident officers led by General José Sanjurjo had revolted in August 1932, but they did not gain popular support and Sanjurjo was arrested. The general's failure hardly discouraged resistance from the army, which was abetted by conservative religious groups and wealthy landowners. Indeed, the coalition of right-wing elements won a substantial victory in the elections of November 1933 and abrogated the more objectionable laws that affected their interests. However, during October 1934, in the province of Asturias, increasing conservative rule produced a general strike, which turned violent and was suppressed by military force amid mutual charges of atrocities and terrorism.

The physical and psychological scars of the October crisis helped to unite the liberals and radicals of different political loyalties against the conservatives. In 1935, the Communist International devised a new alliance to combat fascism by creating a Popular Front composed of various left-of-center groups. Spain's small Communist Party imitated the appeal being made by the Communist Party in France and called for the unity of republicans, socialists, anarcho-syndicalists, communists, and Catalan and Basque separatists. In the February 1936 elections, the Popular Front candidates won a majority of the seats in the Cortes (parliament). Manuel Azaña was elected president on May 8 and, to the dismay of the conservatives, resumed the earlier liberal program. A fratricidal struggle soon divided the nation, with agrarian disorders, urban rioting, and terrorism activity seemingly out of control. General Francisco Franco y Bahamonde joined other officers to stage the July 1936 coup, pledging to restore order and guarantee freedom to the people.

Most army units supported the revolt, but the navy and air force generally remained loyal to the government. Since the navy temporarily con-

**General Francisco Franco helped
start the Spanish Civil War when he
joined other officers to stage
a coup in July 1936 against the
Popular Front government of
Manuel Azaña, elected on May 8.**

trolled the Straits of Gibraltar, Franco requested that Germany and Italy provide aircraft to transport his troops from Spanish Morocco to Seville. Simultaneously, the Azaña government turned to France and Great Britain for its military needs and also appealed to the League for political support. Avenol was apprehensive that League intervention could lead to the further alienation of Germany and Italy. He therefore welcomed the decision of France and Great Britain to attempt to limit foreign involvement in the Civil War through an agreement reached outside of League chambers.

The International Non-Intervention Committee

On July 20, the republican government tried to purchase arms from France, whose premier, the socialist Léon Blum, was sympathetic to Azaña. Blum learned, however, that the British government was opposed to aiding the Republic because of reports concerning the growing strength of left-wing socialism and the apparent influence of Soviet communism in Spain. English businessmen associated with multinational corporations were expressing uneasiness over the new militancy of their Spanish workers and the specter of forced expropriation. British Prime Minister Stanley Baldwin therefore urged Blum to reconsider his decision, and in the aftermath of the German reoccupation of the Rhineland, it was necessary for France to cultivate British goodwill and to appease royalist and clerical sentiment in France. On the other hand, Blum was aware that Italy and Germany were already furnishing aircraft to Franco so that he could ferry his troops from Morocco to Seville. Blum feared a Spanish state allied to Rome and Berlin emerging below the Pyrenees, but the French parliament was more fearful of stumbling into war with the fascist powers because of Spain. In light of these domestic and foreign considerations, Blum prohibited the sale of French arms to the Republic and proposed a non-intervention agreement to bar all foreign aid or involvement in the Civil War.

Across the English Channel, the British Foreign Office viewed the struggle as a no-win situation for the United Kingdom—a communist-oriented government would threaten England's economic position in Spain and propagate communist ideology on the peninsula and in France, but victory by Franco would strengthen Italian and German influence at the expense of Britain's strategic position in the western Mediterranean. The best that could be hoped for was to avoid the development of "any serious grudge" against England by either side. Thus, the French policy of non-intervention commanded support, and Foreign Secretary Anthony Eden recommended that all nations be invited to participate in such an agreement. On September 9, 1936, representatives of twenty-six European nations met in London to inaugurate the International Committee for the Application of the Agreement for Non-Intervention in Spain.

Avenol realized that this Non-Intervention Committee could serve as a substitute for the League in action concerning Spain, and he hoped that since Germany and Italy joined the group, their cooperation with nations that were also members of the League would lead to reintegration in the world body. The republicans, however, as the recognized government officials of Spain, continued to hold their League posts and used them as platforms to protest fascist aid to Franco. To avoid exacerbating the difficulties between the League and Franco's supporters, Avenol blocked an attempt in September by Spain's foreign minister, Julio Álvarez del Vayo, to raise the issue in the Assembly. The secretary-general continued this obstructionism throughout the conflict.

Following the French refusal to sell it military equipment, Madrid turned to the United States, apparently unaware that the State Department shared Britain's reservations concerning the Azaña government. Reports of violence, communist influence, and possible seizure of American property colored Washington's response, and on August 5, Secretary Hull recommended that the United States also adopt the policy of non-intervention; Spanish Ambassador Luis Calderón was so advised. The existing Neutrality Act of 1935 did not apply to civil war, so the administration called upon American business firms to observe a "moral embargo" on the sale of military supplies. When the Spanish government tried to purchase aircraft from the Glenn L. Martin Company, the firm was informed that the sale would violate administration policy. President Roosevelt enjoyed the support of both isolationists and internationalists—the former because the United States was avoiding involvement in the Spanish Civil War, and the latter because the administration was cooperating with the Non-Intervention Committee. In an election year, the "moral embargo" enabled the president to cultivate the important pacifist vote, and his speeches stressed his commitment to keeping the United States out of war. He warned that those who sought the "fool's gold" of wartime profits would compromise the United States' neutrality. When a New Jersey firm applied for export licenses to fill a $3 million order from the loyalists for aircraft and engines, Roosevelt described the company's action as legal but unpatriotic. The president then requested that Congress enact an arms embargo applicable to the Spanish Civil War. There was only one dissenting vote to the law, which was passed on

January 6, 1937, and public and press reaction was favorable at the time. Yet in succeeding months, the legislation generated considerable debate, as pro-Franco and pro-loyalist groups emerged in the United States.

Spanish republican authorities considered both the Non-Intervention Agreement and the American embargo unjust because they treated the republicans and rebels as equals. The republican authorities argued that international law permitted assistance to an established government but barred aid to those seeking to overthrow it. Aside from the theoretical argument, there was also the more dangerous practical consequence arising from the fact that the Western democracies obeyed the agreement but the fascist states did not. Foreign Minister Álvarez del Vayo asked Great Britain and France to reconsider the policy. Some British officials conceded the legal case but continued to express fear that the Azaña administration would be replaced by a communist regime. This deep-rooted anticommunism appeared again when Blum wanted to relax the French arms embargo because of Italy's violations of the Non-Intervention Agreement. The British Ambassador to Paris, Sir George Clerk, repeated the warnings concerning Bolshevik influence in the Republic. But while the specter of communism preoccupied the American and British governments, Italian and German troops continued to reinforce Franco's army. Republican protests concerning these violations of the Non-Intervention Agreement received grudging consideration from Avenol as he resisted action by the League that would antagonize Mussolini and Hitler.

Foreign Intervention in the Civil War

In the summer and fall of 1936, Franco's troops advanced northward from Seville, captured Badajoz and Toledo, and prepared for an assault against Madrid. Insurgent troops also gained control of the northwest except for an enclave around Bilbao. However, when Franco's attack against Madrid in November failed after a ten-day battle, the city became a symbol of republican resistance. Germany and Italy had intended to use the fall of the capital as the occasion to announce their recognition of Franco's government, but despite their disappointment, Mussolini and Hitler still established diplomatic relations with it at its temporary seat in Burgos. Both countries also continued to send military aid to the insurgents despite professing observance of the Non-Intervention Agreement. Foreign Minister Galeazzo Ciano assured a British representative of Italy's "one hundred per cent neutrality," while a British War Office report dated November 23, 1936, indicated that Franco had received some 125 to 135 aircraft, about 100 tanks, and an undetermined number of gas cylinders from Italian sources. Mussolini viewed the Civil War as a means of enhancing Italy's military prestige and of gaining political leverage in the western Mediterranean.

The German ambassador to Rome, Ulrich von Hassell, informed his Nazi superiors on December 29, 1936, that 3,000 of Mussolini's Black Shirts and 1,500 technicians had sailed from Italy. Two weeks later, another 4,000 troops left for Spanish service, and before February 1937, over 50,000 men were part of the Corpo Truppi Volontarie, the Italian expeditionary corps technically described as volunteers. To correspondents attending the Nazi Party Congress in Nuremberg in September 1936, Hitler stressed his concern with Bolshevism's expansion to the West and insisted that Germany could not be indifferent to Spain's fate: "We do not live on the moon. What happens in Europe does concern us." Hitler did not deploy as many men as did Mussolini, but he did provide specialists and cadres for training rebels, especially in air, armor, artillery, and communications. Some 6,500 Germans debarked at Cádiz in November 1936, but the total number of Nazi troops posted to Spain during the conflict probably amounted to little more than 10,000. British intelligence estimates in late November 1936 traced 60 aircraft, 4,000 incendiary bombs, and 500,000 rounds of aircraft ammunition to German sources. Joachim von Ribbentrop, who represented Germany on the Non-Intervention Committee, suggested that it should have been renamed the Intervention Committee.

There had been little Soviet reaction when the Civil War had first begun and the prospects of the Republic had appeared good. However, once the evidence of broad Axis aid to Franco had appeared, thousands of "spontaneous" public demonstrations in Soviet factories and on collective farms began making contributions to the loyalists. Like Germany and Italy, the USSR had formally accepted the Non-Intervention Agreement, but it was difficult for the Soviets to stand aside while German and Italian assistance contributed to Franco's victory. Almost 40 Russian ships carried food, clothing, and military supplies to Spain every month from October 1936 to March 1937. In addition, British sources estimated that at least 75 Soviet aircraft, over 100 tanks, and several thousand tons of munitions had reached the Republic by mid-November 1936. In March 1937, the U.S. State Department reported that the Soviet Union had supplied over 400 aircraft, in addition to almost all the tanks and heavy artillery used by the loyalists. There were, however, few Soviet troops in Spain, probably no more than 1,000, and like the Germans, they were essentially specialists and advisers. Attached to the staffs of republican leaders, Soviet generals—under false identities—actively commanded operations, and agents of the NKVD, the Soviet secret police, worked openly for republican victory.

With the war in its fifth month in November 1936, Álvarez del Vayo called for a special session of the League Council to examine the continued aid to Franco by Italy and Germany. He found, however, that neither the French nor British representative wanted the session convoked. France's foreign minister, Yvon Delbos, thought that the division of opinion among the members precluded any League action, and he shared Avenol's concern that it would further strain relations between Italy and the world body. Eden concurred, but he did not think there was any way to prevent the Council from meeting. Avenol suggested some ground rules: Invitations would be issued to Germany, Italy, and Portugal, the parties accused of aiding Franco, with the understanding that the Council would prescind from consideration the question of their possible "aggression" against Spain. Since the Council's objective would be mediation, representatives of the insurgents would also be invited to attend. As in the Ethiopian crisis, the secretary-general wished to avoid any confrontation with Italy, and since he still harbored the illusion of Hitler's return to the League, he did not want to offend Germany.

When the Axis powers recognized Franco on November 18, 1936, Avenol committed himself to a policy of obstructing League aid to the Republic.

On December 4, 1936, Pablo de Azcárate, Spain's ambassador to the Court of St. James, discussed with Eden the possibility of the Council debate producing a resolution supporting the Non-Intervention Agreement. If the Council also provided for supervision, Azcárate said, the Spanish government would consider endorsing it. Eden then raised the issue of what he termed the "so-called volunteers," foreigners entering Spain to serve in the war. Some of these foreigners had been coming as individuals, enlisting in the republican militias or forming units with their own nationals, while others had been coming as part of organized bodies, such as the España Squadron, an international group of pilots. The French Communist Party, with the aid of Italian political refugees, had been organizing some of these volunteers and transporting them from France to Spain, where they were integrated into international brigades. In January 1937, the British Foreign Office listed over 47,000 foreigners as serving under republican command. Some later studies documented more conservative figures—about 15,000 foreign volunteers by February 1937 and 30,000 by the end of that year. Scarce and unreliable records make precision difficult, but the majority of volunteers appear to have been French, with Germans, Italians, Poles, English, Americans, Belgians, and Balkaners represented in substantial strength, that is, contingents of 2,000 to 5,000 men. Supporting Franco's army were some 6,000 Germans and 14,000 Italians, according to British intelligence, but other accounts put the Italian buildup at 50,000 to 70,000. The original Non-Intervention Agreement did not prohibit foreign personnel from volunteering to serve in the war, and Azcárate believed that there should be a distinction made between civilian individuals or groups coming on their own to support the Republic and the organized military units being sent by foreign governments to fight for Franco. He believed,

The Spanish Civil War attracted troops from many nations. Here, an international brigade is welcomed as it marches into a town.

however, that his government would accept a Council decision to ban all foreign personnel.

At the Council meeting on December 11, 1936, Álvarez del Vayo accused the fascist powers of exploiting the Civil War and emphasized the need to make the Non-Intervention Agreement effective. The British parliamentary under-secretary of state for foreign affairs, Lord Cranborne (Robert Cecil), admitted that there was "leakage," but he insisted that corrective steps were underway and that jurisdiction would be expanded to prevent non-Spanish combatants from entering the war. The Council recommended that the members of the League who were also serving on the Non-Intervention Committee should "spare no pains" to make the control "as stringent as possible." Secretary-General Avenol used Álvarez del Vayo's reference to the Non-Intervention Committee to propose that the League transfer primary responsibility for containing the Civil War to the committee. Many of the nations on the Council were also members of the committee and could maintain a liaison between the two bodies. Avenol undoubtedly recognized the advantage to Germany and Italy of having the Non-Intervention Committee handle problems emerging from the Civil War, since they were represented on the committee and the republican government was not. The arrangement was acceptable to the loyalists because in December, the Non-Intervention Committee had announced its intention to police Spanish ports and frontiers in order to prevent violations of the agreement and to halt the flow of volunteers to Spain. The republicans believed that if Franco's foreign support ended, they could crush the rebellion.

The interdiction policy was approved by the Non-Intervention Committee on February 16, 1937, and a naval patrol comprised of units from the British, French, German, Italian, Portuguese, and Russian fleets took stations in designated zones and border guards manned positions along Spain's land frontiers. In Great Britain, Ambassador Azcárate impressed upon Eden his government's desire to see all foreign forces evacuated, a point that was underscored in March 1937, when at least four Italian divisions were identified in action during the battle of Guadalajara. The capture of Italian troops with documents indicating their military units prompted another loyalist appeal to the League to condemn fascist aggression. Foreign Minister Dino Grandi furnished unexpected support to Azcárate's argument when he undiplomatically exclaimed at a meeting of the Non-Intervention Committee that "not one single Italian volunteer will leave Spain until Franco is victorious!" Despite Grandi's blunder, the French foreign minister still tried to discourage Álvarez del Vayo from approaching the League, since the League would not take any effective action. Delbos recommended letting the Non-Intervention Committee continue to deal with the situation. Avenol found Blum and Delbos apprehensive over the Italian role in Spain and fearful for France's strategic position in the Mediterranean. Eden also attempted to dissuade the Spanish foreign minister from invoking the League, which he believed would only create political problems and "poison the atmosphere." Understandably, Álvarez del Vayo was not as averse as were the other men to raising embarrassing issues, and at the end of March, he gave Eden over 100 pages of documentation proving Italian military presence, a flagrant violation of the Council resolution adopted in December 1936.

Frustrated by the continued inactivity of the Non-Intervention

Committee, the Spanish foreign minister brought his charges against the Italian government to the Council on May 28. The ruthless destruction of Guernica by German air attack on April 26 and the bombing of other cities added to the urgency for League action. Delbos and Eden both assured Álvarez del Vayo that the Non-Intervention Committee was studying the air operations, but Maxim Litvinov caustically observed that those opposing League response were entertaining an "ideal of the League [as] a universal mummy." On May 29, the Council passed a unanimous resolution calling for the immediate and complete withdrawal of all non-Spanish forces from the Civil War. It asked the Council members who were also sitting on the Non-Intervention Committee to reinforce the resolution through that body. Eden then proposed consideration of an armistice, which would be needed to facilitate the evacuation of foreign personnel.

While this was under study, the Non-Intervention Committee's naval patrol suffered a loss on May 30, when two unidentified aircraft bombed the *Deutschland*, killing twenty-two members of the crew and wounding twenty. Ribbentrop blamed the attack on "Red bombing aeroplanes of the Valencia authorities" and announced a retaliatory shelling of the Spanish port of Almería, which was carried out by the pocket battleship *Admiral Scheer* and two destroyers. The German government notified the committee that it was withdrawing from the naval observation assignment until guarantees against another such incident could be provided; Italy gave similar notice. France believed that British and French ships should fill the positions in the naval screen previously occupied by German and Italian units to maintain the integrity of the supervision of shipping in Spanish waters. When Rome and Berlin objected, the French Foreign Ministry interpreted the situation as a test of strength, but the British Cabinet refused to be drawn into the trial. Instead, on July 14, Eden submitted a compromise

The Spanish city of Guernica was ruthlessly destroyed on April 26, 1937, by German bombers aiding Franco. This prompted the Council on May 29 to pass a unanimous resolution calling for the immediate and complete withdrawal of all non-Spanish forces from the Civil War.

proposal, which included replacing the existing naval patrol with inspection officers stationed in Spanish ports, resuming suspended border surveillance, recognizing the belligerent status of both sides in the Civil War, and providing for the withdrawal of foreign volunteers. Italy and Russia found portions of the plan objectionable, and the deadlock continued into the summer months. Finally, it was overshadowed by a new naval crisis, which spurred Great Britain and France to launch a multinational patrol in the Mediterranean to protect ships carrying supplies to the Spanish Republic. At the same time, republican officials renewed their requests for support by the League but encountered both resistance from Avenol and divided sentiment among the members.

The Nyon Conference

Unidentified submarines operating throughout the Mediterranean were attacking vessels of the Spanish Republic and also neutral vessels carrying cargoes intended for the loyalists. Although merchant vessels were the usual victims, a British destroyer, H.M.S. *Havock*, narrowly escaped a torpedo attack on August 31, 1937, and countered with depth charges. Italy's Foreign Minister Ciano confided to his diary that the submarine was the *Iride* and that maritime tension was rising. Finally, on September 10, the British and French governments called for a conference of all the Mediterranean powers (Italy, Yugoslavia, Albania, Greece, Turkey, and Egypt), the Black Sea nations (the USSR, Rumania, and Bulgaria), and Germany. To encourage Italian and German attendance, the site selected was the Swiss town of Nyon rather than Geneva, but neither country accepted the invitation. Their absence undoubtedly facilitated progress, since those attending agreed to have the British and French conduct regular patrols along the major trade routes linking the Dardanelles and Suez with Gibraltar. The eastern Mediterranean nations assumed the responsibility for the security of their own territorial waters. Operational orders authorized firing upon any submarine attacking a non-Spanish ship, and a supplemental agreement extended protection against attack by surface vessels and aircraft. Apparently surprised by the militancy of the Nyon Conference powers, Italy belatedly joined, leading Eden to believe that the attacks would cease, since Rome now realized the perils of continuing the underwater piracy.

Appearing before the League on September 16, Spanish Prime Minister Juan Negrín argued that the Nyon Agreement should also protect vessels of Spanish registry and called for the public identification of Italy as the nation responsible for the maritime losses. Avenol prepared a draft resolution; but it was intended to placate Italy and Germany, and Azcárate criticized it as weak. After revision, the Council resolution of October 5 adopted Spain's demand for the protection of its ships by condemning attacks against "any merchant vessels." Negrín also presented the Spanish case to the Assembly, asking that the League acknowledge the aggression of Italy and Germany against Spain; allow his government access to supplies, in conformity with international law; secure the evacuation of foreign personnel from Spain; and permit the Republic to join the Nyon powers in their naval patrols. Álvarez del Vayo reiterated the charges against the Axis states and argued that the Non-Intervention Agreement should be either enforced or abandoned. Eden conceded that it was not perfect but maintained that "a leaky dam may yet serve its purpose." He considered the Nyon Agreement open to any Mediterranean power that wished to participate and reaffirmed his commitment to seeking peaceful solutions through collective action. Litvinov supported Negrín's proposals and complained that some members were treating the League like "a gentle maiden" instead of a vigorous force to repel aggression. Delbos refused to be goaded into strong action and submitted a moderate resolution that expressed regret for the violations of the Non-Intervention Agreement and the delay in evacuating volunteers from Spain. The resolution did conclude with a warning that unless the intent of the committee and the League was fulfilled, "the whole policy of non-intervention would be called into question." Álvarez del Vayo wanted the resolution to contain an explicit reference to the aggression against Spain and to the right of the Republic to secure arms and munitions. Italy's involvement was apparently greater than ever, with its aircraft mounting regular raids against major cities and its army playing an increasing role in Franco's offensives. Units of the Italian surface fleet cruised off the Spanish coast, and unmarked submarines harassed vessels transporting supplies to the Republic. As Eden struggled to preserve the Non-Intervention Agreement, Mussolini publicly asserted that Italian troops were fighting in Spain to save civilization from communism. They already had saved Ethiopia from barbarism.

Avenol and Álvarez del Vayo clashed over the wording of the resolution for the Assembly. After rejecting two weak versions, Álvarez del Vayo finally accepted a compromise draft that admitted the failure of the Non-Intervention Committee to secure the withdrawal of foreign personnel: "There are veritable foreign army corps on Spanish soil which represent foreign intervention in Spanish affairs." If the evacuation of the foreigners was not secured in the near future, the League members who were parties to the Non-Intervention Committee would consider terminating the agreement. Presented to the Assembly on October 2, the resolution failed to receive the necessary unanimity for passage when Albania and Portugal voted against it. Thirty-two states were in favor, but fourteen abstained. The British delegation informed Eden that considerable pressure had been exerted on Albania and Portugal to abstain, but their missions remained immovable.

Eden found himself the target of British critics who attributed the failure of the League's initiative in the Civil War to his interference. Eden reminded the Opposition that the League had shown little inclination to exert leadership in the crisis and twice had referred the handling of it to the Non-Intervention Committee. The vote, with its fourteen abstentions, he said, indicated the sharp division among League members, many of whom favored Franco and would oppose any substantive steps to affect his fortunes or limit the actions of his supporters. Eden and Delbos tried to portray the thirty-two affirmative votes as a show of moral support and requested a meeting with Mussolini to discuss the evacuation of non-Spanish forces from the peninsula. The Italian leader rejected the overture, confident that Eden's hardline policy toward Italy was not shared by British Prime

Minister Neville Chamberlain, who had succeeded Stanley Baldwin on May 28, 1937.

Chamberlain, Mussolini, and Franco's Victory

Shortly after his appointment, Neville Chamberlain had received a letter from Mussolini expressing regret over the strained relations between their two countries and assuring the new prime minister that while he favored Franco, he had no political or territorial interests in Spain. In his response, Chamberlain had referred to the "highest regard" his late brother, Sir Austen Chamberlain, had held for Mussolini and his own "most friendly feelings toward Italy." An entry in Chamberlain's diary recorded that he did not show his letter to Eden because he suspected the foreign secretary "would object to it." Clearly, he was right. In an address on October 15, 1937, Eden insisted that it was necessary to understand the distinction between non-intervention and indifference. Great Britain would avoid interference in the internal resolution of the Civil War, but it would act to protect British interests that could be affected by the conflict. He believed that negotiations with Italy must be conducted on the basis of reciprocity, with the Duce matching any concessions that Chamberlain might offer. Perhaps Mussolini's desire to secure British recognition of Italian sovereignty over Ethiopia would provide an opportunity to request the end of Italy's role in the Spanish Civil War. Chamberlain, however, did not wish to offend Mussolini by insisting on a quid pro quo and informed the Cabinet of his differences with Eden.

Neither Chamberlain's gesture of conciliation nor Avenol's long-standing deference to Mussolini deterred the Duce's dramatic announcement to 100,000 Black Shirts on December 11 that he was abandoning the "tottering temple" of the League, whose earlier sanctions still rankled him as "an opprobrious attempt to throttle the Italian people." Ironically, as Chamberlain moved toward formal recognition of Italy's conquest of Ethiopia, Mussolini complained that no nation had offered, or wished to offer, a "gesture of reparation." But while Chamberlain and Avenol pondered an appropriate act of contrition to earn the Duce's forgiveness, Eden continued to express concern over the record of broken promises by Italy and had his suspicions confirmed when two British ships were sunk in the Mediterranean during February 1938. The Nyon naval patrol was resumed at full strength, and Eden warned Grandi that British destroyers would attack any submarine detected. The display of force apparently impressed the Italian government, and Grandi expressed interest in removing the Spanish "stumbling block" in their relations. Eden intended to move cautiously, but Chamberlain pressed for an early agreement. Eden complained that the prime minister was convinced that he was the "man of destiny" who would preserve European peace.

While the British foreign secretary and prime minister debated policy toward Spain and Italy, Hitler prepared to annex Austria. In a British Cabinet meeting, Eden contended that Mussolini must have approved Hitler's move, but Chamberlain accepted Grandi's word that there had

Lord Halifax (Edward Wood) became the new British foreign secretary on February 20, 1938, after Anthony Eden resigned in protest against Prime Minister Neville Chamberlain's conciliatory policy toward Italy. Two months later, he signed the Anglo-Italian Pact, which recognized Mussolini's defeat of Ethiopia.

been no agreement between Rome and Berlin regarding *Anschluss* ("annexation"). Eden argued that an announcement of the opening of formal negotiations with Mussolini would be interpreted as "another surrender" by England to Italy. Since Chamberlain remained committed to formal talks, Eden submitted his resignation on February 20, 1938. Ciano noted in his diary the "general cheer" in Roman circles at the news of Eden's fall. Two months later, the new foreign secretary, Lord Halifax (Edward Wood), signed the Anglo-Italian Pact, which included recognition of Mussolini's defeat of Ethiopia.

In northern Spain, nationalist troops mounted a major offensive, which broke through to the Mediterranean at Viñaroz in mid-April 1938. The military disaster spurred new attempts by the republicans to secure Council action, and on May 11, Álvarez del Vayo called for an end to the "sham" of non-intervention. However, Lord Halifax and the French foreign minister, Georges Bonnet, refused to abandon the agreement. In the Council vote of May 13, only the USSR voted with Spain; Poland and Rumania joined France and Great Britain in opposition, and eight states abstained. On July 24, the loyalists launched a surprise offensive across the Ebro River, which achieved initial success. They then fought a three-month battle against Franco's counterattacks and gained foreign admiration. In early September, the republican government tried to exploit the situation to gain a compromise peace, but Franco refused to negotiate. European attention was then diverted to the Sudeten crisis and the highly publicized steps that would lead to the Munich Agreement. During that month, however, the loyalists made another attempt to involve the League by requesting that the Assembly supervise the withdrawal of the non-Spanish troops who were serving with the Republic. Negrín hoped that if the League confirmed the evacuation, it would then exert pressure on Franco to allow a similar observer role with respect to the Italian and German forces under his command. Aware of the embarrassment this would create for the nationalists, Avenol joined with Italy's supporters in trying to block the motion. To his disappointment, the Assembly and the Council approved Spain's request. In October 1938, the international brigades were officially disbanded, and the Council created a commission to investigate the status of foreign troops in republican areas. Its report, submitted on January 16, 1939, verified the withdrawal of over 12,500 non-Spanish troops from combat units; 4,600 had already left Spain, and 350 Canadians plus 1,500 "stateless" men were awaiting embarcation. But the League action had no effect on Franco, since he simply denied its accuracy. Equally ineffectual was a British report to the Council on January 20, 1939, which found nationalist bombing "contrary to the conscience of mankind and to the principles of international law." The republican delegate, however, was somewhat more successful in securing League aid for the millions of refugees who crowded the areas still under loyalist control. The British and French governments, the American Red Cross, and some private agencies provided help, as League officials confirmed the ongoing crisis. These token gestures by the world body coincided with Franco's last major offensive. Barcelona fell on January 26, and by February, the nationalists completed the occupation of Catalonia. Madrid was occupied at the end of March, and the last republican armies surrendered on April 1.

In the weeks that followed, Avenol joined several nations in extending formal diplomatic recognition to Franco's government. It was an appropriate climax to the support that he had provided to the nationalist cause by cooperating with the British and French delegates to the League in obstructing the repeated appeals by the Spanish Republic for assistance from the world body. The creation of the Non-Intervention Committee had enabled the secertary-general to shift the responsibility for limiting foreign involvement in the Civil War away from the League. And when Italy and Germany had flagrantly violated the Non-Intervention Agreement, Avenol had weakened the League resolution condemning their actions. It must be conceded, however, that the delegates in Geneva were divided in their sympathies for the nationalists and republicans, and it is uncertain that a more forceful secretary-general could have secured an effective response from the Council and Assembly. Despite his support of Franco, however, Avenol apparently received no gratitude for his service. On May 9, 1939, Franco announced that he was withdrawing Spain from the League, dealing a final humiliation to Avenol's bankrupt Civil War policy of supporting the nationalists and avoiding conflict with Italy and Germany. Now all three nations spurned the world body.

The Spanish Civil War was one of several European political crises that held the world's attention during the 1930s. It had drama, intrigue, and conflict. But those who were not fully absorbed by the European crises could watch another one—the undeclared Sino-Japanese war—inflame the Far East, and again there would be no evidence of effective intervention by the League.

Mr. Matsuoka, chief Japanese delegate to the League, making his last speech before the assembly on February 24, 1933.

The League in Disarray | 5

Humiliated by its failure to defend Ethiopia against Italy and reduced to a nominal role in the Spanish Civil War, the League was disorganized and unprepared to meet the new tests of collective security arising in Asia and Europe. Encouraged by the successful conquest of Manchuria, Japanese expansionists pressed their demands for further territorial concessions from China, which ignited an undeclared war in July 1937. In addition, the following year, Hitler's threat to unleash the German army brought both Austria and the Sudetenland of Czechoslovakia under Nazi control. To the dismay of League supporters, the world body proved to be a hapless spectator as these fateful events carried the post-Versailles world toward its end.

The Undeclared Sino-Japanese War

After creating the puppet state of Manchukuo in 1932, Japanese expansionists gradually pushed into Inner Mongolia and also crossed the Great Wall into northern China. Although the Tangku Truce of May 1933 created a demilitarized zone between Manchukuo and China, Tokyo nevertheless encouraged the five northern provinces of China to secede from their motherland. By 1936, the ultranationalism of the Japanese military was being reinforced by the chauvinism of civilian leaders like Prime Minister Koki Hirota, who sought substantial concessions in northern China. Chiang Kai-shek desperately tried to consolidate his political control but encountered continued resistance from Mao Tse-tung and the communists, who were firmly established in the provinces of Shansi and Shensi, where their economic reforms had peasant support. Mao's armies were conducting guerilla warfare against their numerically superior opponents while at the same time denouncing Chiang's efforts, turning brother against brother instead of uniting all Chinese against the Japanese. The appeal touched some of Chiang's own subordinates, who took him prisoner in Sian in December 1936 and demanded that he stop fighting the communists. With this forced resolution of the civil war, there came a new determination among the people to "fight Japan to save China."

China and the League

After Chinese and Japanese troops clashed at the Marco Polo Bridge, west of Peiping, on July 7, 1937, all attempts to bring about a cease-fire failed. By the end of July, heavy fighting had engulfed the north, and it spread to

Shanghai the following month. China appealed for League assistance on September 12, and three days later, the British consul in Geneva, C. A. Edmond, met with Secretary-General Avenol, French Foreign Minister Delbos, and Wellington Koo, the Chinese delegate to the League. Edmond's objectives, shared by Delbos and Avenol, were to dissuade China from seeking sanctions against Japan and to have the Marco Polo Bridge incident referred to the Advisory Committee on the Sino-Japanese Dispute, a body orginally set up in February 1933 in the wake of the Manchurian crisis. One reason for transferring the matter to the Advisory Committee was that the United States belonged to the group, which might provide a convenient way to enlist American cooperation with the League. Koo was also advised that strong League action might goad Japan into a formal declaration of war, which would force President Roosevelt to apply American neutrality legislation and suspend arms shipments to both belligerents. This would have an especially adverse effect on China, Koo was told. Koo argued that the United States was already curtailing the use of American vessels in the arms trade and that China considered it more important to secure League condemnation of Japan's aggression. The conference, however, apparently convinced the Chinese delegate of what Edmond described as the "manifest limitations" of the League, and Koo finally agreed to submit the issue to the advisory body. Edmond discovered, however, that Koo was not about to sign a blank check. Koo expected the Advisory Committee to acknowledge Japan's aggression, embargo military supplies and terminate credits for Japan, prohibit the importation of Japanese goods, and arrange economic aid to enable China to purchase arms and munitions. Delbos was disturbed by the scope of China's demands but estimated that it was probably expecting about one-fifth of what it was requesting. He recommended that arms shipments to China be allowed to continue and that Great Britain and France review the granting of loans to Japan.

Prior to the public meeting of the Advisory Committee on September 27, 1937, there was a private session in Avenol's quarters attended by the British, Chinese, and French representatives. Koo intended to pursue the several objectives he had outlined on September 15, until Delbos indicated that some of the requests would require the imposition of sanctions. Lord Cranborne pointedly reminded Koo of the lessons of Ethiopia. Unless the members were prepared "to go to all lengths," economic sanctions were ineffective, he said, and the British Foreign Office did not believe that the members would support the Chinese proposals. With respect to Koo's assertion that world opinion expected some positive action by the League, the British representative insisted that the more promising alternative was to submit the issue to a conference of Pacific powers that could "help her [China] quietly." In the interim, he said, condemnation of the bombing of civilian areas and increased medical assistance seemed possible. When the British and French insisted on the need for American cooperation, Koo objected to any attempt to link the League's decisions to the policy of the United States. The Chinese were dismayed to learn that Washington's collaboration was "absolutely essential" and that the Advisory Committee would do nothing without prior American commitment. Cranborne made it quite clear that he did not expect the League to take "any immediate action," although Delbos said he was willing to support condemnation of air attacks.

Avenol then proposed that the Advisory Committee be allowed to proceed without any specific instructions.

Appearing before the League on September 27, Koo reluctantly conformed to the guidelines set by Avenol, Cranborne, and Delbos. He did not request sanctions and confined himself to asking for a discussion of air bombardment. Cranborne then moved that general discussion of the Far East crisis be delayed and that only the bombing issue be reviewed. China wanted the attacking aircraft identified in the resolution as Japanese and had to overcome British opposition before this specification was inserted. The Assembly unanimously adopted the resolution in this form on September 28, and the Chinese delegation interpreted the vote as indicative of likely support for a stronger resolution. Koo subsequently called for the recognition of Japanese aggression and the application of Article 10. Once again Cranborne tried to discourage him from submitting an intemperate resolution, since only the smaller nations without Far Eastern interests would support it. His superiors instructed him to have Koo's statement "toned down" in order to avoid adding complications in the Far East to Britain's other international problems. The Admiralty added its own objections to involvement in Asia unless a firm commitment could be obtained from the United States for joint military cooperation. However, when Eden explored the possibility of American collaboration "in some form of economic boycott" against Japan, the prime minister altered the conclusion of his message to Secretary of State Hull to suggest that the British government doubted whether such a policy could succeed. Washington quickly used the opportunity to reject the probe.

On October 1, the Advisory Committee appointed a subcommittee—composed of Australia, Belgium, Ecuador, France, Latvia, the Netherlands, New Zealand, Poland, the Soviet Union, Sweden, and the United Kingdom—to hear Koo's resolution on Japanese aggression. The United States participated only as an observer and watched Cranborne succeed both in deleting the word "aggression" from the resolution and in modifying the other Chinese proposals that necessitated collective League support for China. The British delegate was also successful in deleting Koo's motion that the League bar aid to Japan, as well as in weakening the recommendation for assistance to China. In the final resolution, members were simply asked to avoid actions that might injure China's resistance and to consider aid to that country on an individual basis.

More importantly, Britain also succeeded, by October 6, in shifting the debate from the League to the nations associated with the Nine Power Treaty of 1922. This accord, accepted by Japan and other powers at the 1921–1922 Washington Conference on the Limitation of Armaments, pledged the signatories to respect the territorial and administrative integrity of China. Koo resisted this abdication of responsibility by the League, but the representatives from Belgium, the Netherlands, and Sweden advised him that the League could not provide him with any real assistance. On the other hand, Japan and Italy also were signatories to the Nine Power Treaty, which could provide a forum for their participation in discussions of the situation. Equally significant was the fact that the United States was a party to the convention.

The United States and the Brussels Conference

From the beginning of the crisis, the League had hoped to enlist American participation, and Secretary of State Hull issued statements that suggested closer ties with the world body. Much more impressive was President Roosevelt's "Quarantine the Aggressors" address of October 5, 1937, which coincided with Avenol's invitation to the signatories of the Nine Power Treaty to meet in Brussels in November. Roosevelt asserted that:

> The peace-loving nations must make a concerted effort to uphold laws and principles on which alone peace can be secure. . . . There is no escape through mere isolation or neutrality . . . [and] the epidemic of world lawlessness is spreading. When an epidemic of physical disease starts to spread, the community approves and joins in a quarantine of the patients in order to protect the health of the community.

The optimistic interpretation of the speech was that the United States intended to take some action supportive of China and the League; but the British prime minister feared that the speech might be no more than "ballyhoo," and the Foreign Office described it as "a new 'Sermon on the Mount'—Mount Blank." The other concern, expressed by Eden, was that the president might be mistakenly assuming that the Japanese government would peacefully submit to economic sanctions. Under-Secretary of State Sumner Welles quickly denied that the United States had any intention of translating "quarantine" into an active policy, and the American ambassador to the Court of St. James, Robert W. Bingham, confirmed this on the eve of the Brussels Conference.

The Brussels Conference opened on November 3, 1937, but Japan refused to attend. The eight remaining powers discussed possible actions, and the American delegate, Norman Davis, spoke at various times of embargo, nonrecognition, and boycott. Eden impressed upon Davis that effective sanctions carried out by the League involved the risk of war and thus Great Britain and France had to have the guarantee of American support. Conflict with Japan, he said, would require the deployment of French and British military forces from Europe and the Mediterranean, which might tempt Hitler and Mussolini to commit new aggressions. In addition, Japanese retaliation would expose the imperial possessions in Asia to attack. Hostage to these considerations, the League members looked to the United States, but the discussions proved meaningless. On November 13, Welles described Davis's proposals as exploratory and indicated that the administration would not ask Congress for legislation authorizing sanctions. The conference then concluded on November 24 with an innocuous report that called for an end to the fighting and for the use of "peaceful processes."

The American government demonstrated its unwillingness to take strong action when, on December 12, 1937, Japanese aircraft sank the U.S.S. *Panay*, a clearly identified American gunboat assigned to the Yangtze River patrol. The British were suffering similar attacks and invited Washington to develop a joint policy of protest. Hull, however, was apprehensive of isolationist reaction to any indication of Anglo-American cooperation and dispatched the American note separately. Japan moved quickly to reduce the tension, and Ambassador Hiroshi Saito expressed "deep regrets" for "a completely accidental and great mistake." Roosevelt told British Ambassador Sir Ronald Lindsay that he was considering a joint naval blockade of Japan if the incidents continued. Lindsay described this as one of Roosevelt's "worst 'inspirational' moods" but said that his "horrified criticism" had no effect on the president, who refused to concede that a blockade was an act of war. On a more practical level, Roosevelt suggested conversations between naval personnel of both nations to organize future cooperation. Captain R. E. Ingersoll arrived in London on New Year's Day 1938 to inaugurate an exchange of information on subjects that included Pacific war plans, fleet dispositions and tactics, and codes and signals. These peripheral developments brought no relief to suffering China, and Koo looked in vain for an effective response from the League.

An End to Collective Security

By the end of 1937, Japanese troops were occupying north and central China in the still undeclared war. The fall of Nanking in December 1937 made the nationalist capital the unfortunate symbol of Japanese brutality, as its inhabitants suffered murder, rape, and robbery for several weeks at the hands of rampaging troops. *Time* accused the Japanese of committing "modern history's greatest mass rape" and estimated that 20,000 Chinese prisoners of war and civilians had so far been killed. Chiang Kai-shek moved his government to Hankow while his soldiers fought delaying actions, and the people adopted a scorched-earth policy to deprive the invaders of supplies.

Japanese troops celebrate with a cheer of "*banzai!*" after capturing the gate to Nanking on December 13, 1937. *Time* magazine accused the Japanese of committing "modern history's greatest mass rape," estimating that 20,000 Chinese prisoners of war and civilians had so far been killed.

A Chinese victim cries amid the ruins of her house. She lost her husband and children when the Japanese bombed Chengtu in 1939.

Against this background, Koo met with Eden, Cranborne, Delbos, and Litvinov at the end of January 1938 to beg for League action. Delbos and Eden continued to assert that the United States was the key to sanctions, and Koo protested the vicious circle—the League would not act without the United States, and the American government would not move until the League did something. Koo insisted that the time had come for the League to take the decisive step and depend upon the United States to follow. If the full League would not do anything, he said, perhaps a group of interested members could be formed to consider practical ways of helping China. The British and French were unhappy with this suggestion but preferred it to Koo's more extensive demands. In its final form, the League resolution called attention to the Assembly's expression of moral support for China, made on October 6, 1937, and its recommendation that members consider on an individual basis how they might help. The new resolution also asked member states to give the previous agreement their "most serious attention" and to consult among themselves and with other interested parties on "the feasibility of any further steps" to achieve a just peace in the Far East. Addressing the Council on February 2, Koo expressed disappointment with the League's failure to respond to Japan's second aggression against China. Although he accepted the current resolution, he considered it inadequate and reserved the right to a future appeal.

Koo's concern was well founded, as his efforts to secure independent aid from Great Britain demonstrated. An interdepartmental committee reviewed his request for munitions, military transport, loans, and credits for China and an embargo on arms sales, loans, and credits for Japan. The only items that received favorable consideration were the supply of a limited number of weapons and some ammunition to China and the discouraging of new loans to Japan. The arms release was not implemented, and the committee never again met as a whole.

The British pattern was typical because, on May 10, Koo complained to the Council that its resolution was being ignored. His reward was another resolution, expressing sympathy for China and confirmation of the earlier motions. Koo made his fourth bid to the Council in the autumn of 1938 while the Japanese were threatening Hankow. He reminded the members that it was now fourteen months since his first appeal for help and little had been done to deter Japan. "The people of China," he declared, "cannot understand why . . . the League of Nations has taken no effective steps to discourage the invaders by proclaiming against them an embargo of arms, aeroplanes, financial credits, and the essential materials for their war effort." Admonishing those nations that chose neutrality, Koo maintained that "China has a right to ask for everything that can be done collectively by the League as an entity." His persistence yielded minor results. On September 30, the Council authorized its members "to adopt individually the measures provided for in Article 16" but expressly stated that collective action would not be taken. Japan immediately warned that any nation employing sanctions would face reprisals. It also announced its resignation from the League's social and technical groups in which it had continued to participate, charging them with "slandering at every turn" Japanese policy in China.

Avenol must have felt misgivings as this final tenuous link between the League and Japan was severed and Japan denounced the Council's report as proof of the "irreconcilability between the positions of Japan and the League." There was little prospect of intervention by League members in the Far East, for while deploring the suffering of the Chinese people, the Council referred in its report to the "grave international tension" in Europe. Earlier in the year, the League had watched silently while Germany had absorbed Austria, and the fate of Czechoslovakia found the world body continuing its ostrich-like policy. "Never yet," Álvarez del Vayo told the delegates, "has the League of Nations held its meetings in so painful an atmosphere of indecision and impotence. While the god of war is knocking brutally at the very door of this hall, we are being invited to become mere spectators. . . ."

Austria and Czechoslovakia

Japan's alienation was the second blow during 1938 to Avenol's policy of reconciling former members with the League. On February 20, Hitler had shattered the prospects for Germany's reunion with the world body when he told the Reichstag that "Germany has not the slightest intention of ever returning to the League, especially now that Italy has left it." He attacked the world body as an instrument created to preserve the "insane and unreasonable" terms of the Treaty of Versailles. Its history, he said, also revealed a failure to face the realities of political changes from Manchuria to Ethiopia, behavior that resembled a "well-known large bird," rather than a responsible organization. Hitler's disdain for the League was not surprising, but it was followed by an attack from an unexpected quarter when British Prime Minister Chamberlain expressed his own reservations concerning the world body's ability to safeguard the existence of its smaller member states. The pronouncement could only have encouraged Hitler as he prepared to move against Austria and Czechoslovakia.

Anschluss With Austria

On the same day that Hitler described the League as a political ostrich, Eden resigned as British foreign secretary in protest against Chamberlain's policies. League advocates expected some weakening of the British support for the world body as a consequence, but they failed to anticipate the extent of the retreat. Brushing Eden's opposition aside, the prime minister told the House of Commons on February 22, 1938, "We must not try to delude small weak nations into thinking that they will be protected by the League against aggression and acting accordingly, when we know that nothing of the kind can be expected." Shortly afterward, Chamberlain confessed that his faith in the "mutilated, halt and maimed" world body had been "profoundly shaken" by the events of the past few years. He probably had also expressed these views to Avenol during the secretary-general's visit to London earlier in January. Avenol himself favored limiting the members' responsibility to impose sanctions by excusing those nations whose interests were not affected by the particular crisis under consideration. He appeared to be encouraging regional pacts under the League umbrella, rather than general responsibility for collective security. Chamberlain observed that this would revive the old alliance system with its dependence on military power, which the League had been intended to replace.

Given Great Britain's lack of confidence, a feeling that was shared by other nations, it was not surprising that the League did nothing when Hitler announced Austria's unification with Germany on March 12. Two years earlier, on July 11, 1936, Hitler had pledged in a treaty to respect Austrian sovereignty and Austria had affirmed its character as a "German state." A secret clause had required the release of Nazi political prisoners held by Vienna and the appointment of some Austrian Nazis to public office. Ignoring this treaty now, Berlin encouraged public disturbances and terrorist activity by Austrian Nazis to undermine the authority of Chancellor Kurt von Schuschnigg. On February 12, hoping to resolve the situation, Schuschnigg met with Hitler at Berchtesgaden, only to find himself presented with an ultimatum. Threatened with military invasion by Hitler, Schuschnigg capitulated. Back in Vienna, however, he and other officials decided to resist and scheduled a plebiscite on the Anschluss for March 13. Infuriated by the chancellor's decision and facing possible defeat at the polls, Hitler ordered his army to prepare to invade Austria. Rather than risk the loss of life that resistance would exact, Schuschnigg cancelled the plebiscite on March 11. German troops crossed the frontier unopposed, and Hitler soon conducted his own plebiscite, reporting that 99.7 percent of Austrian voters favored union with Germany.

Unlike the coup attempt in 1934, this coup saw no Italian troops deployed on the Austrian border, and Schuschnigg's call to Mussolini went unanswered. A grateful Hitler received the Duce's acceptance of Anschluss and assured his ally, "I shall never forget this." France, in the midst of a Cabinet crisis, was without a government until the union was a *fait accompli.* Chamberlain registered a formal protest, but the German Foreign Office denied that Great Britain had any right to intervene, since it was a matter of domestic concern between Berlin and Vienna. With respect to the League, British Foreign Secretary Lord Halifax cautioned against the adoption of ineffective resolutions that could only add to its humiliation, and Chamberlain claimed that even the Opposition in Parliament realized there was no collective security to save smaller nations such as Austria. Chamberlain denied that he was disloyal to the League. "True disloyalty," he asserted, "lies in pretending that the League today is capable of functions which are clearly beyond its power."

Schuschnigg made no appeal to London, Paris, or Geneva, and Austria disappeared as a separate, independent nation without a word of protest from any of its sister states or the secretary-general. Many nations felt little sympathy for Vienna because of its alignment with Italy during previous crises, but the League's weakness was once again graphically demonstrated. Avenol's critics noted that the secretary-general spent his time working in the gardens of the Palais des Nations while the German army marched into Austria.

The image of Avenol tending the palace gardens was shocking and scandalous to League supporters. It was true, nonetheless, that one of the secretary-general's responsibilities since 1933 had been the overseeing of the construction and furnishing of the League's new home, the Palais des Nations. Avenol brought a personal interest in design and decoration to the project, and the garden incident may have been part of his ongoing concern with the palace and grounds, rather than a deliberate slighting of Austria's plight. (For a discussion on the League's new home, see "The Palais des Nations," page 76.)

As Hitler's central European policy unfolded, France and Great Britain again sought Mussolini's help in forming a common front against Germany, just as they had at the Stresa Conference in April 1935. On April 16, 1938, Chamberlain and Lord Halifax completed the Anglo-Italian Pact, which permitted Italy to retain troops in Spain until the civil war there was over and committed Great Britain to recognizing Italian sovereignty over Ethiopia. Avenol did not believe these concessions could split the Rome-Berlin Axis, and the following month, Hitler's visit to Rome produced a week of military demonstrations and cultural events, which served as a background for mutual affirmations of Italo-German unity. In fact, Mussolini boasted that their two nations had "left behind them the Utopias to which Europe had blindly committed her destinies."

Nonetheless, the secretary-general encouraged British efforts to win Italy's favor, and he consulted with London on implementing League consideration of the Ethiopian question. Avenol devised the formula by which Lord Halifax offered a "declaration" to the Council, rather than a resolution that would require a vote. The foreign secretary noted that five members of the Council—Belgium, Ecuador, Latvia, Poland, and Rumania—acknowledged Italian sovereignty over Ethiopia, while other nations did not. Since Avenol had recommended that each member should be free to decide the recognition issue independently, he must have enjoyed some perverse satisfaction in seeing Great Britain finally accept his position on Ethiopia and court

The Palais des Nations

Although news of the affairs of state usually dominated the press coverage of the League, there were periodic references to the planning and construction of a new residence for the world body. During the 1920s, the League used the Hôtel National, located on the shore of Lake Leman, to accommodate the Secretariat, the Council, and the library. Since there was no room for the Assembly in the hotel, Assembly meetings were held in the Salle de la Reformation, which was located on the other side of the lake. To end this awkward separation, the delegates decided, in 1924, to erect a hall for the Assembly on property adjacent to the Hôtel National.

The Assembly invited architects to submit plans for the new building and appointed an international jury to select the best design. However, the immediate reaction of the jurists was that the plot for the intended hall was too small, so the League purchased sixteen acres of land, with frontage on Lake Leman, to house all of its divisions. Architects were again invited to submit designs for the new edifice, and an unexpected 377 plans were entered in the competition. Unfortunately, the jurors found it difficult to select a single winner, and instead, they resorted to naming nine first-place, nine second-place, and nine third-place winners. To resolve this impasse, a committee of five League delegates chose a basic design from the twenty-seven winning plans and entrusted Henri Nenot of Paris, Julien Flegenheimer of Geneva, Camille Lefevre of Paris, Giuseppe Vago of Rome, and Carlo Broggi of Rome with the responsibility of developing a master plan.

A further complication arose when John D. Rockefeller, Jr., offered $1 million for the construction of a League library. The five architects soon concluded that the sixteen-acre site would be inadequate for the palace that they were now envisaging.

In 1928, Geneva's local government provided a solution by offering to exchange its sixty-two-acre Ariana Park for the smaller League property. Within this spacious park, the architects planned a complex shaped like a horseshoe that would have a 1,200-foot-long center section that would house the Assembly, with a 250-foot-long right wing for the Council chamber and Secretariat, and a comparable left wing for the library.

Among the impressive ceremonies marking the tenth anniversary of the Assembly in September 1929, the then secretary-general, Sir Eric Drummond, welcomed the representatives of fifty-three nations to the laying of the cornerstone of "their house of peace and international collaboration." The president of the Council, Prince Mohammed Ali Khan Foroughi of Persia, linked the historic monuments of the Near East and the common heritage that they inspired as "the cradle of civilization" with the new palace that was to be "the common property of peoples [of all nations] united in the same sentiments."

Four years later, the final stone was put in place, and it was now Secretary-General Joseph Avenol who presided over the convocation as workers "put the bouquet" on the roof, the traditional conclusion of the rough exterior construction. Given the size of the palace, the usual bundle of evergreen boughs was replaced with a large fir tree. A nearby crane was decorated with the flags of fifty-seven nations, including the flag of the United States in recognition of the Rockefeller gift. The Japanese and German colors were also displayed, a probable sign of Avenol's commitment to securing their return to the League.

The sanctions against Italy during the Ethiopian crisis interrupted the supply of marble for the interior, but by early 1936, the work was nearing completion. Journalists such as Clarence R. Streit of *The New York Times* were impressed. "It stands today," he wrote on February 23, 1936, "the greatest edifice perhaps, that has been built anywhere on earth during the Depression, and [is] certainly one of the greatest monumental buildings of all time." The completed structure conformed generally to the earlier horseshoe design, facing Lake Leman, with Mont Blanc visible in the distance. The façade of the white marble palace was only a few yards shorter than the Palace of Versailles and housed the Assembly hall. The Council chamber was located at the corner where the Secretariat wing began. In the opposite arm was the library, described as "the most modern on earth" and designed to hold 2 million volumes.

Some commentators and illustrators expressed their reservations. One suggested that the white marble structure might become a mausoleum rather than a home for the League. Another portrayed the palace with a foreground of antiaircraft weapons casting ominous shadows across the stark white façade. The caption, "Shadows of War Over the League Building," was an appropriate lead-in to the feature article by Clarence R. Streit, "For the League: Life or Death," in *The New York Times Magazine*, December 6, 1936. The Spanish Civil War was putting the League to another test, but Streit remained hopeful that France and Great Britain, assisted by the United States, could rally the democracies in support of the League.

And there was no sense of foreboding among Avenol's 1,400 guests, who had celebrated the opening of the Council chamber two months earlier. The problems of Spain and Ethiopia were set aside as officials, guests, and members of the press admired the splendid tan marble walls and grey ceiling, or looked through the huge windows at placid Lake Leman. Even more striking were the enormous murals, a gift commissioned by the Spanish Republic in happier times. The work had been entrusted to José María Sert y Badia, a native of Barcelona and a member of the Catalan avant-garde. After studying the Renaissance masters in Italy, he had devoted his career to murals and decorative art, gaining international recognition for his modern baroque style.

On the wall that the members of the Council would face from their seats, Sert developed the theme of peace, not as the customary angel or white-gowned woman but as five men, representing the continents, slinging a bow in a common effort to show the power of unity. The artist depicted, on the right-hand wall, the age-old struggle by the masses for human liberty and economic freedom. On the opposite wall, he portrayed both the achievements of man and the goals yet to be reached, especially the end of warfare. In the ceiling mural, the courtyard of the College of Salamanca recalled the sixteenth-century jurists who had attempted to substitute the rule of law for the violence of war. Five giants clasped hands across the courtyard, again conveying the unity of the continents. The Spanish delegate, Angel Ossorio y Gallardo, judged Sert's work to be "striking proof" of Spain's enduring creative genius. The president of the Council, Manuel Rivas Vicuna of Chile, described the murals as "the greatest wonder of our new building" and an expression of the artist's faith that man could overcome even war.

The artist's faith was challenged, however, by the civil war in his own country. The opening celebration was interrupted by the Spanish government's distribution of charges concerning Italian, German, and Portuguese aid to Franco in violation of the Non-Intervention Agreement. Franco's supporters circulated countercharges relating to the atrocities committed in Madrid by the Republic. And when the Council members took their seats for the first time, one chair was conspicuously empty—the Italian delegate was boycotting the session in retaliation for Ethiopia's continuing presence and recognition as a League member.

The following year, on September 25, 1937, the Assembly celebrated the opening of its new hall with a lavish reception for 2,800 guests, hosted by its president, the Aga Khan III of India, one of the richest men in the world. Square in design, the hall had a capacity of 3,000. The interior color scheme was predominantly tan and deep blue, with the walls crowned by a ceiling featuring a large golden skylight. One journalist acknowledged Avenol's contribution to "the remarkable exposition of modern interior decoration and color harmonies," noting that the secretary-general had a "hobbyist's interest" in the field. The first of two balconies was reserved for the press, and the second, for the public. On the roof, visitors could enjoy the services of a restaurant and an open-air café with breathtaking views of Lake Leman and Mont Blanc.

A jarring note of reality was rung in the midst of these sumptuous surroundings when one critic took note of the early departure of the Chinese representative from the gala party. "How heartless," the journalist commented, "to have music and dancing at a dedication while women and children were being slaughtered at Nanking and other Chinese cities by Japanese aerial bombardment." In an earlier piece for *The New York Times*, Frederick T. Birchall had concluded on a pessimistic note:

If the completion [of the palace] should mark a climax in a disintegration [of the League] that would leave only a name and a memory, we would be close to a world calamity. . . . And the greatest danger of its happening is that nowhere is the imminence of that danger less realized than in Geneva itself.

As Birchall feared, the speeches of the delegates continued to fill the League's chambers, but just as Chancellor Otto von Bismarck had mocked the nineteenth-century German Reichstag as a *schwatzbude* ("talk shop"), so, too, would the Axis leaders contemptuously dismiss the debates in the Palais des Nations.

The Council meets in its new home on January 28, 1938.

Italian support. The Anglo-Italian agreement encouraged Chamberlain to enlist Mussolini's assistance in convening a conference to resolve the clash between Germany and Czechoslovakia over the Sudetenland. There was also a surprising, if fruitless, proposal from Avenol concerning a League initiative in the issue.

The Sudeten Crisis

The September 1938 meeting of the Assembly coincided with the Czechoslovakian crisis. In an unusual departure from his previous willingness to accept a passive role for the League in political affairs, Avenol informed French Foreign Minister Georges Bonnet that the world body could exercise effective power if France and Great Britain would support it. Having weakened the principle of collective security with his earlier policies, including the emasculation of Article 16, he now insisted that "contemporary international life [was] essentially collective." Although the Czech question was not on the agenda of the Assembly, Avenol sought an expression of opinion by that body, which he believed could have an influence. Avenol's point had merit, but it assumed that the Assembly could provide a decisive expression of opinion by an overwhelming majority of its fifty delegations. Avenol himself admitted that the League was divided between those who feared the Axis and those who hoped for renewed leadership by France and Great Britain. Unfortunately, the upcoming conference at Munich would demonstrate the futility of the latter.

To discourage possible intervention by the Prague government during the Austrian Anschluss, Hitler had assured its minister to Berlin, Vojtech Mastny, that Germany was no threat to the independence of Czechoslovakia. As usually happened, however, such assurances signalled renewed tensions. In the case of Czechoslovakia, it involved agitation by the Sudeten Germans against their alleged Czech oppressors and a torrent of propaganda calling for the recovery of the *irredenta* that was directed at German and foreign audiences. Hitler portrayed the over 3 million Germans incorporated in the Czech state as historic victims of World War I peacemaking; in increasingly strident speeches, he demanded their reunion with the fatherland. The 1.5 million Nazis attending the Party Conference in Nuremberg in September heard Hitler warn that "the talks and half-promises of Beneš cannot go on any longer. The Sudeten Germans are neither defenseless nor deserted." Behind the street violence and propaganda attacks in the Sudetenland were military preparations for an invasion of Czechoslovakia scheduled for October 1. But, unlike Austria, Czechoslovakia enjoyed a strong defensive position, with a miniature Maginot Line along the German frontier, a well-trained army, and an excellent munitions industry. Moreover, Czechoslovakia had alliances with both France and the Soviet Union, and expected that Great Britain would provide aid if war came.

As the tension mounted, Chamberlain offered to consult with Hitler, and in Berchtesgaden on September 15, the prime minister agreed to the cession of the Sudetenland to Germany. France also accepted this plan, and when the Czechs objected to the terms being imposed on them, Paris and London warned that no aid would be provided in the event of war. The Czech government finally bowed to the pressure on September 21, but when

Chamberlain presented Hitler with the fruits of his negotiations, he was shocked to learn that the Fuehrer no longer considered the concession satisfactory. Now Hitler wanted an immediate occupation of the Sudetenland. On September 22, the Czech government mobilized and appealed to France to honor its treaty. Paris informed London that it intended to aid Czechoslovakia and asked for Great Britain's position. Facing revolt within the Cabinet over further yielding to Germany, Chamberlain reluctantly pledged support to France.

In the midst of mobilization, Hitler, Chamberlain, Mussolini, and French Premier Édouard Daladier met in Munich from September 29 to 30. The terms discussed at the conference were drafted by the German Foreign Office but were presented by the Italian government. Czech officials were not allowed to participate and only learned of the outcome afterward. When they protested, a British representative advised them that if they rejected the settlement, they would have to face Germany alone. After the conference, Chamberlain met privately with Hitler, and the Fuehrer signed a note expressing "the desire of our two peoples never to go to war with one another again." Waving the paper to the cheering London crowds, the prime minister assured them of "peace with honor" and "peace in our time." The House of Commons registered its approval with a 366 to 144 vote, but a brooding Winston Churchill contended in Parliament that "we have sustained a total and unmitigated defeat."

Avenol was among those who praised Chamberlain and Daladier for their work in Munich, just as he supported the policy of Great Britain and France toward the undeclared war in Asia. Regarding Asia, the secretary-general resisted China's repeated petitions for League condemnation of Japan. China received token expressions of moral support, but League members generally ignored the Council's invitation that they consider, on an individual basis, the extension of aid to China. Avenol's circumspect guidance of the world body failed to mollify Japan, and Tokyo finally abandoned its last ties to the League.

During the weeks of the European crisis, the secretary-general insisted that his Council members, especially the smaller European states, also would avoid involvement in the Sudetenland controversy. The Assembly, whose opinion he had recently contended could be influential, listened to Litvinov defend Czechoslovakia's right to determine its own fate, but the delegates actually did nothing in the end to prevent the loss of the Sudetenland. Apparently convinced that the political developments of the time were beyond League control, Avenol now intended to revive the League—as he told the Argentine delegate Carlos Pardo—by suspending its political activities and concentrating instead on the social and economic services that it could offer.

British Prime Minister Neville Chamberlain, who has just arrived home from Munich, waves a note signed by Hitler expressing "the desire of our two peoples never to go to war with one another again."

The League: "And to think that I once posed for that!"

1939 political commentary cartoon.

Economic and Social Institutions | 6

At the opening session of the Council in September 1937, Spain's prime minister, Juan Negrín, and Chile's representative, Augustin Edwards, contrasted the intensity of the League's technical activities with the sterility of its political achievements. They echoed Avenol's hope that manifest success in the service areas would encourage continued support by the present members and the return of former associates. In a decade suffering from the Depression, the League tried to assist in the revival of international trade. It sought to improve the well-being of people by encouraging governments to participate in programs sponsored by the League in such fields as nutrition, housing, public health, and rural life. These activities complemented the goal of the League's sister association, the International Labour Organisation (ILO), to improve the condition of the working class. Other League committees dealt with subjects ranging from academic cooperation among international scholars to the suppression of the illicit traffic in drugs. Of special importance during the 1930s was the expansion of League services for the victims of racial and religious persecution, especially by Nazi Germany. In these economic and social endeavors, the League frequently encountered the same obstacle—national self-interest—that obstructed its efforts in the political realm.

The League and the World Economy

Although conceding that the political atmosphere made collective economic action difficult, officials of the Economic Committee insisted that their studies of trends in international commerce and trade were a unique resource for those overseeing the planning of national policy. They emphasized the mutual responsibility of nations to restore the global economy to health and reiterated the secretary-general's warning to countries that believed they could alleviate domestic problems by barring foreign commodities from their markets. Bans against importing goods impeded recovery from the Depression, they said, and had to be replaced by a "really enlightened self-interest" that recognized the reciprocal nature of international trade. Acknowledging the difficulty of securing ratification of broad international agreements after the collapse of the London Economic Conference of 1933, the Economic Committee drafted "model rules" to serve as guidelines for nations that were negotiating commercial treaties. These regulations offered the contracting parties the experience of the League in handling such subjects as customs, bills of exchange, and commercial arbitration.

With this tactical change concerning treaty negotiations also came a broader concern for the consequences of economic agreements. "International trade should not be regarded as an end in itself," said one official, "but rather as a means towards enabling the citizens of each country to attain a standard of living higher than they could reach by relying on their own resources." A committee report underscored the point: "It is not enough to consider commercial policy as a problem of inter-State negotiations. The aim of all commercial policy and of all international economic relations should be to create conditions as favourable as possible to the life of man." The League's humanitarian efforts to improve standards of living could also have a political impact. Australian delegate Stanley Bruce pointed out that when governments tried to liberalize trade policy, they frequently faced not only opposition from vested interests that would be adversely affected but also the indifference of a general public for whom the tedious and technical negotiations were of slight interest. However, if the discussions could be shown to be important for the welfare of the individual citizen, then popular support for governmental policy would be generated. Bruce spoke from a background in social welfare. His commitment to social welfare had begun in 1935, when he had proposed a broad-based study of nutrition by several agencies of the League. A two-year investigation resulted in a report, *On the Relation of Nutrition to Health, Agriculture and Economic Policy*, which appeared in the summer of 1937 and became the leading publication of the League. This pioneer work discussed the causes of malnutrition and provided dietary lists for different age and occupational groups. It described the correlation between poverty and poor health, and suggested steps that governments could take to improve the nutrition of their people. The producers of the report encouraged the creation of comparable committees within individual countries that would work to implement the League's findings; thirty such national committees were organized within four years.

Sharing the interests of the Economic Committee was the International Labour Organisation. In January 1919, the Paris Peace Conference had appointed a commission to study the conditions of labor and to design a permanent agency whose purpose would be to seek international cooperation in addressing the problems of the working class. Under the chairmanship of Samuel Gompers, president of the American Federation of Labor, the commission drafted a convention that was eventually incorporated as Part XIII of the Treaty of Versailles. The convention also became the constitution of the International Labour Organisation, which set as its objectives the securing of maximum hours and a living wage, full employment, medical assistance for work-related injury and illness, protection for working women and children, and safeguards for those employed in foreign countries. It also sought recognition of the right to unionize and the establishment of vocational and technical educational institutions. The ILO became the model for later international agencies, since it possessed an autonomous status despite being linked to the League. It had its own director-general and a governing structure that was separate and provided for equal representation of national governments, employers, and employees. Its annual Geneva conference, whose chief business was to discuss draft conventions and make recommendations for submissions to the member states, permitted each country to appoint four delegates—two representatives of the government, one chosen by employers, and one chosen by workers.

Director-General Albert Thomas, a French socialist, conceded that the early progress of the ILO was hampered by national prejudices, economic apprehension, and public indifference, yet despite these obstacles, some thirty conventions were ratified during the first ten years. Even in the absence of formal approval, convention discussions frequently led to practical implementation of resolutions. A sampling of the early conventions indicates actions on hours of work, unemployment, maternity protection, night work by women and children, minimum working age, workman's compensation, and seamen's rights. The Depression naturally slowed the group's progress, but another thirty conventions were negotiated by 1939 that expanded the areas of earlier coverage and introduced agreements on old age and survivors' insurance.

Social and Cultural Committees

In addition to its work in international economics, the League also investigated other areas of social and intellectual concern. A variety of committees embraced a range of subjects from the commonplace to the challenging—from improving housing to suppressing the illegal drug trade. The Housing Commission examined such subjects as cooling and heating, insulation, noise, and lighting, and their effects on public health. Influenced by the League committee, France established its own National Housing Committee.

In 1931, the Health Committee's European Conference on Rural Hygiene concluded that studies on specific concerns could not be isolated from general economic and social factors. Acting on the committee's recommendation to study rural life in its entirety, Avenol invited all European countries to participate in a conference scheduled for July 1939. The secretary-general asked each nation to develop reports covering demography, land-tenure systems, agricultural methods, cooperatives, credit and insurance, education, and medical and social programs. The response was very favorable, but unfortunately, the conference became yet another victim of the approaching war.

Faced with the militant nationalism of the Axis nations in the 1930s, the task of the Committee for Intellectual Cooperation was hopeless. Established in May 1922, this committee promoted international contacts among the professions and encouraged greater understanding of cultural diversity. Quartered in Paris, its members included Henri Bergson, who was the first chairman; Marie Sklodowska-Curie; Albert Einstein; Sigmund Freud; and Aldous Huxley. The presence of such luminaries prompted Sir Alfred Zimmern, a well-known British authority on the League, to suggest that the committee become the faculty of a "world university," and he encouraged the formation of national groups as adjuncts to the League's International Institute for Intellectual Cooperation, located in Paris, or the Paris Institut, as it came to be called. The American "college" was organized in 1926 by Dr. Robert A. Millikan, who won the Nobel Prize for Physics in 1923; he was joined by Raymond Fosdick and Elihu Root. Root's presidency of the Carnegie Endowment for International Peace assured funding for the Paris Institut, as did the generosity of John D. Rockefeller, Jr. These American contributions helped to support international conferences conducted by the committee on contemporary political issues, a project that was encouraged by Columbia University President Nicholas Murray Butler, who succeeded Root as the head of the Carnegie Endowment. Butler believed the committee should foster the development of the "international mind"—a mind that possesses a universal set of values culled from transnational experience. His Columbia colleague James T. Shotwell emphasized the study of common cultural elements to replace the national emphasis on political and economic conflicts. One of the committee's academic goals involved the revision of history textbooks to eliminate national bias.

Although French and German cooperation ended after Hitler's accession to power, the committee continued its attempts to offset growing intellectual nationalism. It encouraged university faculties and secondary educators to develop syllabi for general education that would provide a common foundation of learning for students. The committee also called for the scientific study of international questions and sponsored an international studies conference in 1938 whose theme was economic policy and peace. To foster scientific collaboration, the International Council of Scientific Unions invited biologists, chemists, and physicists to regular meetings on topics such as "Theories of Modern Physics," which was discussed in Warsaw in June 1938.

Evaluations of the committee's achievements were mixed. In a report appearing in *International Conciliation* in April 1941, James Shotwell and Edith Ware offered a favorable assessment and argued that intellectual cooperation is as important as economic and political cooperation in maintaining

Albert Einstein (left) was a member of the Committee for Intellectual Cooperation, organized in May 1922 and headquartered in Paris. Robert A. Millikan (right) organized the American "college" of what committee members hoped would become a "world university."

peace. However, Frank P. Walters, a former deputy secretary-general, contended that the committee was always hampered by the lack of League funding and by the difficulty of steering the individualism of the intellectuals toward a common purpose.

Obstacles of a different kind challenged the Advisory Committee on Opium and Other Dangerous Drugs, which sought to control the illicit trade in narcotics during the interwar years. Reformers hoped to restrict the cultivation and manufacture of drugs to the quantities required for medical and scientific use. During the 1920s, however, it was not unusual for those nations that derived substantial revenues from the drug trade to obstruct limitation. The committee included states both directly and indirectly involved in the growth and manufacture of drugs—India, China, Japan, Siam, Yugoslavia, and Germany—and the four European nations with Far Eastern colonies—France, Great Britain, the Netherlands, and Portugal. Bitter debates between the committee members and reformers interested in curbing drug traffic therefore punctuated the years. The First Geneva Opium Conference, held from November 1924 to February 1925, illustrated the reluctance of the delegates from the nations associated with the Far East to suppress the use of prepared opium and thus help eliminate opium smoking. Anglican Bishop Charles H. Brent expressed the frustration of reformers by describing the work of the conference using Horace's line: *Montes parturiunt, nascetur ridiculus mus* ("The mountains are in labor, a ridiculous mouse is born"). However, the Second Geneva Opium Conference, meeting concurrently with the first, ran smoother. It addressed a broader range of narcotics problems, and representatives of forty-one nations agreed to include substances such as coca leaves, Indian hemp, and the new manufactured drugs among the items subject to import and export regulation. Revelation of substantial increases in the manufacture and distribution of morphine, heroin, and cocaine by firms in the Netherlands, France, and Switzerland aroused public concern in Western Europe. Alarmed by the expansion of the drug trade, fifty-seven nations attended the Conference for Limitation of the Manufacture of Narcotic Drugs in Geneva from May 27 to June 13, 1931, and pledged to restrict their manufacture of drugs to the quantities required for domestic medical and scientific purposes and to fill scheduled export orders. The Twelfth Assembly of the League found the agreement an important development in international law, since it was the first time that "an industry has been brought under international regulation and that manufacture in its economic aspect has been wholly subordinated to higher humanitarian and moral aims." Cooperation among the participants made the agreement an effective instrument, and by 1936, the production and distribution of the five principal drugs—morphine, diacetylmorphine, codeine, dionine, and cocaine—were stabilized.

The curtailment of drug manufacturing in Western Europe, however, stimulated the rise of new production centers in the Balkans and especially in China, where 90 percent of the world's raw opium was grown. The shift to Asian manufacturing added a new challenge to the legislative and popular programs being initiated by Chiang Kai-shek to suppress poppy cultivation and opium smoking in China. Reports reaching the Advisory Committee indicated that Japan was sponsoring the drug trade in Manchuria and occupied China, while Hong Kong and Macao were serving as conduits in the flow of narcotics to Europe and the Western Hemisphere.

Dr. Hoo Chi-tsai, China's delegate to the Advisory Committee, attributed the worsening drug situation to the Japanese occupation forces, whom, he charged, were using the trade both to destroy the will to resist among the Chinese people and to obtain funds. There were 3,840 licensed opium saloons and 8,400 licensed heroin dens in Manchuria and Jehol; the human toll in Harbin alone during the first seven months of 1937 was 1,500 lives. Members of the Advisory Committee repeatedly complained to their Japanese colleague, who was at times embarrassed by the reports, but there was little possibility that he or his civilian superiors in Tokyo could change the policy of the Japanese military command in China.

Prior to the Sino-Japanese conflict, the Advisory Committee had responded to demands for more effective policing of the narcotics trade by convening the Conference for the Suppression of the Illegal Traffic in Dangerous Drugs, which met in Geneva during June 1936. Among the provisions agreed upon by the forty-two countries that participated were punishment for actions in violation of existing treaties; arrest and trial in a nation of attempted refuge, or extradition; and cooperation among the agencies engaged in controlling the drug trade. Advocates of the agreement saw it as another important step toward international criminal law; it was also an acknowledgement that some surrender of national sovereignty was necessary to protect the international community from the ravages of the drug trade.

In addition to the need for international cooperation for the success of these programs, the economic and social committees also required the support of the Council, which supervised their activities. Unfortunately, this support was not always forthcoming, and the situation led to a major reform in their status.

The Bruce Report

The history of the League's technical agencies reveals an increasing readiness of professional staff members to criticize member government policies and challenge political authority. The need for careful research and independent scholarship in the preparation of reports and conference papers steadily widened the role of the academics and professionals, who generally enjoyed a greater freedom from bureaucratic control than did those employed by governments. The relationship between the technical agencies and the Council, which established and supervised the committees, often was testy, since the Council exercised extensive control over the subjects investigated, the research reports generated, and the distribution of the finished studies. The political and diplomatic officials who composed the Council were frequently ill prepared to evaluate economic or social findings and tended to defer these questions if political issues were on the agenda. Because of this, Stanley Bruce, who played a major role in the nutrition report, joined with several others involved in the social and economic committees to propose that the Council be replaced as the authority over the committees by a new League administrative body comprised of technical experts. In July 1937, King Leopold III of Belgium advanced an even more radical suggestion. Like Avenol, he hoped to restore some kind of relationship with Hitler and Mussolini but was convinced that they would not cooperate with any organization connected with the League. He therefore recommended completely separating the social and economic agencies from the League.

In 1938, the Assembly invited nonmember states to join the debate on the future relationship between the technical services and the League. The presumption was that if Germany, Italy, or Japan was interested in participating in these activities, it would express support for the extra-League arrangement. None of these powers responded, however, and the major nonmember that did answer—the United States—favored keeping the technical services within the League. Interestingly, the role of the United States was one of the considerations prompting the examination of the Council jurisdiction. As a member of almost all the economic and social committees, the United States provided support but had no voice in the formation of policy. Reformers wanted to provide a format in which the United States could be a full participant in the technical agencies without becoming a League member. Not all the member nations welcomed the prospect of an expanded American influence, however. The Argentine delegate, Carlos Pardo, feared that Washington would in time monopolize the technical fields and discourage other League members. But Secretary of State Hull promised continued American support under the existing arrangement and generously credited the League with being "responsible for the development of mutual exchange and discussion of ideas and methods to a greater extent and in more fields of humanitarian and scientific endeavor than any other organization in history." Hull's remarks helped to decide the issue in favor of keeping the technical services within the League.

Avenol then proposed the establishment of a committee under Stanley Bruce to develop a new structure for the agencies. The secretary-general envisioned the creation of an executive committee responsible for planning and operating the agencies. Although still a part of the League, the new administrative board would be relatively autonomous, and the supervisory role of the Council would be ended. He indicated, however, that Bruce's committee would be free to develop a model of its own choosing. Deliberations produced a plan that resembled Avenol's proposal, with a central committee for economic and social questions exercising the control formerly granted to the Council and Assembly. The committee members would be drawn from the existing social and economic ministries of nations and would thereby provide an expertise hitherto lacking. The Bruce Report appeared on August 22, 1939, and despite the imminence of war, Avenol succeeded in having it passed by the Assembly. It bore fruit in the formation of the Economic and Social Council of the postwar United Nations.

Avenol, however, did not demonstrate the same initiative and persistence in improving the League's assistance to refugees. The situation was exacerbated during the 1930s by the plight of Germany's Jewish community and the secretary-general's desire to avoid League action that Nazi leaders might consider objectionable.

Aid to Refugees

During the 1920s, the League extended limited aid to the victims of World War I, but it generally regarded its responsibility as essentially legal and hesitated to accept broad financial and administrative obligations for the relief and resettlement of refugees. Under the leadership of Dr. Fridtjof Nansen of Norway, the League solicited the cooperation of individual nations in accepting the victims of the Russian revolution and of the political upheavals that shook the Balkans and the Ottoman Empire after the First World War. Nansen, whose name became synonymous with aid to refugees, developed the "League of Nations passport," or, as it was popularly known, the "Nansen passport," which gave its holder legal status in over fifty countries. The passport enabled refugees to move from more densely settled countries to those providing greater opportunities for permanent residence and employment. As a general rule, however, the League could not assume the fiscal responsibility for the care of refugees and depended on contributions from private institutions, appropriate government agencies in the countries accepting the refugees, and sources developed by Nansen himself.

After Nansen's death in the summer of 1930, the Assembly created an international relief office, named in Nansen's honor, to continue the humanitarian aspects of refugee relief, while reassigning the legal aspects to the Secretariat. In practice, however, the Nansen International Office for Refugees assumed both functions. Despite the prospects of long-range refugee problems, the Assembly in addition specified that the Nansen Office's operations would end on December 31, 1938. As that date approached, Judge M. Michael Hansson of Norway, the last president of the Nansen Office, indicated that some 300,000 Russians, 120,000 Armenians, and 4,000 Saarlanders were still looking to the League for assistance, which now would never come.

Also among those Hansson could no longer help was the new wave of refugees created by the racial policies of Nazi Germany. In October 1933, the Council had reached what *The New York Times* described as a "fragile compromise" in dealing with the German objections to having the refugee issue handled directly by the League. In addition to creating the office of High Commissioner for Refugees (Jewish and Others) Coming From Germany, the Council established a governing office, called the Governing Body of the High Commission, that theoretically would be outside the League. Jewish leaders expressed "much dissatisfaction" with the solution, but the Dutch delegation believed that the plight of the German Jews required urgent action and encouraged acceptance of the arrangement. The choice of an American, James G. McDonald, as High Commissioner was welcomed in European circles, where he was known through his chairmanship of the Foreign Policy Association. Relations between McDonald and Avenol were strained, however; the High Commissioner described the secretary-general as "a cautious and bureaucratic official" who pointedly reminded him of the separation between the League and the Governing Body to which he reported. Money advanced to the Governing Body was designated as a loan to be repaid, rather than as operating funds. In addition, McDonald interpreted the selection of Lausanne instead of Geneva as the site of the Governing Body's meetings as further evidence of Avenol's desire to distance the group from the League. The secretary-general's purpose was to avoid offending Germany, and the entire matter was handled in such a way that the German delegate to the Assembly could assert that there was no intended criticism of his country's domestic policies in the League's actions.

The first meeting of the Governing Body, in December 1933, also revealed the obstacles McDonald would encounter in finding countries willing to accept refugees from Germany. Many delegates from Europe and the Western Hemisphere pleaded financial difficulties arising from the Depression and, in some cases, physical limitations on how many refugees they could accommodate. But despite these constraints, McDonald—with the aid of Jewish and other private organizations—managed to resettle 60,000 of those fleeing Germany between 1933 and 1935. The passage of the Nuremberg laws in September 1935, however, increased the number of refugees and strained the resources of the Governing Body. With no significant protest against Germany's persecution of the Jews being voiced by the international community, McDonald contended that the League should become that voice. Frustrated by the lack of response from Avenol and the members of the world body, McDonald resigned in December 1935, pleading for the League to assert its moral authority and "avert the existing and impending tragedies."

On February 14, 1936, the Council appointed Sir Neill Malcolm, a retired British Army general, as High Commissioner for Refugees Coming From Germany and placed the office under the League's jurisdiction. The Council confined Malcolm's role to negotiations concerning the legal status, employment, and residency of refugees with the countries providing sanctuary. Unlike the outspoken McDonald, Malcolm deferred to his superiors:

> I have no policy, but the policy of the League is to deal with the political and legal status of the refugees. It has nothing to do with the domestic policy of Germany. That's not the affair of the League. We deal with persons when they become refugees and not before.

As in the past, the League did not budget relief funds for the endeavor.

When Malcolm's office was terminated in December 1938, the Council recommended that a single organization replace both Nansen's office and that for the refugees from Germany. The primary responsibility of the new High Commissioner for Refugees would be to arrange for the legal status of refugees. The office might coordinate humanitarian assistance, but again, the League refused to help with funding. The arguments raised against direct financial assistance included the League's concern with arousing the hostility of the nations from which the refugees were coming; the competition and jealousy among refugee groups for the limited funds available; and the administrative costs of supervising the program.

There was an air of unreality surrounding these debates as the annexation of Austria and the threat to Czechoslovakia and Eastern Europe swelled the ranks of the refugees. When some of the European states that had been receiving refugees again expressed concern about their ability to absorb new groups, even on a temporary basis, President Roosevelt convoked a conference of thirty-two nations at Evian en Bains in July 1938 to plan an organized resettlement program. It was anticipated that, in addition to the approximately 129,000 refugees that had already fled Germany between 1933 and 1937, another 700,000 could be expected in the future from Germany and Austria. Aware of the League's sensitivity to the creation of a competing agency, the United States emphasized its concern with resettlement but also argued that a new group might be able to open negotiations in Berlin, where the League had been rejected. Unfortunately, none of the nations, including the United States, proved willing to make any substantial changes in its immigration policy except for the Dominican Republic, which made a generous but unrealistic offer to take 100,000 refugees.

At a second meeting in London during August, the new group, the Intergovernmental Committee on Political Refugees (IGC), named an American, George Rublee, as its director and an Englishman, Earl Winterton, as its chairman. Rublee quickly discovered that London preferred to leave the refugee problem in League hands, but he succeeded anyway in negotiating a controversial agreement in February 1939 with German authorities that allowed Jewish emigration financed by the confiscated wealth of resident Jews and by a bond raised by "world Jewry." Outraged Jewish leaders condemned the extortion plot and the dangerous example to other nations with Jewish minorities; Zionists added their objections to the diversion of economic support from Palestine. The funding arrangement was not completed until the American Jewish Joint Distribution Committee allocated $1 million and the Coordinating Foundation was organized in June 1939.

The previous month, the British government had formalized the position it had been taking since the beginning of the Evian Conference, namely, that Palestine was not to be the solution for resettlement. On May 17, the British White Paper on Palestine restricted further Jewish immigration to 75,000, with Arab approval required for any entry beyond that. Instead of a Jewish National Homeland, the British proposed the erection within ten years of a Palestinian state with an Arab majority.

The outbreak of the Second World War created additional problems for refugees, as Great Britain and France urged the suspension of the IGC mission, since all potential emigrants from Germany would have to be classified as enemy aliens. The United States, however, favored the IGC's continued activity, and Roosevelt predicted that 10 to 20 million refugees would be created by the war. He invited the IGC delegates assembled in Washington on October 16 to think in terms of enormous resettlement developments. In the context of the immediate crisis of 1939, many delegates criticized the president's message as visionary and impractical. Instead, to accommodate the present refugees, the delegates turned to considering British Guiana, Alaska, the Philippine Islands, the "United States of Africa" (parts of Rhodesia, Kenya, and Tanganyika), Angola, and Ethiopia. None of these proved viable, however, and tragically, the hope of resettlement turned into the horror of the "Final Solution."

In 1957, a study by the Brookings Institution, an independent research organization, commended the "rich experience" of the League's economic and social agencies, which had become a part of the organization's valuable legacy to the United Nations. It was, in fact, a legacy that the founders of the League had not anticipated, yet in retrospect, one official of the Secretariat concluded that some of the agencies fell "far short" of their potential. In the case of the economic groups and the International Labour Organisation, that judgment must be tempered by recognition of the impact of the Depression. The highly qualified staffs of the economic and financial organizations produced special studies on subjects ranging from agriculture to tariffs, but the London Economic Conference of 1933 demonstrated their failure to convert government leaders to the pursuit of international, rather than national, economic development.

Regarded as the most successful of the technical services was the Health Organization, whose work in disease control alone brought the League's name to corners of the world where it would otherwise have been unknown. Its work reflected the growing emphasis on assistance to individuals in addition to governments, and the widely circulated nutrition study of 1937 exemplified this concern with human welfare. As might have been anticipated, the attempt to harness the world's intellectual leadership proved difficult for reasons that varied from funding to personalities, yet there were noteworthy conferences on the humanities and sciences. The League's commitment to suppress the illegal drug trade was compromised by some of the member states involved in the traffic, but by the mid-1930s, important progress had been made in limiting the manufacture and distribution of drugs in Western society. Unfortunately, conditions in the Far East made it impossible to secure the international cooperation necessary for effective control.

When the staffs of the technical services complained that the members of the Council were exercising undue control over the agencies, Avenol supported their bid for autonomy; in August 1939, the Bruce Report proposed the creation of a committee for economic and social affairs independent of the Council and Assembly. However, the secretary-general did not display the same initiative in responding to the refugee crisis of the 1930s. The policy of limited responsibility for refugees adopted by the League during the 1920s was partially offset by the heroic efforts of Dr. Fridtjof Nansen, but by December 1938, the office named in his honor faced dissolution, with some 425,000 victims still seeking aid from it. In 1933, the Council created a separate organization for refugees from Germany, but it failed to elicit strong League support—moral, political, or fiscal—the most fateful breakdown of responsibility by the Council and Assembly to sustain a League agency. But Avenol could remind his critics of the lack of response by non-League members, especially in the Western Hemisphere, to his appeal in 1935 for expanded immigration quotas and of the apparent failure of Roosevelt's Evian Conference of 1938 to win major concessions for refugee resettlement. This distribution of guilt, however, was no consolation to the victims. On the horizon, moreover, was the fulfillment of Roosevelt's prediction of millions of refugees, as Hitler plunged Europe into the Second World War.

Hitler addresses his troops at Bernau in 1933.

Denouement— The League and World War II

7

A former League official described the world body in April 1938 as being on its deathbed. The fate of Czechoslovakia and then of Albania the following spring confirmed for Avenol his earlier judgment that the League should avoid involvement in the international situation. In turn, the major powers ignored the League as they revived the alliance system that the world body was supposed to have replaced. The greatest surprise in the new alignment of nations was the Russo-German Nonaggression Pact, an agreement that contributed to the outbreak of World War II and that led to the partition of Poland by Hitler and Stalin.

Avenol's abstention from political affairs was abruptly interrupted when the Soviet Union invaded Finland. The secretary-general actively sought the League's condemnation of the USSR and the first and only expulsion of a member state from the world body. Concern for Finland was quickly displaced, however, as the German spring offensive of 1940 first overran Denmark and Norway, and then crushed Holland, Belgium, Luxemburg, and France. The defeat of his native France overwhelmed Avenol. There was a painful interlude before he resigned during which he lost the confidence of his subordinates due to his erratic planning for the wartime status and activities of the League. There was little hope for a miraculous recovery for the organization, but it was strange to see the secretary-general serving as a pallbearer at its funeral.

The Coming of World War II

On March 15, 1939, Hitler rode triumphantly into Prague as Germany absorbed Bohemia and Moravia, while a second predator, Hungary, claimed the Ruthenian portion of Czechoslovakia. Former Czechoslovakian President Beneš appealed to the League, but since he was no longer a member of the government, Avenol tried to deflect his request on technical grounds. Five days earlier, Avenol had told the American consul to Geneva, Howard Bucknell, Jr., that this was "no time [for the League] to make political pronouncements or to undertake political manoeuvers." When Deputy Secretary-General Sean Lester pressed for some kind of League response, Avenol insisted that Council agreement could not be reached and that a defeated resolution would adversely affect France and Great Britain.

After the annexation of Czechoslovakia, Bucknell reported that League officials were anticipating new German advances in Eastern Europe that the smaller states would be hesitant to resist unless England and France offered firm commitments. There was, however, "much pessimism" in the Secretariat regarding the ability of London or Paris "to take such a strong stand that they could not recede therefrom at the last moment." Lester confided to his diary the secretary-general's belief that most of the members considered the League "politically dead," a judgment that was confirmed shortly afterward when Great Britain and France supported Avenol's rejection of Albania's request for assistance following the Italian invasion on April 7. A scornful Mussolini added to Geneva's humiliation by forcing the hapless Albanian government to resign from the League six days later.

However, Hitler's callous violation of the Munich Agreement did arouse British public opinion, and Parliamentary pressure finally spurred Chamberlain to offer broad guarantees of British aid to Poland on March 31, 1939, and to Greece, Turkey, and Rumania on April 13, 1939, if they were attacked. Foreign Secretary Lord Halifax described these new obligations as being consistent with "the spirit of the Covenant," an assertion that was difficult to sustain. The Covenant required the submission to the League of an issue threatening the peace, judgment by the Assembly and Council of the alleged aggression, and collective response by the members in applying sanctions. The British treaties bypassed the League, placed the decision for war directly in the hands of the signatories, and had no provision for collective action. Negotiated outside of League auspices, the alliances returned the involved parties to the pre-League world of international relations. With the League emasculated, a condition to which Great Britain had contributed, there was no alternative but to go backward in search of security.

London's turn eastward also provided the USSR with an opportunity to strengthen its position against Germany. At the time of the Munich Agreement, the Soviet press had denounced Great Britain and France for their shameful betrayal of Czechoslovakia and desertion of the League's principle of collective security. The Soviets interpreted the Munich settlement as an Anglo-French decision to settle their differences with Germany and to turn Hitler against the Soviet Union. However, Chamberlain's unexpected commitment to Poland and the Balkans encouraged Moscow to propose, in April 1939, a new triple entente for mutual military assistance. Churchill, who had once refused to grasp "the bloody paws" of the Bolsheviks, now insisted that the USSR's alliance with the West was vital to British defense interests. However, Chamberlain was hostile to the Soviet overture, and Sir Alexander Cadogan of the British Foreign Office minimized the USSR's military power. Bucknell reported that among the officials of the Secretariat, Soviet military capability also remained a "big question mark." Like many Western leaders, they believed that the purge trials of 1937 had decapitated the leadership and demoralized the survivors, rendering the Red Army unfit for a major war. When the Soviet initiative went unanswered, Stalin replaced Litvinov, who had been a defender of the League and of close relations with France and Great Britain, with Vyacheslav M. Molotov. When this new Commissar of Foreign Affairs failed to attend the May session of the Council, there was inevitable speculation of a shift in Soviet policy, since economic talks between Germany and the USSR were known to be underway. Daladier had told American Ambassador William Bullitt in March that "Stalin was panting" for an agreement with Germany; an agreement, he said, "would not take a half hour" if Hitler made an overture. In fact, Molotov believed that Munich had exposed the impotence of the West and that Soviet security lay in a settlement with Germany.

Although the commissar's assessment was unknown to them, British and French authorities were apprehensive of a detente between Berlin and Moscow. With France's endorsement, the British proposed, on May 25, a mutual defense agreement that would be in compliance with League principles. Molotov objected to the invocation of the Covenant, but more importantly, he demanded a free hand for the Soviet Union in the defense of the Baltic States and for a military convention that would precede the political agreement. Neither London nor Paris would surrender the Baltic nations, but nevertheless, a diplomatic mission under Sir William Strang, chief of the British Foreign Office's Central European Division, was sent to Moscow in mid-June. Soviet critics noted that Chamberlain himself had visited Hitler and interpreted the appointment of Strang as indicative of a lesser importance attached by the British to the Soviet negotiations. The French and British military mission did not arrive until August 11, and by then, a diplomatic revolution was imminent.

To prevent the revival of the Triple Entente of the pre–World War I period, Hitler authorized exploratory talks with the Soviet Union beginning on May 30. There was little progress made in June and July, but on August 23, Ribbentrop and Molotov stunned the world with the announcement of a Nazi-Soviet nonaggression pact. The shock would have been greater if the secret terms were known—Poland was to be partitioned between Germany and Russia; Estonia, Latvia, and Finland were to come within the Soviet sphere of influence; and Lithuania was to be assigned to Germany. Fortified by this Russian "blank check," Hitler ordered final preparations for the invasion of Poland. A new barrage of propaganda attacks against Warsaw's mistreatment of the German irredenta in the Polish Corridor was coupled with charges of repeated military provocations along the frontier, and on September 1, 1939, German troops launched their assault. When Hitler failed to respond to ultimata from France and Great Britain on September 3, Paris and London declared war against the Third Reich. Although the Council met from September 10 to 16, the Allies did not call on it for assistance. Given their previous failures to resist aggression as part of the League, they were obviously embarrassed to solicit help for themselves from the League. Polish authorities simply filed protests with the League after Germany and the Soviet Union divided their defeated country. The inactivity of Avenol and the League delegates in these weeks as Europe plunged into war stood in marked contrast to their readiness to intervene when the USSR invaded Finland on November 30, 1939.

The Russo-Finnish War

Soviet Commissar of Foreign Affairs Vyacheslav M. Molotov is greeted upon his arrival in Berlin.

In the negotiations with France and Great Britain in the spring of 1939, a persistent objective of the Soviet Union had been the recognition of Eastern Europe as a Soviet sphere of influence. Chamberlain had rejected the request, commenting that the USSR was "both hated and suspected" by many of the states, including Finland. However, what the British prime minister had refused to concede, Hitler had consented to, and Stalin had moved quickly to exploit the concessions made in the Nazi-Soviet nonaggression pact. To strengthen its position in the Baltic, the Soviet government had occupied bases in Estonia, Latvia, and Lithuania as a prelude to absorbing

The remains of a Russian convoy destroyed during the Russo-Finnish War testify to the Finns' gallant effort to repel the invading Russians.

these countries. It also had made similar demands on Finland, including a thirty-year lease of the port of Hanko and territory in the isthmus of Karelia. Finland had made some concessions to the Soviet Union but held out on these two points. So the Soviet Union, having learned the political lesson of the 1930s, had decided to take by force what it could not obtain by diplomacy.

As Soviet forces invaded Finland, Moscow named a Finnish communist, Otto Kuusinen, as the head of the Democratic Republic of Finland. When the United States tried to intervene, Molotov stated that there was no war between Russia and the Finnish government under Kuusinen. After meeting with Avenol in Paris, Ambassador Bullitt informed the Finnish minister, Harri Holma, that the secretary-general wanted the League to act in this war. When Holma referred to Avenol's record of inaction, Bullitt insisted that the secretary-general viewed this Soviet aggression as a different kind of challenge. Avenol assured Rudolf Holsti, Finland's delegate to the League, that he was anxious to bring the issue before the world body and believed that the USSR should be expelled from the League.

When the Soviet government refused to negotiate with the Finnish government, Finland appealed to the League on December 3. Avenol promptly scheduled the Council to convene on December 9, with the Assembly to gather two days later. Finland's request for League assistance created a temporary dilemma for Denmark, Norway, and Sweden, who had joined Helsinki in forming the Oslo Group in 1935. The four countries had reserved to themselves the decision to employ sanctions under the Covenant, and it was now possible that the League might invoke Article 16. To the relief of the other Oslo nations, Finland's foreign minister, Väinö Tanner, proposed that they seek only the removal of Soviet troops from Finnish territory and assistance with peace negotiations; neither sanctions nor the expulsion of the Soviet Union was desirable, he said. When Holsti informed Avenol of his instructions, the chagrined secretary-general unsuccessfully tried to enlist the United States in persuading Tanner to change his position. More encouraging for Avenol was the word from Paris, where the USSR's expulsion was viewed as the minimum sanction, and although the British Foreign Office preferred a mild resolution of censure, it yielded to France and the need for Allied solidarity. Under Avenol's guidance, the Assembly voted expulsion on December 14, and the Council approved the decision the same day, with China, Greece, Yugoslavia, and Finland abstaining. It was the first and only time the world body exercised this power—an irony not lost on those who had been the victims of aggression by Japan, Italy, or Germany. The secretary-general also offered the League's technical services to Finland and encouraged aid from nonmember states as well as from the League, which were steps he had resisted for Ethiopia and China. However, despite the gallant Finnish resistance, which surprised the Soviets as much as it impressed the world, the overwhelming numerical superiority of the Soviet armies triumphed in March 1940.

In his study of Avenol's tenure as secretary-general, James Barros speculated about the different world that might have evolved if Avenol had demonstrated the same "initiative, skill and daring" in the early 1930s that he did in securing League action against the Soviet Union. There were, however, substantive differences affecting his reactions to the aggressions. Although he had not opposed the entry of the Soviet Union into the League, Avenol's anticommunism had always been a prominent element of his political character, and he did not have similar ideological differences with the Axis powers. In addition, unlike during previous crises, the secretary-general knew that he could count on an almost unanimous reaction from anticommunist League members. Also, the Helsinki government and Finnish people enjoyed the respect of the international community and evoked, as Paul-Boncour stated, "this somewhat tardy awakening of the universal conscience." Finally, the Nazi-Soviet nonaggression pact represented for many nations the USSR's betrayal of the West and the "green light" for Hitler's invasion of Poland. The secretary-general shared the bitterness of his countrymen and their Allies for Stalin's desertion. Expulsion was a punishment for past sins as well as for the present offense. Avenol and the League won this battle, but it proved to be a Pyrrhic victory, as the Soviet Union later refused to recognize the League of Nations as the post–World War II international organization.

There was little time to sympathize with the Finnish people. The uneasy winter quiet along the Western Front, which was called the "sitdown war" (*Sitzkrieg*) or the "phony war," was shattered by the German offensive of 1940. Denmark fell with token resistance on April 9, and Norway succumbed on June 7 after an abortive Anglo-French expedition to assist it. The West was shaken by this sudden German coup but had yet to face the worst. In May, Nazi forces slashed through Holland, Belgium, and Luxemburg, bypassing the Maginot Line. This time, there was no Miracle of the Marne to save

France. Survivors of the British Expeditionary Force fell back to Dunkirk and were evacuated. As the French Army desperately tried to regroup, Mussolini struck at both the Alpine frontier and the Riviera on June 10. Six days later, Premier Paul Reynaud resigned, and his successor, Marshal Henri Pétain, called for an armistice on June 17.

Overwhelmed by the disaster to his homeland, the secretary-general found a scapegoat for his anger and humiliation in Great Britain, which he blamed for France's plight. He alternated between outbursts against the British and still extravagant praise for Mussolini and Hitler. Outraged by the British attack on French naval units in North African waters on July 3, Avenol attempted to contact Wolfgang Krauel, the German consul general in Geneva, which gave rise to rumors that he was preparing to surrender the League to the Axis. Deputy Secretary-General Sean Lester recorded that Avenol discussed with Marius Viple, chief of the Information Section of the International Labour Organisation, the rise of a "new France," which would join with Germany and Italy in creating a Europe from which England would be barred. Avenol told Lester that he was unsure of Hitler's attitude toward preserving the League but thought that Mussolini would want to maintain it as a balance against Germany. In a letter to Arthur Sweetser, an American attached to the League's Press and Information Section, Avenol portrayed a world on the brink of a "great revolution" that would emulate the progressivism of Germany and Italy. On the other hand, Avenol insisted to Harold Tittmann, the American consul general in Geneva, that reports concerning his betrayal of the League were untrue.

The possible relocation of the League's offices and agencies also aroused controversy between Avenol and his staff members. The secretary-general expected Switzerland to request the League's departure in order to preserve its neutrality. Originally, Avenol had intended to anticipate the request by using France as an interim sanctuary, but in August 1939, he decided to stay in Geneva until the Swiss government formally requested the evacuation. When Germany's spring offensive overran the Netherlands and Belgium, Switzerland finally did ask Avenol to transfer the League. Fittingly, Avenol selected France and received permission to move to Vichy. But members of the Secretariat complained that Avenol was less than candid with them and that there were unnecessary delays and confusion in planning the move. The Swiss government then compounded the confusion by reversing itself and asking the League to remain in Geneva when it became concerned over the adverse effects the sudden departure of the world body would have on its citizens. Avenol next considered relocating some of the technical sections abroad, while still retaining the senior Secretariat officials in Geneva. He contemplated, for example, moving the Economic and Financial sections to the Western hemisphere. After extended negotiations with the U.S. State Department, Princeton University, the Institute for Advanced Study, and the Rockefeller Institute for Medical Research, Sweetser forwarded an invitation to the League on June 12, 1940, for the Economic, Financial, and Health sections to take up residence at Princeton during the war. Only then did the secretary-general announce that he preferred to keep the Secretariat together in Geneva. However, when the prospective refuge in Vichy became instead the seat of the new government of defeated France, the League documents already sent there were either hurriedly returned to Geneva or destroyed. A severe loss to historians was the destruction of a part of the archives, including the papers of Secretary-General Drummond, to prevent them from falling into German hands.

Discussing the Princeton offer with Tittmann, Avenol indicated that he had declined it to keep the League from being accused of deserting its post. He pointed out that the American offer did not provide for an international status for League officials and that transfer would require approval by the world body. Yet only a week later, on June 21, he shifted his position about keeping the technical units in Geneva. The International Labour Organisation was planning to leave, and he suggested that the technical groups be temporarily attached to that body. His reversal may have been influenced by pressure coming from the British government and from Carl Hambro of Norway, chairman of the Twentieth (and last) Assembly, in favor of the American offer. The secretary-general repeated his concern that there was no guarantee the American government would recognize the international status of League officials residing in the United States. Moreover, Secretary of State Hull still hesitated to extend a formal invitation to the League because of opposition from isolationist elements in American congressional and public quarters. Hambro suggested that the problem could be solved if the settlement at Princeton was treated as a temporary seat of operations while a Secretariat group in Geneva continued to staff the permanent home of the League. The transfer would simply facilitate the maintenance of vital activities associated with the League and would also demonstrate the organization's continued viability. Avenol resisted the transfer until the day he resigned.

The secretary-general's procedures for reducing the staff of the Secretariat also generated criticism. Some resignations were voluntary, as men were called to active duty by their countries, but suspicion arose that Avenol was using the situation to purge officials who did not share his political sympathies. Lester expressed concern about the absence of non-European representation on the staff but found the secretary-general unreceptive to change. Avenol saw little contribution that non-Europeans could make on a continent dominated by Germany and Italy. He told Tittmann that he intended to reduce the staff to about forty and to close the main buildings of the Palais des Nations, except for office space in the library. Despite his assertions that he was determined to preserve at least a nucleus of the League, Avenol tried to end its operations completely once his own resignation became imminent. Noting that the war prevented regular meetings of the budgetary committee and of the Assembly, he said that there could be no way to validly appropriate funds. Without a budget, he said, all activities would end. And, Lester realized, although there would be no formal interment, Avenol's decision would bury the League. Lester was shocked and bypassed Avenol by submitting the question to the Supervisory Commission, a seven-member committee serving as an adviser on financial and administrative matters. Acting in the emergency situation, the commission approved a budget and circulated it to the members, who approved the procedure.

Avenol's actions were undoubtedly influenced by his own relationship with the League. On July 4, 1940, he wrote to Pétain, professing his support for the Vichy government and offering to resign his post. His explanation for the decision can be found in a letter to Eden dated January 5, 1941: *Dans ces moments si douloureux, j'ai trouvé l'apaisement du devoir le plus simple: être fidèle à mons pays* ("In this heartbreaking hour, I found ease in the simplest duty: being faithful to my country"). Typically, however, and despite his expressed desire to leave the post, Avenol had second thoughts. He developed a plan whereby Under Secretary-General Thanassis Aghnides would assume the post of acting secretary-general, while he retained the real power of the office. To remove Lester from the scene, Avenol intended to offer the deputy secretary-general unlimited, compensated leave of absence. Aghnides recalled a long interview during which the secretary-general became increasingly angry as Aghnides rejected the proposal and recommended instead the succession of Lester. Avenol maintained that Lester's homeland of Ireland would be excluded, together with the rest of the Anglo-Saxon world, from the new Europe.

Only on July 25 did Avenol finally submit his resignation as secretary-general, accompanying it with a self-laudatory review of his accomplishments. Appropriately, he gave a prominent place to his efforts to recall to membership the nations that had withdrawn from the League. But he still did not leave physically. Disturbed by the delay in Avenol's retirement, Pétain called the president of the Council, Adolfo Costa du Rels, to Paris and expressed to him his desire for the secretary-general's early resignation. Avenol continued to procrastinate for a while but finally did leave the Secretariat on August 31. Vichy immediately expressed its willingness to have Lester succeed Avenol, which was a judgment widely shared by League members, and on September 2, Lester became the acting secretary-general. (For a further discussion of Sean Lester's tenure as secretary-general, see "Sean Lester and the Last Years of the League," on page104.)

Avenol, after his retirement, lived in a small village in Haute-Savoie, France. In December 1943, he sought and obtained asylum in Switzerland after learning that the Nazis were about to arrest him and deport him to Germany. In 1944, he completed *L'Europe Silencieuse*, in which he expressed his views on postwar Europe. Although he believed that the nation state would retain its sovereignty, he recommended the creation of a council of Europe to coordinate economic policy and an international police force to combat aggression. Now conceding that the Axis would lose the war, Avenol reversed his recommendation of May 1942 for close ties between France and Germany. His secretary in France maintained that many Frenchmen shared Avenol's belief in 1940 that their country had no option but collaboration with Germany. However, many other Frenchmen demonstrated their patriotism with continued resistance to the Nazis, and from these countrymen, Avenol could expect no sympathy.

Avenol's former associates in the League also proved unforgiving, and despite several overtures from him for expressions of approval similar to those extended to Lester, he received none. The final meeting of the Assembly in 1946 heard the Czech delegate, Jaromír Kopecký, denounce the "nefarious tendency and state of paralysis" to which Avenol's tenure had reduced the world body by 1940. Succeeding years did not soften the judgment of his critics, and his death—on September 1, 1952, the thirteenth anniversary of the outbreak of the war that the League was to have prevented—attracted little public attention.

Sean Lester and the Last Years of the League

In June 1940, Sean Lester wrote to Arthur Sweetser, an American colleague in the Secretariat: "The world is crashing round our ears but [we] are keeping our heads up, if our hearts are broken. . . ." The sentence suggests something of the courage and self-sacrifice in the midst of trial that Lester's staff would witness during World War II, when, as acting secretary-general, Lester doggedly manned his post in Geneva, attempting to ensure the survival of the League.

Born in County Antrim, Ireland, on September 27, 1888, and educated in Belfast, Lester combined a journalist's career with a commitment to securing Irish independence from Great Britain. He was a member of the Sinn Fein ("Ourselves Alone") party, and after the Irish Free State was established in 1921, he entered his country's Department of Foreign Affairs. His association with Geneva began in 1929, when he was appointed permanent delegate of the Irish Free State to the League. His outspoken advocacy of a League role in settling the international disputes of the early 1930s brought commendations from the organization's supporters, although major powers were embarrassed when he accused them of failing to provide effective leadership for the world body. From 1934 to 1937, he distinguished himself as the League's High Commissioner to Danzig, a post in which he resisted attacks by local Nazis on the League's administration of the Free City. Impressed by Lester's service in Danzig, Secretary-General Avenol appointed him deputy secretary-general. However, Avenol's failure to initiate strong League action during the political crises occurring in Asia and Europe in 1937 to 1939 alienated Lester, and by 1940, the secretary-general, in turn, had virtually isolated himself from his deputy. Relations between the two officials further deteriorated when Lester began to suspect that Avenol was trying to dissolve the League before his resignation as secretary-general became effective on August 31, 1940. But Lester emerged from the internecine struggle enjoying the support of the League community, and he was named acting secretary-general in September 1940.

By the time Lester assumed his new office, Europe had fallen to the Nazis, so his immediate problem was continuing the operations of the Secretariat in Geneva. He needed to maintain contact with those elements of the League that had relocated, secure economic support for the world body, and preserve contact with foreign governments to ensure political support for a postwar revival of the League. Severe reductions in the League staff had begun with the outbreak of the war in September 1939, as civil servants returned to their countries, entered military service, or were dismissed. Eventually, only about 100 officials remained to staff the Secretariat during the war. Nevertheless, Lester and his colleagues continued to prepare modest budgets and to issue annual reports and statistical studies. The acting secretary-general also corresponded regularly with the League units functioning in the United States, Great Britain, and Canada.

In Princeton, New Jersey, the Secretariat's Alexander Loveday supervised the activities of the Economic, Financial, and Transit sections, which had accompanied him from Geneva. These sections continued to produce specialized studies and participated in several conferences held by Allied governments during the war. With Lester's support, the Princeton group continued to publish the *World Economic Survey, Statistical Year-Book,* and *Monthly Bulletin of Statistics.* Princeton also served as a liaison center with Geneva for the Opium Supervisory Body and the Permanent Central Opium Board, which had relocated to Washington, D.C. Both the League treasurer and the High Commissioner for Refugees had moved their offices to London, while the International Labour Organisation had shifted its activities to Montreal. Despite the geographical separation and the uncertainties of wartime communications, Lester provided coordination and direction for these far-flung operations.

Since both the Assembly and Council were unable to convene due to the war, League political activity was suspended, and the Secretariat avoided raising political issues in deference to Switzerland's vulnerable neutrality. A major exception to this rule was allowed when the Vichy government of France announced its intention to withdraw from the League. Lester invoked the aid of the United States, which secured a declaration from both General Henri Giraud and General Charles de Gaulle, co-presidents of the French Committee of National Liberation, that nullified the Vichy action and continued France's membership in the League.

Although Lester's responsibility for political matters was reduced, raising funds to support the League remained a constant concern. Many former member states were unable to make their regular contributions, but Great Britain and the other members of the Commonwealth provided generous funding from 1940 to 1945. The overall decline in revenue, however, forced the budget to go from 28 million Swiss francs in 1939 to less than half that amount in 1940; in 1945, the budget was about 10 million Swiss francs. Lester found it difficult to reduce wages and impose other economies on his staff, but he shared the sacrifices and justified the privations as helping to preserve the League. Similarly, he hoped that the flow of reports from Geneva and Princeton would remind the world that the League was still functioning. He believed that the League agencies in their temporary overseas sanctuaries were visible signs of the viability of the organization and that the research studies of the Princeton group on postwar reconstruction and trade policy, and the participation of its staff in wartime meetings like the Bretton Woods Monetary Conference, would convince the Allied governments of the experience and expertise of the League. He hoped that when the Allies began to plan for peace in the postwar world, they would turn once again to the League.

After the United States entered the war in

December 1941, President Franklin D. Roosevelt established the Advisory Committee on Post-War Foreign Policy, chaired by Secretary of State Cordell Hull. Hull was a longtime advocate of Wilsonian internationalism and wanted to ensure American public and congressional support for participation in an international organization. The League, however, bore the stigma of its repeated failures to curb aggression and, in the United States, revived memories of the bitter ratification struggle of 1919. Roosevelt and his advisers thought that a new organization might encounter less resistance than the League, and from July 1942 to June 1943, Hull's Advisory Committee undertook a detailed examination of the League's Covenant to evaluate its strengths and weaknesses. The United States was emerging as a superpower, and there is no indication that it ever seriously considered retaining the League. At the Dumbarton Oaks Conference in 1944, when a draft proposal for a new world organization was submitted for consideration by China, the Soviet Union, the United Kingdom, and the United States, it became evident as the delegates reached general agreement, except on voting procedures, that the League was doomed.

The British government had always suggested international cooperation, but, as Prime Minister Winston Churchill explained during the Third Washington Conference in May 1943, it no longer believed the League to be adequate. Churchill concluded that only those countries whose interests were directly involved in a particular crisis could be expected to take action. Therefore, he recommended that three regional councils—located in Europe, the American hemisphere, and the Pacific—be created to hold primary responsibility for resolving local disputes. Above them would be a Supreme World Council, consisting of the Soviet Union, the United Kingdom, the United States, and, possibly, China and a few other nations, which would possess the ultimate responsibility for preserving peace. Clearly he felt comfortable with the idea of a greater policing role for any new creation.

An even more formidable obstacle to restoring the League stemmed from its alienation of the Soviet Union, which had been expelled in December 1939 as a result of its aggression against Finland. Having suffered a humiliation unique in the history of the League, the USSR had no interest in the Geneva body. The resentment of the Soviet government was still evident at the Yalta Conference in February 1945. When discussion of the new international organization arose, Stalin pointedly reminded Roosevelt and Churchill that during the Russo-Finnish War, France and Great Britain had led the League's condemnation of the Soviet Union and had secured its expulsion from the world body. Stalin wanted guarantees that a similar situation could not recur. Roosevelt therefore proposed that in the new world body, substantive actions by the Security Council require the unanimous assent of the permanent members, China, the Soviet Union, the United Kingdom, and the United States. Stalin was assured that the USSR could protect itself by simply exercising the veto, although he indicated that he preferred stronger safeguards. The episode demonstrated the impossibility of securing Soviet support for a reconstituted League.

Unaware of these developments, Lester remained hopeful that the League would be "the central foundation" of a new international body. But by the time the military reconquest of Europe enabled him to leave Geneva in late 1944, the issue had been decided by the Allied coalition. Instead of planning a revival of the League, Lester was asked to prepare for the transfer of League properties and personnel to the new United Nations. The acting secretary-general and other League officials were invited to attend the San Francisco Conference in April 1945 that would prepare the United Nations Charter, but because of objections raised by the Soviet Union, the United States classified Lester's party as "unofficial representatives." Despite Lester's expectations that his experts would be consulted by the committees involved in drafting the new charter, they were virtually ignored, and Lester was not invited to address a single group.

At the last formal meeting of the General

Assembly of the League, held in April 1946, Lester received recognition for his wartime service. A resolution was passed that made him officially the third secretary-general of the League, with an effective appointment from September 1, 1940. It was nonetheless a disappointing end to his six years of personal sacrifice and professional dedication to the ideal of the League, but he graciously extended his cooperation to the United Nations. He served with the League Board of Liquidation and the United Nations committee responsible for the transfer of League personnel and assets. Lester was particularly concerned about the placement of former League staff, and he took satisfaction from the fact that over 200 members of the Secretariat found employment within the United Nations structure. Their presence, he believed, would assure the new organization a leaven of experienced officials. In 1947, Lester refused political appointments offered by the Irish government and by the United Nations, and he returned to Ireland in retirement.

Sean Lester provided an appropriate concluding note for the transition from the League to the United Nations. Responding to an award given him by the Woodrow Wilson Foundation for his commitment to the principles of the Covenant, Lester alluded to the monument of President Wilson in the Court of Honour in Geneva. He reflected that the terrible war that had just ended might have been prevented if the "sublimely commonsense vision" of Wilson had been followed. His words were both an indictment of the elders and a warning to the young of the world. "The peoples are now rebuilding that which they destroyed by timidity and neglect," he said, and it was now the task of the United Nations to prevent such suffering from happening again.

Looking Back | *8*

In an address prepared for the ceremonies marking the opening of the League of Nations Pavilion at the New York World's Fair on May 2, 1939, the secretary-general anticipated the judgments that future historians might offer concerning the world body. They will discover, Avenol mused, "a fruitful theme in discussing whether the League has been gradually paralyzed in the performance of its fundamental task of preserving peace because the obligations for which it provided were too rigid or too extensive, because it was not universal, or because its members shrank from the risks of today without foreseeing that those of tomorrow would be inescapable and far greater." These lines can well serve as an epitaph for the League because later studies determined that each of the factors mentioned contributed to its demise. What Avenol did not anticipate was the critical assessment that historians would make of his own role as secretary-general. Most accept Lord Cecil's judgment that Avenol was "wholly unsuited to the job . . . [and] was evidently out of his element."

Avenol assumed office shortly after Japan resigned from the League rather than accept censure for its aggression in Manchuria. Several months later, Germany joined Japan in rejecting Geneva when Hitler denounced the failure of the World Disarmament Conference to grant equality to the Third Reich. The commitment of the secretary-general to winning the return of these nations prevented him from advocating effective responses both to Japan's aggression against China and to Hitler's repeated violations of the Treaty of Versailles. Avenol also desired good relations with Italy and hesitated to confront Mussolini in the Italo-Ethiopian conflict. Prior to the outbreak of that war, Avenol had tried to secure concessions from Ethiopia for Italy and to prevent France and Great Britain from clashing with Mussolini. When Italy invaded Ethiopia and the League imposed sanctions, Avenol's support for the League's action was lukewarm, and he later endeavored to encourage the League members to recognize the Italian conquest of the African nation. The secretary-general minimized the role of the League in the Spanish Civil War and proved reluctant to act in the crises provoked by Germany's union with Austria, the dismemberment of Czechoslovakia, and the invasion of Poland. By courting the very governments whose conduct violated the League's Covenant, Avenol weakened the prestige of his office and the performance of the world body.

Not all historians accept this verdict without qualification. In his review of *Betrayal From Within*, Christopher Thorne noted the judgment of the book's writer, James Barros, that the secretary-general contributed "in no small way" to the breakdown of peace yet also conceded the difficulty of imagining how Avenol could have changed "the course of events." Thorne warned against divorcing Avenol's policies from the political spirit of the 1930s and holding him alone responsible for the failures of the League. In a recent study of the League, F. S. Northedge argued that the concept of collective security was too radical a formula for statesmen accustomed to the balance-of-power theory. The failure of the London Economic Conference in 1933 demonstrated that even in a major crisis like the Depression, national interests were stronger than the League's appeal for international cooperation. The limited response of League members to China's request for aid during the Manchurian crisis revealed the weakness of collective security. Despite the failure of the balance of power to prevent World War I, the traditional formula seemed inescapable. It was in the capitals of Europe, not in Geneva, where decisions that would shape the political future were made. A former under-secretary of the League, Vladimir Sokoline, maintained that the foreign policies of France and Great Britain limited Avenol's room to maneuver and lessened his responsibility for the League's fortunes. These points are well taken, but it can be argued that the secretary-general was obliged to uphold the Covenant, not compromise it; to punish its violators, not cooperate with them. One may concede that his resistance would have been unavailing, but it would have preserved the integrity of his office and avoided his becoming a partner in the undermining of the League.

Avenol insisted that by the late 1930s the organization was politically dead and that he was trying to preserve it by developing its social and economic services. At the time, it was generally believed that this was another attempt by him to re-enlist the Axis powers, but he later contended that his primary objective was the greater involvement of the United States. When the Second World War began, however, he steadfastly opposed moving the technical services to Princeton. But one important result of his interest in the economic and social organizations was the formation of the Bruce Committee, whose report incorporated Avenol's conception of separating the technical sections from the predominantly political Council. The secretary-general did secure adoption of the report by the Assembly, although its implementation was prevented by the war. The Bruce Report became the basis for the United Nations Economic and Social Council and represents Avenol's most significant contribution to international organization.

Unfortunately, the secretary-general's considerable experience in fiscal matters was not matched by a similar command of political affairs; he never undertook the rigorous study of political matters that his office required. Colleagues complained of his ignorance, indolence, and inability to offer or accept advice. Lack of confidence in his qualifications necessarily limited his influence in both the formal and informal functions of his office. He seldom addressed the Council or the Assembly, and his infrequent public speeches, like his press conferences, tended to be bland and uncontroversial. These were not necessarily bad qualities in a trained diplomat, but the belief prevailed that personal ignorance rather than caution inhibited Avenol's speech. Drummond's tenure had featured many informal meetings with members of the Secretariat and representatives posted to the Assembly and Council. He enjoyed their confidence because of his grasp of international affairs and their respect because of his impartial judgments as an officer committed to serving the world community. Avenol never developed this rapport with his colleagues.

More serious are the charges that Avenol subordinated the interests of the League to those of France and Great Britain. This seems inconsistent with his own description of the obligations of League officials. "We are," he said in May 1938, "required to discharge our functions and to regulate our conduct with the interests of the League alone in view. . . . It is our duty not to take advantage of the means placed at our disposal . . . in order to assert our own personal sympathies. They should be used with the idea that we are in the service of all." In a postwar interview, he maintained that he had acted independently of the French government, and his private secretary, Vera B. Lever, observed that the many personnel changes in the foreign ministry, representing a variety of political views, would have made it difficult for the French authorities to control Avenol. However, the evidence indicates that Avenol failed to conform to his own high standards of international service. During the prewar years, his policies toward Japan, Italy, and Germany closely paralleled those of the French government, and the military success of Germany from 1939 to 1940 apparently convinced him that resistance was futile. Avenol always denied rumors that he proposed turning over the League's properties to the Axis diplomats in Berne, but other suspicions were aroused by his delay in transferring the technical services from Geneva. Finally, on the eve of his resignation, he tried to suspend the operations of the League.

The circumstances surrounding Avenol's resignation were confusing. He insisted that his action was voluntary, but other accounts attributed the final step to pressure from the government of Marshal Pétain. Avenol cited several considerations that affected his decision, including the constitutional difficulties arising from the inability of the various League organs to meet, the wartime disruption of the economic and social programs, and the embarrassment of retaining his position while other personnel were being discharged. The most important factor, however, was probably his patriotism, stirred by France's defeat at Germany's hands and by the British naval attack against the French fleet at Mers-el-Kebir. Resignation, he wrote, was now a "point of honor." Despite his many years of service as an official of the League, his loyalty to France remained undiluted. Many people expected the secretary-general to exercise greater control over his nationalist sentiments, but Eden recognized the human reaction and cautioned those whose own countries had not been invaded against passing judgment on Avenol.

Historians speculate about what the fortunes of the League might have been under a secretary-general fully committed to the Covenant and its enforcement. The temptation is to compare the leadership of Drummond, who guided the world body through the foundation years, with the performance of Avenol, who presided over its decline. Drummond, however, had the good fortune to serve in the flush of enthusiasm and optimism that marked the birth of the League, and his diplomatic background served him well in his relationships with the Secretariat staff, League delegates, and government ministers. His previous service enabled him to work behind the scenes without displaying a vigorous public leadership. Avenol admired the active role developed by Albert Thomas as director of the International Labour Organisation but noted how difficult it was to change the fourteen-year model of the secretary-general created by Drummond. Drummond also left the ongoing Depression, the floundering disarmament conference, and the consequences of the Manchurian crisis to his successor. In addition, Hitler's rise to power produced a political challenge for Avenol unlike any that Drummond had encountered. Revealingly, the secretary-general confessed that he turned not to the League, but to Louis Barthou, the French foreign minister, to provide the counterbalance to the German chancellor.

Political inexperience undoubtedly inclined Avenol to defer to the French Foreign Ministry, but it was a costly dependency that made him no stronger in dealing with aggression than his countrymen at the Ministry. In an address entitled "The Future of the League of Nations," delivered at Chatham House in December 1933, Avenol had warned that it would be "useless and imprudent, indeed dangerous, to abandon the careful conservation of assets that still remain to us . . . in exchange for what is unknown and uncertain." Unfortunately, caution and careful conservation were inadequate in a turbulent decade that demanded a secretary-general who was courageously committed to the ideals of the League and its Covenant.

An aerial view of the League of Nations complex in Geneva, Switzerland, May 1936.

Chronology

1929

JANUARY

1 The Chinese Nationalist government of Chiang Kai-shek extends its control into Manchuria, where both the USSR and Japan also have economic and political interests.

3 Bolivia and Paraguay submit their border dispute over the Gran Chaco to a Commission of Inquiry and Conciliation, composed of Colombia, Cuba, Mexico, the United States, and Uruguay, and created by the International Conference of American States on Conciliation and Arbitration.

5 King Alexander I suspends the constitution of Yugoslavia in the wake of clashes between Croats (Catholic and federalist) and Serbs (Orthodox and centralist).

15 The U.S. Senate ratifies the Kellogg-Briand Pact (Pact of Paris), whose signatories renounce war as "an instrument of national policy."

24 Continuing the rapprochement established by the Rapallo Treaty in 1922, Germany and the USSR sign a treaty of conciliation. The USSR wishes to prevent Germany from being drawn into a possible anticommunist coalition of Western European nations, and Germany hopes that British and French concern over the Berlin-Moscow tie will lead to revision of the Treaty of Versailles.

31 Leon Trotsky is banished from the Soviet Union as Joseph Stalin consolidates his control of the Communist government.

FEBRUARY

6 Germany signs the Kellogg-Briand Pact.

Yugoslavia proposes reopening its border with Bulgaria and creating a mixed commission to resolve any frontier controversies between the two nations.

9 Estonia, Latvia, Poland, Rumania, and the USSR sign the Litvinov Pact, which renounces war.

11 Italy and the Vatican sign the Lateran Accords, which acknowledge papal sovereignty over Vatican City and recognize Victor Emmanuel III as king of Italy. The treaty ends the rupture between the Papacy and the House of Savoy, which began in 1870 with the capture of Rome by Victor Emmanuel II and Pope Pius IX's self-imposed status as "Prisoner of the Vatican." Benito Mussolini wins praise from Catholics at home and abroad.

Chiang Kai-shek's Chinese Nationalist government extended its control into Manchuria on January 1, 1929.

27 Secretary-General Sir Eric Drummond discourages the publication of a report by the League High Commissioner to Danzig on the political situation in the Free City to avoid offending Germany. He does so again on March 9 and March 21.

MARCH

3 –April 3 A rebellion against the Socialist and anti-Catholic government of President Emilio Portes Gil is suppressed by General Plurtarco Elías Calles, a former president who holds the real political power in Mexico.

4 Responding to Germany's charges of Polish violations of German minority rights in Upper Silesia, the Council sets up a Committee of Three (Great Britain, Japan, and Spain) to review the situation.

23 The League's Communication and Transit Organization seeks to improve communications between Poland and Lithuania.

28 Japan ends several months of military intervention in China's Shantung Province and withdraws its troops.

Ecuador adopts a new constitution, which ends the military regime established in 1925 but leads to conflict between President Isidro Ayora and the legislature.

APRIL

15 –May 6 The Preparatory Commission to the World Disarmament Conference prepares a draft proposal, which is criticized by the German delegate because it does not call for any substantial arms reductions.

27 Having secured the agreement of Belgium, Denmark, Italy, Portugal, and Spain to end extraterritoriality rights, China asks Brazil, France, Great Britain, the Netherlands, Norway, and the United States to allow their nationals to be tried in Chinese courts.

MAY

20 **–22** United after World War I to preserve their gains from the dissolution of the Austro-Hungarian Empire, the nations of the Little Entente (Czechoslovakia, Rumania, and Yugoslavia) discuss economic cooperation and extend their alliance for five more years.

27 Chinese authorities raid the four Soviet consulates in Manchuria and charge Soviet officials with spreading Communist propaganda in violation of a 1924 agreement.

30 Great Britain's general election gives the labourites 287 seats in Parliament; the conservatives, 261; the liberals, 59; and others, 8.

JUNE

1 The body of Sun Yat-sen is moved from Peiping to Nanking in a state funeral.

3 After the failure of earlier mediation efforts by the United States, direct negotiations between Chile and Peru resolve the long-standing dispute over Tacna-Arica by awarding Tacna to Peru and Arica to Chile. Since 1920, Bolivia had unsuccessfully pursued claims to the provinces through the League, the United States, and Argentina, but Chile does grant Bolivia a rail outlet to the Pacific.

5 James Ramsay MacDonald forms a labour-liberal coalition and becomes prime minister of Great Britain.

7 The Young Committee, meeting since February 11, completes its report on the final settlement of Germany's reparations payments, which are substantially reduced.

10 **–15** The Committee of Three's report on Poland's treatment of

German minorities in Upper Silesia rejects Germany's request for a change in the League's procedure for handling complaints. The German Foreign Office is "surprised and disappointed" by the report, but the Council approves it.

13 Italian forces conquer the last native resistance in Cyrenaica.

14 Eleven nations sign an agreement at the Geneva Conference on Transit Cards for Emigrants.

18 The United States appoints an Interoceanic Canal Board to study a transit route across Nicaragua.

21 Mexico and the Vatican announce an agreement to end their conflict.

29 General Augusto César Sandino, leader of antigovernment and anti-American insurgents in Nicaragua, flees to Mexico.

JULY

2 Ultraconservative Japanese leaders protest the Kellogg-Briand Pact as an affront to the emperor, since it describes rulers as "representatives" of their people. General Giichi Tanaka and his ministry resign after Tanaka's compromise wording fails to satisfy the extremists. Osachi Hamaguchi, whose Liberal Party has been attacking Tanaka's militant policy toward China, succeeds him.

17 Great Britain initiates steps to resume diplomatic relations with the Soviet Union, which were severed in 1927.

17 **–20** China and the Soviet Union break relations after Chinese authorities in Manchuria seize the Chinese Eastern Railway and arrest over 200 Soviet personnel. The major powers denounce the action as an indefensible violation of Soviet rights, which were secured by a treaty with China in 1924.

24 American President Herbert Hoover proclaims the Kellogg-Briand Pact in force among the fifteen original signatories following Japan's ratification

of it. Forty-three additional nations will also adhere to the treaty.

26 By a narrow margin of 8 votes (300 to 292), the French senate ratifies a bitterly debated war-debt agreement to pay the United States nearly $7 billion over a sixty-two-year period.

27 Aristide Briand succeeds Raymond Poincaré as premier of France when illness forces the Lion of Lorraine to retire.

AUGUST

6 **–31** The Hague Conference reaches agreements on the reduction of German reparations under the Young Plan and for the end of the Allied occupation of the Rhineland by no later than June 30, 1930.

11 Iran and Iraq sign a treaty of friendship.

13 The USSR attacks Chinese positions in Manchuria as the conflict over the Chinese Eastern Railway continues.

16 Fighting between Jews and Moslems erupts at the Wailing Wall in Jerusalem and spreads to other Palestinian cities, leaving 196 dead and 305 wounded.

Illness forced Raymond Poincaré, the Lion of Lorraine, to retire as premier of France on July 27, 1929.

Aristide Briand once again took over the reins of France when he succeeded Raymond Poincaré as premier on July 27, 1929.

SEPTEMBER

2 **–25** Representatives of fifty-three nations celebrate the Assembly's tenth anniversary and pass resolutions on a tariff truce, drug traffic, and armaments.

5 Briand proposes a European federal union to provide economic, social, and political links among the nations. German Foreign Minister Gustav Stresemann endorses the plan.

12 Bolivia and Paraguay accept a conciliation resolution prepared by the Commission of Inquiry and Conciliation, also known as the Washington Commission of Neutrals, to settle the Chaco dispute of December 1928.

14 British troops begin their withdrawal from the Rhineland, which has been occupied since the end of World War I. They will complete their evacuation by December 13.

OCTOBER

3 Great Britain and the Soviet Union resume diplomatic relations; the Soviets agree to stop spreading communist propaganda in India, and the British agree to defer discussion of the USSR's debts to England.

7 Prime Minister MacDonald issues invitations to France, Italy, Japan, and the United States to join Great Britain for a five-power naval disarmament conference to be held in London.

24 **–November 1** The Economic Committee drafts the Tariff Truce Convention.

29 The collapse of the U.S. stock market signals the onset of the Depression, which affects much of the 1930s.

30 **–November 4** With the political tension between Italy and Yugoslavia rising, Secretary-General Drummond meets with Mussolini and King Alexander I. He describes his visits as "distinctly useful" in resolving the crisis.

NOVEMBER

3 André Tardieu, conservative protégé of Poincaré and staunch defender of the Treaty of Versailles, becomes premier of France following the resignation of Édouard Daladier, leader of the Radical Socialists.

17 Nikoli Bukharin is dismissed from the leadership of the Communist International, as Stalin eliminates the right-wing advocates supporting concessions to the peasants.

21 France and Germany begin discussing economic investments in the Saar, where a plebiscite will be held in 1935 to decide whether it will return to Germany, become a French possession, or remain under League administration.

30 French and Belgian troops evacuate the Coblenz area of the Rhineland, leaving the French units in the Mainz zone as the last Allied occupation force.

DECEMBER

2 **–4** France, Great Britain, Italy, and the United States invoke the Kellogg-Briand Pact in memoranda to the Soviet Union and China concerning their conflict in Manchuria. Moscow rejects intervention in the dispute, but Nanking agrees to mediation, as Soviet troops drive 200 miles into Manchuria.

4 **–10** Antigovernment rioting in Haiti threatens American residents and property, so the U.S. High Commissioner, using authority provided by a 1916 treaty, orders 700 marines stationed there to restore order.

5 The Third International Conference for the Abolition of Import and Export Prohibitions and Restrictions opens in Paris.

6 Italy celebrates "the day of reconciliation," as King Victor Emmanuel III and Queen Elena become the first members of the House of Savoy to visit the Vatican. Their reception by Pope Pius XI

French troops leave the Coblenz area of the Rhineland on November 30, 1929.

King Victor Emmanuel III helped end nearly sixty years of alienation between the papacy and Italian monarchy when he visited Pope Pius XI on December 6, 1929.

ends the nearly sixty years of alienation between the monarchy and the papacy.

22 A German referendum supports the adoption of the Young Plan.
The Sino-Russian Peace Protocol restores joint control of the Chinese Eastern Railway, provides for the withdrawal of Soviet troops from Manchuria, and arranges for the reopening of consulates.

28 –30 A Chinese mandate declares that all foreigners must observe Chinese laws as of January 1, 1930, but the government then agrees to consider foreign powers' reaction to its termination of extraterritoriality.

29 Achmed Sukarno and other leaders of the Indonesian National Party are arrested by Dutch authorities.

1930

JANUARY

1 The British government announces that it will regard the process to abolish extraterritoriality "commenced in principle," a phrase designed to "save face" for China after the Western powers and Japan rejected the Chinese mandate of December 28, 1929.

3 –20 Dr. Hjalmar Schacht, president of the Reichsbank, nearly disrupts the second session of the Hague Conference by denouncing the Young Plan as "morally wrong" because it allows sanctions against Germany for default on reparations payments. However, Foreign Minister Julius Curtius commits Germany to the agreement.

6 Stalin, with a speech, "Destroying the *Kulak* or Rich Farmer as a Class," launches a campaign against those resisting the compulsory collectivization of agriculture demanded by the Five Year Plan.

16 –23 Paraguay reports a new clash with Bolivia in the Gran Chaco, and the Council calls upon both parties to seek a settlement. Secretary-General Drummond wishes to avoid direct League involvement and to leave the issue in the hands of the Washington Commission of Neutrals.

21 The Five Power Naval Conference convenes in London amid discouraging reports of Anglo-American controversy over cruiser ratios, Japanese demands for parity with Great Britain and the United States, and Italo-French competition for superiority in the Mediterranean.

23 Convinced that recent anti-Mexican demonstrations in Washington, Buenos Aires, and Rio de Janiero were ordered by Moscow, Mexico breaks diplomatic relations with the USSR.

28 The six-year rule of Miguel Primo de Rivera as *dictature* ("dictator") of Spain ends when King Alfonso XIII appoints another military officer, General D'Amaso Berenguer, as his successor.

FEBRUARY

5 –April 28 The Committee on Eastern European reparations meets to prepare an agreement for Hungary.

6 Mussolini signs a treaty of friendship with Austria.

7 President Herbert Hoover sends a commission to Haiti to investigate charges of misconduct by Haitian President Louis Borno. The commission recommends replacing Borno, holding general elections and restoring the Republican government, and ending the United States' control as exercised through a High Commissioner and marines.

17 –March 24 Twenty-nine nations attend the Economic Conference in Geneva and defeat a British proposal for a tariff truce because of the Depression and the rise of protectionism in the United States and Europe.

MARCH

8 The United States–League of Nations Commission reports the existence of slavery in Liberia. It estimates that some 5 million people are in bondage throughout Africa and the Middle East.

12 Mahatma Gandhi, the revered leader of India's independence movement, continues his campaign of civil disobedience with a "march to the sea" to challenge the British salt monopoly.

13 –April 12 The Conference on International Law adopts conventions on nationality and statelessness.

25 Bulgaria arrests leaders of the International Macedonian Revolutionary Organization when the group's terrorist acts threaten relations between Bulgaria and Yugoslavia.

30 Heinrich Bruening, leader of the Catholic Center Party, succeeds socialist Hermann Mueller as chancellor of Germany after a dispute over an unemployment-insurance fund divides Mueller's supporters.

31 The British government's Shaw Commission reports that Palestinian fighting between Arabs and Jews in August 1929 was initiated by Arabs and that its "fundamental cause" was Arab frustration over "their political or national aspirations and fear for their economic future."

APRIL

2 Austria enacts antiterrorism legislation to curb the power of socialist trade unions.

3 Ras Tafari becomes emperor of Ethiopia with the title Haile Selassie I.

4 Bolivia and Paraguay agree to resume diplomatic relations and to settle the Chaco dispute under the terms of the resolution drafted by the Washington Commission of Neutrals.

9 The London Naval Treaty continues the Anglo-American superiority over Japan in all ship categories except submarines. It also contains an "escalator clause" that allows a signatory to build beyond the limitations of the agreement if it is threatened by the construction program of a nonsignatory nation. France and Italy agree to the capital ship "holiday" but refuse the other limitations; they do agree to continue the negotiations, however.

18 Great Britain signs a convention returning Weihaiwei to China.

MAY

1 Sir John Hope Simpson undertakes a study of immigration, land settlement, and economic development in Palestine for the British government.

6 Japan acknowledges China's tariff autonomy.

8 The negotiations for an Anglo-Egyptian treaty break down over the Sudan issue.

15 The Council establishes the Wailing Wall Commission to visit Palestine and investigate the clashes between Arabs and Jews.

16 China and France sign a commercial agreement regarding Indochina.

24 Courting the favor of Germany and its former allies, Mussolini calls for a revision of the Treaty of Versailles.

JUNE

3 **–21** The seventeenth (extraordinary) session of the Permanent Mandates Commission criticizes the Shaw Commission's failure to link Arab leaders to the Palestinian incidents and to recognize the extent of the Arab opposition to British rule. The commission also charges the British authorities with failure to provide sufficient men and equipment to control rioting. The Council's adoption of the commission's report leads to the first time a major power submits to censure by a League body.

8 Although he had previously renounced the throne in favor of his son Michael, Prince Carol returns to Rumania and deposes his son, beginning a ten-year reign as King Carol II.

10 Despite the centuries-long animosity between them, Greece and Turkey reach an agreement on refugee exchange.

10 **–28** The International Labour Conference adopts agreements on forced labor and on working hours in commerce and offices.

13 Greece and Hungary sign a convention on Greek war claims.

17 The U.S. Congress ignores an appeal from over 1,000 economists and adopts the highly protectionist Hawley-Smoot tariff, which leads to a new wave of increased rates abroad.

24 Sir John Simon's report on India recommends ending the dyarchy system of divided authority between British and native personnel but with the British viceroy continuing to control the military and resuming complete power in an emergency. The report does not mention Dominion status and deliberately ignores Gandhi and his civil-disobedience movement. Held incommunicado in prison, Gandhi cannot comment, but Pandit Motilal Nehru declares that the Indian National Congress will not pay "the slightest heed" to the report.

27 General Blanco Galindo replaces Hernando Siles as president of Bolivia.

30 Great Britain recognizes the independence of Iraq, a World War I mandate.

The Allied military occupation of the Rhineland ends, as the last French troops leave.

JULY

16 Finland and the USSR exchange charges over the Finnish deportation of communist agents.

21 Maxim Litvinov becomes the foreign minister of the Soviet Union.

AUGUST

16 General Rafael Leonidas Trujillo becomes president of the Dominican Republic after a revolution forces Horacio Vásquez to resign.

27 Long-time dictator Augusto Bernadino Leguía is overthrown in Peru by Colonel Luis Sánchez Cerro after alienating both the conservative Peruvians and the Indians.

SEPTEMBER

2 Italy and Great Britain settle claims that arose from incidents on the Somaliland border.

5 General José Félix Uriburu becomes president of Argentina after a revolt deposes the senile despot Hipólito Irigoyen and brings large landholders and business interests back to power.

9 **–October 4** The Assembly elects Guatemala, the Irish Free State, and Norway to the Council.

11 Sixty-six Indian delegates accept invitations from the British government to attend the October Round Table Conference on India, but no followers of Gandhi are invited.

12 The Council agrees to withdraw French and Belgian railroad guards from the Saar.

18 The Council proposes bilateral negotiations between Lithuania and Poland over frontier incidents after Poland refuses to submit the dispute to the League.

30 Promising to make Germany politically, economically, and militarily strong again, the charismatic Adolph Hitler leads the Nazis to nearly 6,500,000 votes and 107 seats in the Reichstag, transforming the party from the ninth and smallest to the second largest.

OCTOBER

1 –November 14 The Imperial Conference in London adopts the Statute of Westminster, recognizing the equality and autonomy of the Dominions.

3 In contrast to previous policy, the United States announces that it will not intervene in Cuba despite opposition threats to President Gerardo Machado y Morales.

5 Albania, Bulgaria, Greece, Rumania, Turkey, and Yugoslavia convene the First Balkan Conference.

14 The International Institute of Agriculture holds its tenth general assembly and calls for closer relations with the League.

20 Baron Passfield (Sidney James Webb), British Minister for Colonies and Mandates, recommends the continued suspension of Jewish immigration to Palestine, strict supervision of sale of Arab land to Jews, and increased British military forces in Palestine. Joining the Jewish outcry, Dr. Chaim Weizmann, president of the World Zionist Organization, resigns in protest, and other Jewish spokesmen condemn the "grotesque travesty" at which the Jewish people "stand aghast."

23 A League commission calls for freedom of domestic slaves of native tribes in Liberia.

27 A preliminary meeting of drug-manufacturing states convenes in London.

NOVEMBER

3 Getulio Dornelles Vargas begins a fifteen-year rule as president of Brazil following a revolution against Julio Prestes.

10 In response to Jewish protests, the British government agrees to issue 1,500 Jewish immigration permits for Palestine.

14 Japanese Prime Minister Osachi Hamaguchi is seriously wounded in an assassination attempt, the motive of which is not revealed by the assailant.

The viceroy of India, Lord Irwin (Edward Wood, who becomes Lord Halifax), recommends the continuation of dyarchy in India but acknowledges the need to move toward Dominion status. British conservatives criticize the overture to Gandhi, but the Indian National Congress rejects it as inadequate.

15 Belgium, France, Great Britain, Italy, the Netherlands, and the United States send representatives to a conference in Nanking on China's domestic and foreign debts.

17 The Geneva Economic Conference begins a study of means to combat world depression.

18 President Hoover's Haitian Commission leads to honest elections for congress and the free choice of Sténio Vincent as president.

British Prime Minister MacDonald concedes that Zionists have rights, and the British Labour Party promises to aid the movement for a Jewish homeland in Palestine.

DECEMBER

4 Secretary-General Drummond leaves for a visit to the Americas.

9 The Preparatory Commission to the World Disarmament Conference reaches an agreement on a draft convention to be submitted to the World Disarmament Conference.

12 Political unrest and an abortive air force mutiny threaten the Spanish government.

16 Bautillo Palma, provisional president of Guatemala, is overthrown by General Manuel Orellana.

Getulio Dornelles Vargas (right) began his fifteen-year rule as president of Brazil on November 3, 1930. Here, he rides in a motorcade with President Augustín Justo of Argentina.

17 China informs Great Britain and other powers of its desire to settle the extraterritoriality issue by negotiation.

1931

JANUARY

2 José Maria Reina Andrade is named provisional president by the Guatemalan assembly after the United States intervenes to end the revolutionary activity and succession of temporary leaders.

12 Representatives from twenty-six nations meet in Geneva to study agricultural problems.

16 –21 The Commission of Inquiry for European Union studies the effects of the Depression on Europe.

18 In response to complaints made by the Free City of Danzig concerning Poland's development of the competing port of Gdynia, a Commission of Jurists impaneled by the League High Commissioner to Danzig, Count Manfred Gravina, rules that Poland must use the port of Danzig, which was detached from Germany to serve Poland's economic needs but that it can also open other ports.

19 –24 German and Polish delegates to the League exchange charges regarding the treatment of German minorities in Upper Silesia, and the Council adopts the report of a League observer calling on Poland to punish assailants and indemnify German victims.

20 The Council discusses the report of the Preparatory Commission to the World Disarmament Conference and sets February 2, 1932, as the opening date of the conference.

21 Honduras and Nicaragua agree to arbitrate their boundary dispute.

26 To win native support for a new British plan to grant India Reserved Dominion status temporarily and Full Dominion status eventually, Great Britain releases Gandhi from jail. However, Gandhi immediately calls for amnesty for all political prisoners and for the end of British "repressive measures." Winston Churchill denounces the British overture to Gandhi: "We will have no truck with lawlessness and treason."

27 Pierre Laval forms a new government in France after a wheat-speculation scandal topples Theodore Steeg's cabinet. Laval appoints Blaise Diagne of Senegal, making him the first Negro to hold cabinet rank in France.

30 President Carlos Ibáñez del Campo assumes dictatorial power in Chile.

FEBRUARY

7 President Gerardo Machado y Morales suspends constitutional rights in Cuba in response to a threat of revolution, as vessels are reported to be carrying munitions to the insurgents.

13 Prime Minister MacDonald suggests that Jewish immigration to Palestine may be resumed.

24 The U.S. Senate ratifies a fisheries treaty with Great Britain.

27 Canada prohibits the importation of Soviet goods because of the use of forced labor in the USSR.

28 –March 3 Great Britain, Italy, and France reach an agreement that brings Rome and Paris into the London Naval Treaty of 1930. The agreement grants Italy parity with France in new ships but gives France superiority in older vessels.

MARCH

4 Gandhi and the viceroy of India, Lord Irwin, agree to the Delhi Pact, which ends Gandhi's civil disobedience campaign and calls for the British to release political prisoners.

8 The USSR and Turkey reach an accord on the reduction of naval strength in the Black Sea.

10 The League convenes the first session of the Nansen International Office for Refugees.

21 Austria and Germany establish a customs union despite protests from Czechoslovakia, Italy, and France, who fear that it will lead to a political union. Briand assures a cheering French senate that the Treaty of Versailles must be "loyally executed" or there can be "no safeguards for the security of Europe."

30 President Machado y Morales of Cuba offers a compromise to his opponents, pledging to restore the constitutional rights he suspended in February if they will halt their bombings.

APRIL

14 King Alfonso XIII goes into exile when republican candidates dominate the first Spanish elections in eight years, and Niceto Alcalá Zamora becomes provisional president of a government dedicated to republican principles.

The USSR and Germany sign an export-credits agreement.

Reijiro Wakatsuki forms a new Japanese government after Hamaguchi fails to recover sufficiently from the wounds he suffered in the November 1930 assassination attempt.

14 –21 President Hoover denounces the killing of nine American citizens by Nicaraguan rebels led by Augusto César Sandino but refuses to commit the U.S. Marine Corps to providing security throughout that country. Despite public outrage at the murders and criticism from American business interests in Nicaragua, the Hoover administration advises American citizens to either evacuate or move to the safer coastal areas.

15 Great Britain grants Austria a two-year deferment on the payment of its war reparations.

Germany agrees to submit the plan for the customs union with Austria to the Council for review.

17 President Machado y Morales announces the restoration of constitutional rule in Cuba.

21 Great Britain reports that European nations oppose the plan for a 25-percent reduction in tariffs, as they abandon economic cooperation during the Depression and seek self-preservation through protectionism.

22 Egypt and Iraq sign a treaty of friendship, the first such agreement between Egypt and an Arab state.

27 Italy and the Soviet Union renew their commercial treaty.

MAY

11 The largest of Austria's banks, Osterreichische Kreditanstalt, founded eighty-six years previously by the House of Rothschild, goes into bankruptcy and triggers an economic collapse in Central Europe.

12 –15 The People's Convention approves a new provisional constitution for China, which becomes effective on June 1.

13 Supported by conservative members of the National Assembly, Paul Doumer upsets the favored Aristide Briand for the presidency of France. Briand's long-time support for Franco-German reconciliation handicapped him as the Nazis gained strength in Germany and Hitler called for the end of the Treaty of Versailles.

15 Pope Pius XI's encyclical *Quadragesimo Anno* calls for a better distribution of the proceeds of labor and capital, and for an end to the "abominable abuses" stemming from the anonymity of corporate ownership. The pontiff denounces the "impious and nefarious character of Communism" and denies that anyone can be both a "sincere Catholic and true Socialist."

18 –23 The Conference of Wheat-Exporting Nations, meeting in London, fails to reach agreement on prices or production control. The leading exporters—Canada, Argentina, and the United States—fear that competitors like the USSR will "dump" wheat and lower prices still further. The United States opposes a quota system to control exports, and the USSR rejects voluntary acreage reduction.

19 Attired in his field marshal's uniform, President Paul von Hindenburg christens the pocket battleship *Deutschland* at Kiel, where the German Home Fleet has assembled for the ceremony.

22 The Council selects Geneva as the site of the World Disarmament Conference and names Arthur Henderson as its president.

27 –July 31 The Conference for Limitation of the Manufacture of Narcotic Drugs hears its president, Louis de Brouchère, optimistically deny the widespread use of drugs among the masses in most nations. Critics describe previous League efforts to control opium as a failure, estimating that some 8,000 tons are produced annually, with only 350 tons supplying medical needs.

28 American-educated Tang Shao-yi denounces Chiang Kai-shek as aspiring to become emperor of China and establishes a rival government in

Arthur Henderson departs London for Geneva, site of the World Disarmament Conference, of which he was named president on May 22, 1931.

Canton. Japan recognizes Tang, but the United States and other major powers continue diplomatic relations with the nationalists.

28 –June 18 The International Labour Conference adopts an agreement on working hours in coal mines.

30 Italy's fascist press charges the League of Catholic Action with plotting to seize political power, and the police close some 15,000 of its centers. Pope Pius XI places the Catholic Action chapters under episcopal and papal jurisdiction, thereby setting the stage for a clash with Mussolini.

JUNE

15 Poland and the United States sign a treaty of friendship, conciliation, and consular rights.

Chiang Kai-shek is reelected president of the Nationalist government.

20 Alarmed by the drain of $250 million in gold reserves from the Reichsbank since June 1 and the danger of Germany's economic collapse, President Hoover proposes a one-year moratorium on Allied war-debt payments to the United States and the suspension of the annual reparations from Germany.

25 The Washington Commission of Neutrals proposes mediation in the Chaco dispute between Bolivia and Paraguay.

27 The killing of Captain Shintarō Nakamura, a Japanese army officer, by Chinese soldiers in Manchuria is memorialized in Japan, and retaliation against China is demanded.

28 Republican and socialist candidates triumph in Spain's general elections.

29 Pope Pius XI challenges Mussolini's continuing suppression of the League of Catholic Action with the encyclical *Non Abbiamo Bisogno*, which attacks fascism's indoctrination of Italian youth with a pagan worship of the state.

Smuggled out of Italy by Monsignor (later Cardinal) Francis J. Spellman, an American member of the Vatican Secretariat of State, the Pope's message draws worldwide attention and infuriates Mussolini.

30 **–July 15** The Seventeenth World Zionist Congress elects Nahum Sokolow as president after denouncing Chaim Weizmann as an "eternal disgrace," a tool of the British government. Sokolow faces pressure from Revisionists demanding creation of an autonomous Jewish state in Palestine.

JULY

2 **–13** A dispute between Chinese and Korean farmers in Manchuria provokes anti-Chinese rioting in Korea, which kills 142 Chinese and injures nearly 400. Nanking charges that Japanese officials failed to protect the Chinese victims, and a boycott of Japanese goods begins in Shanghai.

10 **–12** Norway occupies eastern Greenland, and Denmark asks the Permanent Court of International Justice (PCIJ, or World Court) to review the action.

14 The German government orders the closing of all banks for a "holiday" until August 5.

26 **–29** Student riots sparked by Chilean economic problems and the abrupt dismissal of a popular premier force the resignation of President Carlos Ibáñez del Campo and his immediate successor. José Esteban Montero, another favorite of the students, becomes acting president and secures recognition by the United States.

AUGUST

1 The Bank of France and the U.S. Federal Reserve Bank extend $250 million credit to the Bank of England to offset the heavy drain of its gold reserve.

3 Facing strong European opposition and anticipating a negative judgment by the PCIJ, Austria and Germany dissolve their credit union.

11 Authorized by the Cuban Congress, President Machado y Morales again declares martial law when evidence of a planned coup is uncovered.

16 Joseph Avenol, deputy secretary-general of the League, and Alexander Loveday, director of the Financial Section, begin consultations with Austria over the failure of the Kreditanstalt.

21 The United States joins other nations and the League Public Health Service in offering aid to China after the Yangtze River rises ten feet above flood level and destroys the autumn crop. Some 30 million people are left homeless, and approximately 2 million are killed.

24 Unable to resolve Hungary's economic problems, Count Stephen Bethlen resigns after serving as prime minister for ten years. The regent of Hungary, Admiral Nicholas Horthy, asks Count Julius Károlyi to form a cabinet.

24 **–28** Facing a budget deficit of $583 million and unwilling to reduce welfare costs, MacDonald's Labour government resigns. However, MacDonald is asked by King George V to form a National government and obtains $400 million in loans from French and American banks.

SEPTEMBER

1 Angered by budget cuts affecting sailors' pay, the Chilean navy mutinies, but the air force remains loyal to the government and forces the surrender of the rebels.

1 **–14** After hearing complaints about Polish harassment of the German minority in Upper Silesia, the Council adopts a resolution calling upon Poland to improve its treatment of the minority.

5 The PCIJ rules against the proposed customs union between Austria and Germany.

7 **–29** The Assembly elects China, Panama, and Spain to the Council.

10 Mutiny sweeps through the British Home Fleet when a government economy measure reduces the pay of seamen by 25 percent but leaves officers' pay relatively unaffected.

12 Mexico joins the League of Nations.

18 Japan blames China for an explosion on the tracks of the South Manchurian Railway near Mukden, and its Kwantung Army opens a major offensive in Manchuria.

21 China calls on the League to respond to the Japanese attack in Manchuria.

Because the London market has lost £200 million in gold and foreign currency since July, the British government abandons the gold standard, leading to a collapse of stock prices abroad and the dropping of the gold standard by other nations. To protect their markets against the now cheaper British goods, several countries raise their tariffs.

22 The Council calls on China and Japan to halt their fighting in Manchuria, while the United States reminds Japan of its Nine Power Treaty and Kellogg-Briand Pact obligations.

23 The United States recommends that the League delay its inquiry into the Manchurian crisis to avoid weakening the civilian elements in the Japanese government, but it does ask China and Japan to cease hostilities.

26 **–28** The Assembly adopts a general convention to improve the means of preventing war, while, ironically, public demonstrations in China call for war against Japan.

30 **–October 1** The Council unanimously adopts a resolution calling on China and Japan to restore normal relations. Japan assures the League that it has no intention of annexing Manchuria and that its troops will be withdrawn. China asks for League supervision if such a withdrawal occurs.

OCTOBER

4 José Esteban Montero, acting president, succeeds Ibáñez as president of Chile after defeating Arturo Alessandrie, a former chief executive popular with the working class.

9 Challenged by Hitler's growing power in the Reichstag and by opposition from moderate deputies to his rule by decree, Bruening reorganizes his cabinet to eliminate moderates like Foreign Minister Julius Curtius.

Japan refuses to set a timetable for its withdrawal from Manchuria, and China calls for a League meeting to deal with the expanding Japanese operations there.

10 Hitler has his first meeting with President Hindenburg, which leads to press speculation that he will be named chancellor. In fact, however, Hindenburg is unimpressed by the Bohemian corporal, as he calls him.

11 The United States complains about Japan's failure to fulfill its promise to withdraw its troops from Manchuria.

13 The Spanish Cortes (parliament) calls for the separation of Church and State.

16 An American representative, Prentiss B. Gilbert, attends the Council session on Manchuria, which recommends that members ask their governments to invoke the Kellogg-Briand Pact. The following day, several nations send notes to Japan and China reminding them of their obligations under the treaty; the United States sends a note on October 19.

21 Representatives of the Canton rebels and of the Nationalist government conduct talks to heal the political division in China.

24 The Council calls on Japan to remove its troops from Manchuria by November 16, but the Japanese delegate vetoes the resolution.

25 Laval meets with Hoover to discuss the retention of the gold standard by France and the United States. Hoover calls for progress in the disarmament talks, but Laval insists on safeguards for security before France will agree to arms limitations.

26 Secretary-General Drummond suggests that Japan consider the Chinese pledge to fulfill its treaty obligations as an opportunity to end the Manchurian crisis "without losing face."

27 Voters in Great Britain endorse a coalition government, and Mac-Donald continues as prime minister.

NOVEMBER

1 Fifty-four nations accept the Assembly's resolution calling for a one-year armament truce, which becomes effective immediately.

6 Secretary-General Drummond expresses his belief that the Manchurian crisis is a critical test for the League that requires the major powers to fulfill their obligations to the Covenant.

6 –7 The League again appeals to China and Japan to end their fighting, but Japan informs the Council that it will not withdraw from Manchuria until China accepts a settlement.

7 Mao Tse-tung establishes the Chinese Soviet Republic in the Kiangsi province.

11 The Washington Commission of Neutrals assists the Bolivian and Paraguayan efforts to settle the Chaco dispute.

The League repeats its call for peace in Manchuria. The United States announces that Charles Dawes will not "attend" the Council session but that he will instead act as an observer.

12 A committee of Spain's Constituent Assembly finds King Alfonso XIII guilty of high treason and bans him from returning to Spain.

12 –13 Avenol suggests that Drummond encourage private talks

Mao Tse-tung established the Chinese Soviet Republic on November 7, 1931.

between China and Japan in an effort to avoid the public League sessions. The secretary-general, however, sees no possibility of direct talks because China has already rejected bilateral negotiations while Japan occupies Manchuria. In addition, he does not want to force China into unwanted discussions with Japan.

13 In response to the League's appeal of November 6, China pledges not to use force and invites League observers to visit Manchuria. Japan states that its troops will remain in place unless attacked and also invites an on-site study of the situation.

At a meeting of the Franco-German Economic Committee, the Weimar delegates insist on the reconsideration of both short-term loans and reparations, while the French wish to discuss only reparations.

The Permanent Mandates Commission reports that Iraq is ready for independence.

14 The USSR charges that anti-Soviet propaganda is being disseminated by the Japanese army in Manchuria.

20 China and Japan agree in principle to the League's conducting an on-site investigation of the Manchurian crisis.

24 Japan assures the United States that no military operations will be conducted against Chinchow.

25 The Council reaffirms its resolution of September 30 calling upon China and Japan to restore peace in Manchuria. China requests that League forces occupy a neutral zone between Chinese and Japanese troops; Japan objects, saying that this would interfere with its efforts to resolve the conflict directly with China.

26 –27 The League recommends sending an observer group to Chinchow to monitor Japan's compliance with its earlier pledge, but the Japanese reject the proposal.

27 Right-wing demonstrators disrupt the final ceremonial meeting of the Preparatory Commission for the World Disarmament Conference in Paris.

DECEMBER

2 The League restates its resolution of November 25 and again seeks the evacuation of Japanese troops from Manchuria as soon as possible.

3 Parliament passes the Statute of Westminster Bill to give legal status to the decisions of the Imperial Conference of 1926, which made the Dominions autonomous, equal, and bound by common allegiance to the Crown.

5 Meeting since September, the Second Round Table Conference on India fails to draft a new constitution because the Moslems and Hindus disagree over proportional representation in the parliament. Gandhi and the Indian National Congress call for complete independence.

6 The Pan-Islamic Conference, meeting in Jerusalem, calls for a boycott of Zionist goods and for the formation of an association to purchase Palestinian land. It appeals to all Moslems, not only Arabs, to protect their interests in the Holy Land and to establish a university in Jerusalem.

9 –10 The new Spanish constitution provides for separation of Church and State, nationalization of Church property, and secularization of education. It also grants the government extensive rights of expropriation and nationalization. Niceto Alcalá Zamora becomes the first president of the Spanish Republic, and Manuel Azaña becomes the first premier.

10 The League appoints a Commission of Inquiry, headed by the Earl of Lytton (Victor Lytton) to conduct an investigation in Manchuria.

11 The PCIJ hands down its opinion that Poland does not have the right to send a warship to the Danzig harbor.

Japan abandons the gold standard.

13 Tsuyoshi Inukai succeeds Reijiro Wakatsuki as Japanese prime minister and approves funding for the occupation of Manchuria.

15 Student demonstrations against the government's weakness lead to the resignation of Chiang Kai-shek and his succession by Lin Sen.

29 The Japanese army is reportedly advancing on Chinchow in "antibandit" operations.

1932

JANUARY

3 Japanese troops take Chinchow and drive most of the Chinese forces from Manchuria.

4 The new British viceroy orders Gandhi's third arrest, outlaws the Indian National Congress, and imprisons all of the Congress leaders. Civil disorders erupt, and over 32,000 people are arrested in January and February.

7 U.S. Secretary of State Henry Stimson announces a nonrecognition doctrine in response to Japan's aggression in Manchuria. The United States will not recognize any changes affecting the status of China brought about in violation of open-door policy and the Kellogg-Briand Pact. Japanese leaders accurately appraise the United States' unwillingness to use economic or military sanctions and ignore Stimson's "paper deterrent."

9 The Bruening government welcomes the report of the Young Committee, which justifies Germany's deferring its July reparations payments because of the impact of the world Depression on the German economy.

Emperor Hirohito of Japan escapes an assassination attempt by a Korean nationalist.

18 –20 A clash between Chinese and Japanese groups in Shanghai results in the death of a Japanese national. Japan's consul general in Shanghai demands an apology and indemnity from the mayor of the city.

22 Stalin announces that the Soviet Union's first Five Year Plan, begun in 1928, will be completed in four years, and the second Five Year Plan will begin in January 1933. The new plan's goals will include a 300-percent increase in consumer goods, in addition to similar increases in heavy industry, oil, and electricity.

24 The foreign consuls in Shanghai protest against threats as Japan increases its naval force.

25 Poland and the USSR sign a nonaggression pact.

27 –28 Although the Chinese mayor of Shanghai accepts an ultimatum from the Japanese consul general, Japanese Admiral Koichi Shiozawa orders an occupation of Chapei, the Chinese district of Shanghai.

28 The Council calls for an end to the British mandate over Iraq as soon as a minorities guarantee can be offered and admission to the League can be voted on.

29 Encountering unexpected resistance from the Chinese, the Japanese bomb Chapei. China requests League assistance.

FEBRUARY

2 Representatives of fifty-nine nations gather in Geneva for the long-awaited World Disarmament Conference, but they have to delay the opening session to deal with the Shanghai incident.

2–3 Great Britain asks the League to delay its action on the Manchurian crisis so that France, England, Italy, and the United States can submit a five-point peace proposal to China and Japan. China accepts the plan, but Japan does not.

3 Additional United States army and naval forces arrive in Shanghai to protect American personnel and property.

5 French War Minister André Tardieu submits a plan to the World Disarmament Conference that calls for the transfer of offensive army weapons, capital ships, and large submarines and aircraft to the League of Nations for use as part of an international military force.

A new Japanese offensive in Manchuria captures Harbin.

7 The Scandinavian nations, Belgium, and the Netherlands begin economic cooperation under the Oslo Convention.

16 Laval resigns for the second time in two months when the French senate defeats an electoral-reform measure that includes women's suffrage.

Tardieu becomes premier and foreign minister.

The Council adopts the Stimson Non-Recognition Doctrine and advises Japan that it will not acknowledge territorial changes achieved by aggression.

18 Japan announces the existence of the new state of Manchukuo, which declares its independence from China.

Bruening asks the Disarmament Conference to allow military equality for Germany.

23 In a letter to Senator William E. Borah, chairman of the Senate Committee on Foreign Relations, Stimson indicates that the Nine Power Treaty on China and the Five Power Naval Limitation Treaty of the Washington Conference on the Limitation of Armaments are interrelated.

29 The United States agrees to participate in an international conference sponsored by the Council to end the fighting in Shanghai.

MARCH

2 Great Britain announces that it will not oppose the formation of the new state of Manchukuo.

3 A cease-fire becomes effective in Shanghai after a month-long battle leaves Chapei in ruins.

3–11 The Assembly opens a special session on the Sino-Japanese dispute and calls for an armistice and the evacuation of Japanese troops from Shanghai. It also adopts the Stimson Doctrine and appoints a Committee of Nineteen to report on the China conflict.

9 Japan installs Henry Pu-yi, the former boy emperor of China who abdicated the throne in 1912, as regent of Manchukuo.

Éamon de Valéra is elected president of the Irish Free State. His economic program to diversify agriculture and encourage industry leads to a bitter tariff war with Great Britain.

Sir Samuel Hoare (left) and Neville Chamberlain represented Great Britain at the World Disarmament Conference, which convened in Geneva on February 2, 1932.

13 The German presidential election is forced into a run-off when none of the candidates (Theodor Duesterberg, Paul von Hindenburg, Adolph Hitler, Ernst Thaelmann, and Gustav Winter) wins a majority of the votes.

APRIL

10 Hindenburg wins the presidential election with 53 percent of the votes. Hitler received 36.8 percent, and Thaelmann, 10.2 percent.

11 Hugh Gibson, the American representative to the Disarmament Conference, offers a plan that would abolish land aggressive weapons—tanks, heavy artillery, and gas.

12 –30 The International Labour Conference agrees to bar the employment of children in nonindustrial occupations.

13 Bruening bans the Nazi Storm Troopers as his government begins to weaken.

14 Japan refuses to meet with the Assembly's Committee of Nineteen.

19 Bruening seeks an increase in German troop strength and equipment, but the Disarmament Conference instead adopts a resolution providing for the progressive reduction of armaments.

20 –June 4 The Lytton Commission investigates the origins and development of the Manchurian crisis.

Social democrats listen to speakers at a rally in Berlin.

27 The British government advises that it will invoke the "escape clause" of the London Naval Treaty of 1930 if no agreement on naval disarmament is reached.

MAY

5 China and Japan accept an Assembly resolution that provides for an armistice in Shanghai and the evacuation of Japanese troops.

6 An anticommunist Soviet émigré, hoping to provoke a Franco-Russian war, assassinates French President Paul Doumer. On May 10, the National Assembly chooses Albert Lebrun as Doumer's successor.

15 Radical Japanese junior officers, identifying themselves as nationalists and calling for an end to political corruption, bomb banks and a police station and then assassinate Prime Minister Inukai. The emperor appoints Admiral Makoto Saito as head of the new government, which is completely under the control of the military.

Admiral Viscount Makoto Saito became prime minister of Japan on May 15, 1932, as part of a new government completely under the control of the military.

JUNE

2 Hindenburg names Franz von Papen as chancellor after dismissing Bruening because of his plan to increase taxes by emergency decree.

4 Following the overthrow of the José Esteban Montero government, Cárlos Dávila leads a junta, which adopts a program of progressive socialism, beginning with the nationalization of Chile's industry and foreign trade.

15 Bolivian troops attack a Paraguayan post in the Chaco.

16 Papen lifts the legal ban on Hitler's Brown Shirts.

16 –July 9 The Lausanne Conference on reparations lowers Germany's obligation to $714 million contingent on the United States' reduction of the Allied war debts. However, the Hoover administration is bound by a Joint Resolution of Congress from December 22, 1931, that opposes any concessions on war debts, so the president insists that reparations are a "strictly European problem."

22 Hoover proposes to the Disarmament Conference that the army strength of all nations be reduced by one-third and that comparable limitations be applied to naval power.

30 The American, British, and French ambassadors in Tokyo protest the seizure of Chinese customs offices in Manchukuo by the government installed by Japan.

JULY

12 Norway annexes Frederick VI Land in southeast Greenland.

15 The Council approves a loan to Austria on the condition that it will not join Germany in an economic or political union for twenty years.

18 Belgium, the Netherlands, and Luxemburg sign a convention to reduce their economic barriers.

Foreign Minister Yasuya Uchida indicates that Japan will formally recognize Manchukuo.

Turkey enters the League after a period of alienation from the Western European Allies following World War I and from the League, whose mandate system it viewed as an instrument of Western imperialism. Secretary-General Drummond had encouraged Turkey's entry as a means of improving the League's role in the Near East.

21 –27 Bolivia and Paraguay exchange charges in the Council concerning the Chaco dispute.

21 –August 20 At the Imperial Economic Conference meeting in Ottawa, Great Britain abandons its free-trade policy for the first time since 1849. Imperial preferences favor the Commonwealth members.

22 Germany announces that its continued participation in the Disarmament Conference will depend on the recognition of its equality.

25 Poland and the USSR agree to a three-year nonaggression pact.

26 –27 General Kurt von Schleicher, minister of defense, threatens to reorganize the German army contrary to the Treaty of Versailles if the other nations do not disarm to Germany's level. France protests Schleicher's warning of unilateral action.

29 China embargoes goods from Manchuria in retaliation for the seizure of its customs offices.

30 The Reichstag elections give the Nazis 230 seats, with the social democrats at 133 and the communists at 89 as Hitler's closest rivals.

AUGUST

1 The Council calls on Bolivia and Paraguay to cease fighting in the Chaco and to settle their conflict.

3 Nineteen nations belonging to the Pan American Union advise Bolivia and Paraguay that they will not recognize any territorial changes made by force, as provided by the Stimson Doctrine.

5 The Washington Commission of Neutrals asks Bolivia and Paraguay to agree to arbitration.

10 A monarchist uprising in Madrid and Andalusia fails.

13 Hitler refuses to accept the post of vice chancellor in Papen's ministry.

SEPTEMBER

1 In violation of a cession made by treaty in 1922, Peruvian filibusters take the town of Leticia, which provides Colombia with access to the Amazon River. Popular support for war sweeps both countries, but Colombia asks for League intervention.

3 After losing favor with former President Plurtarco Elías Calles, who remains the dominant political force in Mexico, Ortiz Rubio resigns the presidency and is succeeded by another Calles choice, General Abelardo Rodríguez.

5 A conference on the economic reconstruction of Central and Eastern Europe opens at Stresa.

7 France rejects a German suggestion from August 29 for bilateral talks on disarmament.

10 Great Britain proposes a four-power conference to discuss arms equality for Germany, but France opposes it.

13 –October 30 General Bartolome Blanche replaces Chile's provisional president, Cárlos Dávila, in a military coup. Abraham H. Oyanedel succeeds Blanche on October 1, and Arturo Alessandrie wins the general election on October 30.

14 Secretary-General Drummond defers League intervention in the Chaco conflict and allows the Washington Commission of Neutrals to continue its efforts.
    Germany announces that it will not

The Gran Chaco was the subject of a heated border dispute between Bolivia and Paraguay. However, Secretary-General Drummond deferred League intervention in the dispute on September 14, 1932, in favor of the Washington Commission of Neutrals.

send a delegation to the next meeting of the Disarmament Conference unless it is offered arms equality.

15 Japan signs a treaty of alliance with Manchukuo.

20 Gandhi begins a Fast Unto Death to improve the status of India's Untouchables, and after six days, Hindus of all castes accede to his wishes.

24 Prime Minister Per Albin Hansson heads Sweden's socialist government, a position he will hold until his death in 1946.

25 The home rule granted to the Catalonians by the new Spanish con-stitution of 1931 prompts similar demands from the Basques.

26 The Assembly elects Czechoslovakia, Mexico, and Poland to the Council.

26 –30 The Council forms a Committee of Three to study the Chaco dispute, but the United States urges "patience" while the Washington Commission of Neutrals tries to end the conflict.

28 Argentina's Chamber of Deputies votes to rejoin the League.

30 –October 1 Peru is willing to arbitrate the Leticia incident, but Colombia rejects the proposal.

Per Albin Hansson became prime minister of Sweden on September 24, 1932.

30 –October 4 The Vatican and Mexico clash over the position of the Church in Mexican affairs. The papal legate, Archbishop Leopoldo Ruiz y Flores, is expelled from Mexico.

OCTOBER

2 The League releases the Lytton Report, which is extremely critical of Japan's actions in Manchuria but also acknowledges the grievances of Japan against China.

3 The civil war ends in Brazil; President Vargas adopts one of the rebels' objectives by announcing elections for a constituent congress, with Brazilian women granted the right to vote for the first time.
Iraq joins the League, and the British mandate ends.

4 Great Britain suggests a conference of the major powers to review Germany's demands concerning military equality.
Japan rejects the Lytton Report's peace proposals and refuses to change its Manchurian policy.
Julius Gömbös replaces Count Julius Károlyi as Hungary's premier. He pursues a policy of cooperation with Italy, hoping to secure territorial revision for Hungary.

5 The USSR introduces a five-year plan to promote atheism and to close all places of religious worship by May 1, 1937.

17 The Council appoints Joseph Avenol to succeed Sir Eric Drummond as secretary-general, effective July 1, 1933.

NOVEMBER

6 The Reichstag elections show a decline in Nazi strength to 196 seats, with the social democrats holding 121 seats and the communists increasing to 100 seats.

8 Franklin D. Roosevelt becomes president by a landslide in the United States, with 472 electoral votes to Hoover's 59.

9 –15 Council President Éamon de Valéra expresses concern over the continued fighting in the Chaco, but Stimson is confident that the Washington Commission of Neutrals will end the war.

14 France and Italy reopen their naval talks, which have been broken off since April 1931.

Franklin D. Roosevelt won the American presidential election by a landslide on November 8, 1932.

17 Papen resigns as German chancellor and, on December 2, is succeeded by General Kurt von Schleicher.

29 France and the USSR sign non-aggression and conciliation pacts.

DECEMBER

2 –11 France, Germany, Great Britain, Italy, and the United States reach a formula to restore German participation in the Disarmament Conference.

3 The Financial Committee reaches an agreement with Bulgaria on loan terms.

5 Japan's naval disarmament proposals include the abolition of aircraft carriers and long-range submarines, and the limitation of battleship armaments.

7 The Assembly approves the Lytton Report, and the Japanese delegation walks out of the meeting in protest.

11 Germany returns to the Disarmament Conference.

12 The USSR and Nationalist China resume diplomatic relations.

14 –18 The Herriot government loses a vote of confidence after advocating the payment of a war-debt installment to the United States. France defaults on December 15, and Joseph Paul-Boncour becomes premier on December 18.

15 Mexico believes that money it has allocated for League membership can be better utilized for domestic needs and resigns from the world body. Secretary-General Drummond had requested American intervention in September, when Mexico had first announced its intention to resign. In May 1933, following economic talks in Washington, Mexico withdraws its resignation notice.

15 –17 Belgium, Estonia, Hungary, Poland, and Yugoslavia all default on their war-debt payments to the United States. Hoover sends a special message to Congress concerning the debts and asks President-elect Franklin Roosevelt to collaborate in setting up a conference with the governments involved. Roosevelt refuses to commit the incoming administration, and Congress takes no action.

20 Paraguay rejects the Washington Commission of Neutrals' proposal to settle the Chaco conflict, and its delegate leaves Washington.

24 Alessandrie begins a six-year rule in Chile, during which his government carries out economic and social reforms with the support of both the liberal and conservative parties.

30 The Washington Commission of Neutrals informs the League of its failure to settle the Chaco dispute. However, it still believes the crisis can be best resolved by Western hemispheric nations and suggests intervention by the ABCP powers (Argentina, Brazil, Chile, and Peru).

1933

JANUARY

1 The Soviet Union begins its Second Five Year Plan, as Stalin proclaims that the First Plan, begun on October 1, 1928, is already completed. Although food shortages exist, the USSR now ranks second in the world production of pig iron, oil, and machine building, and third in coal and electricity.

Juan Bautista Sacasa is inaugurated as president of Nicaragua, and the U.S. Marine Corps completes its withdrawal the following day.

Japan's War Minister Sadao Araki dismisses the role of the League in the Manchurian crisis, and Japanese troops threaten Jehol province in northern China.

10 Mao Tse-tung calls for a united effort by Chinese communists and noncommunists against Japan.

13 Hoover vetoes a bill granting independence to the Philippine Islands, but Congress overrides his action. If the Philippine people approve

the measure, a ten-year probationary period will follow.

13 **–14** Secretary-General Drummond initiates Council admonitions of Colombia and Peru because of the Leticia conflict, and the Council calls on Peru "to refrain from any intervention by force in Colombian territory."

30 Hindenburg names Hitler to succeed Kurt von Schleicher as chancellor of Germany.

31 The Disarmament Conference reconvenes, but the French and German delegations disagree bitterly on proposals.

Paul-Boncour's cabinet falls, as the French Chamber of Deputies rejects a reduction in civil-service pay; radical socialist Édouard Daladier becomes premier.

FEBRUARY

4 Hitler issues a decree giving the government control over the press and political assembly.

9 The famous British debating society, the Oxford Union, adopts a resolution stating "that under no circumstances will we fight for King and Country."

14 Colombia breaks its diplomatic relations with Peru over the Leticia dispute.

14 **–16** The Little Entente powers (Czechoslovakia, Rumania, and Yugoslavia) express concern over a possible territorial revision by Germany and Hungary. They establish a standing council to coordinate their policies.

17 Hitler orders the German police to cooperate with his Nazi S.A. (Brown Shirts, or Storm Troopers) and S.S. (Black Shirts) in suppressing domestic opposition.

The Committee of Nineteen reaffirms the Lytton Report on the Manchurian crisis.

24 Japan demands that China recognize Manchukuo's control of

Jehol province, but Chiang Kai-shek refuses.

The Assembly adopts the report of the Committee of Nineteen, which had endorsed the Lytton Report by a vote of forty-two in favor, one opposed (Japan), and one abstained (Siam).

25 Bolivia and Paraguay reject a peace initiative by Argentina and Chile to settle the Chaco dispute.

Palestinian Arabs boycott British goods after High Commissioner Sir Arthur Wauchope rejects their demands for restrictions on Jewish immigration.

27 **–28** Hitler blames a Reichstag fire on the communists, and Hermann Goering warns the public of Red "terror squads preparing to start civil war." At Hitler's request, Hindenburg signs a decree suspending constitutional rights.

MARCH

1 The Council calls for the Peruvian evacuation of Leticia and temporary control of the area by the League using Colombian troops as an international force. Peru rejects the proposal.

Hermann Goering, founder and head of the Gestapo, warned the German public about communist "terror squads" after a Reichstag fire was blamed on them on February 27, 1933.

4 In his inaugural address, President Franklin Roosevelt tells the American people that "the only thing we have to fear is fear itself." He also promises "action now" to end the Depression.

4 –29 To control the Austrian national socialists calling for a union with Germany, Chancellor Engelbert Dollfuss assumes semidictatorial powers.

5 The Nazis and the nationalists form a majority coalition after the Reichstag elections, in which the Nazis win 288 seats; the socialists, 120; the communists, 81; the center, 74; and the nationalists, 52.

6 –13 Responding to the victory of the Danzig Nazis in local elections, Poland lands troops at the Westerplatte munitions depot. The League High Commissioner to Danzig, Helmar Rosting, requests Council intervention, but in order to avoid a public clash between Poland and Germany, Secretary-General Drummond privately exerts pressure on Poland to withdraw its troops.

13 Dr. Paul Joseph Goebbels becomes minister of propaganda and popular enlightenment in Germany. He describes the press as "a great keyboard on which the government can play."

16 Prime Minister MacDonald submits a British plan to the Disarmament Conference that will fix the armies of France, Germany, Italy, and Poland at 200,000 troops, with an additional 200,000 colonial troops for France and 50,000 for Italy. Military aircraft will be restricted to 500 for each major power.

18 –20 MacDonald meets with Mussolini in Rome to discuss the Duce's proposed Four Power Pact, which would coordinate the political and economic affairs of France, Germany, Great Britain, and Italy. Mussolini wishes to increase the independent role of the major powers outside the League structure.

20 Great Britain suspends commercial negotiations with the USSR because of the pending trials of six British subjects charged with sabotage by the Soviets.

23 The Enabling Act gives Hitler dictatorial power for four years.

27 Japan gives notice of its withdrawal from the League.

APRIL

1 Hitler orders a one-day boycott of Jewish businesses and professions. This reflects the increased physical and economic attacks against Jews carried on since his appointment as chancellor.

5 The PCIJ rejects Norway's claim to eastern Greenland.

6 Roosevelt begins a series of meetings with visiting heads of state in preparation for the World Economic Conference.

7 An Aryan law is passed barring any German with a Jewish grandparent from civil-service employment.

8 Manchukuo interrupts the transportation of Soviet goods on the Chinese Eastern Railway.

12 Antonio de Oliveira Salazar promulgates a new constitution that

Dr. Paul Joseph Goebbels became the German minister of propaganda and popular enlightenment on March 13, 1933.

makes Portugal a corporate state under his dictatorial rule.

12 **–22** Of the six British subjects tried for sabotage by the Soviet Union, one is acquitted, three are expelled, and two are sentenced to prison. The United Kingdom embargoes Soviet goods, and the Soviet Union imposes a similar restriction on British trade.

30 Peruvian President Luis Sánchez Cerro is assassinated by a member of the radical APRA (Alianza Popular Revolucionaria Americana) and is succeeded by General Don Oscar Benavides, who has the support of conservative groups.

MAY

2 The Nazi government forces all workers to join the German Labor Front after dissolving all other unions.

The USSR offers to sell the Chinese Eastern Railway to Japan.

3 Peruvian naval units move through the Panama Canal en route to Leticia.

Ireland's Dail (the lower house of the legislature) abolishes the oath of loyalty to the king of England and votes that its legislation no longer needs the approval of the governor general.

5 Germany and the USSR renew their neutrality pact.

8 Gandhi begins a three-week fast to secure the admission of Untouchables to all of India's temples. The British government had released him from jail in Poona, where he had been held since January 1932.

10 Hitler dissolves all socialist parties in Germany.

In a demonstration at Berlin's Humboldt University, students and Storm Troopers "burn the books" judged objectionable by the Nazi government. These include the works of Sigmund Freud, Erich Remarque, Karl Marx, Albert Einstein, and Thomas Mann.

Paraguay declares war against Bolivia in the Chaco dispute.

Mahatma Gandhi (left), shown here with the Aga Khan, began a three-week fast on May 8, 1933, to secure the admission of Untouchables to all of India's temples. He had just been released from jail.

11 Foreign Minister Konstantin von Neurath insists on equal rights for Germany in any disarmament plan.

17 To break the power of the Catholic Church in Spain, the socialist coalition orders the closing of all parochial schools and the nationalization of Church property.

20 The League's Saar Basin Governing Commission bans all political demonstrations.

21 Secretary-General Drummond asks the Council to review complaints against anti-Semitic regulations in Upper Silesia. The American Jewish Congress praises his intervention, and Jewish newspaper editors name him one of the twelve leading Christian defenders of Jews in 1933.

25 Peru and Colombia accept a League proposal to settle the Leticia conflict—Peru will evacuate Leticia, a League commission will rule Leticia for one year, and the issue will be submitted to final arbitration.

26 Austria bans the Communist Party.

28 Local Nazis win a majority in the Danzig senate.

29 Germany imposes a fee of 1,000 marks for tourist visas to Austria.

31 The Tangku Truce ends the conflict between China and Japan, leaving Japan in control of Manchukuo and Jehol province.

JUNE

4 The United States Reconstruction Finance Corporation grants a loan of $50,000,000 to China.

12 Sixty-four nations attend the World Monetary and Economic Conference, which opens in London. Europe's six gold-standard nations hope to establish a currency-stabilization formula based on gold, but Roosevelt unexpectedly refuses to bind the United States to a currency agreement, and the conference collapses.

15 Belgium, France, Estonia, Poland, and Hungary default on their debt payments to the United States, while Czechoslovakia, Great Britain, Italy, Latvia, and Rumania forward partial or token payments. Only Finland makes a full payment.

19 Austria outlaws the local Nazi Party as violence increases.

27 The Washington Commission of Neutrals announces that it is withdrawing from the negotiations to resolve the Chaco War and is leaving the issue in the hands of the League.

27 –July 4 The German Nationalist Front and the German People's Party dissolve themselves when Goebbels warns that the Nazis will "tolerate no other party. We annihilate other parties!"

28 China requests the dispatch of a technical agent to serve as a liaison between it and the League. On July 18, the Council appoints Dr. Ludwik Rajchman.

29 The major powers are unable to agree on a disarmament plan, and the conference adjourns until October 16.

JULY

1 Soviet authorities release the two British prisoners from jail, and British-Soviet trade relations are resumed.

Joseph Avenol becomes the second secretary-general of the League of Nations. Sir Eric Drummond predicts an optimistic future for the world body, which, he says, is in "the best of hands."

3 A special session of the Council appoints a Commission of Inquiry for the Chaco War.

5 The German government prohibits all Catholic political parties.

10 –23 Arthur Henderson, president of the Disarmament Conference, discusses the future of the negotiations with the heads of state of France, Italy, Germany, Czechoslovakia, Austria, and Great Britain.

20 German Vice Chancellor Franz von Papen and Papal Secretary of State Eugenio Cardinal Pacelli sign the first concordat between the Vatican and the government of all Germany. It provides safeguards for the Church and Catholic education but requires the clergy to avoid politics.

26 At the request of Bolivia and Paraguay, the League consents to mediation efforts by the ABCP powers (Argentina, Brazil, Chile, and Peru) in the Chaco War and suspends its own work.

28 The Spanish Republic establishes diplomatic relations with the Soviet Union.

AUGUST

1 Gandhi is arrested again when he begins another march for Indian independence. Sentenced to prison for one year, he begins another fast, and the British authorities release him.

5 Poland reaches an agreement with Danzig that secures protection for its nationals there, while allocating a percentage of its export trade to the port, which has suffered from the development of the new port at Gdynia.

7 Germany states that foreign intervention in Austro-German relations is unacceptable and rebuffs the Anglo-French efforts to refer it to the Four Power Pact of March 18–20.

The United States signs a treaty with Haiti providing for the withdrawal of American troops and the Haitianization of the country's military forces.

11 Cuba's liberal President Gerardo Machado y Morales is deposed in an army officers' coup, and Carlos Manuel de Céspedes succeeds him.

SEPTEMBER

2 Italy and the USSR sign a pact of friendship, neutrality, and nonaggression.

5 –10 Cuban President De Céspedes' proposal to reduce military pay sparks the Revolt of the Sergeants, which is joined by sugar workers seeking higher wages. De Céspedes is replaced by an executive committee, of which one member, Ramón Grau San Martín, becomes president. Roosevelt orders thirty American naval vessels to the area and withholds recognition of the new government.

8 –12 The Azaña government resigns after its defeat in the Spanish elections, and Alejandro Lerroux forms a new ministry without socialist members.

13 In his first interview since taking office, Secretary-General Avenol expresses interest in the "great economic experiment" underway in the United States. He believes that the Disarmament Conference will succeed and is impressed by the increasing global influence of the League as it responds to crises in Asia and Latin America.

18 –29 Negotiations involving France, Germany, Great Britain, Italy, and the United States fail to develop a disarmament plan acceptable to both France and Germany.

25 The Assembly elects Argentina, Australia, and Denmark to the Council and creates a new nonpermanent seat, to which Portugal is elected.

Manuel Azaña and his government resigned after being defeated in the Spanish elections on September 8, 1933.

OCTOBER

1 The mediation effort by the ABCP powers to end the Chaco War fails, and the League sends its Committee of Inquiry to Bolivia and Paraguay, where it arranges a cease-fire beginning in November.

3 Chancellor Dollfuss of Austria escapes the first Nazi assassination attempt against him.

After only twenty-one days in office, Spain's Lerroux government resigns, and conservative Diego Martínez Barrio forms a new ministry, with instructions from President Alcalá Zamora to dissolve the Cortes and call for new elections.

11 The Assembly adopts a resolution to assist Jewish and other refugees from Germany. James G. McDonald will serve as the League's High Commissioner for this purpose.

13 –29 The economic distress of rural Palestinian Arabs along with their opposition to Jewish immigration and land acquisition incites new rioting, which leaves one police officer and twenty-six civilians dead.

14 Germany withdraws from the Disarmament Conference and announces its intention to leave the League.

17 The Saar Basin Governing Commission bans the wearing of political uniforms and badges in the region.

In a conference with President Harmodio Arias, President Roosevelt agrees that Panama's commercial rights as a sovereign nation should be acknowledged in the Canal Zone.

22 The Council agrees to Guatemala's request to have a League expert reorganize its fiscal system.

25 With Brazil serving as mediator, Colombia and Peru open negotiations to end the Leticia dispute.

26 Sean Lester of the Irish Free State is named High Commissioner to Danzig, effective January 15, 1934.

26 –28 Fourteen nations accept the Council's invitation to serve on the Governing Body advising the High Commissioner for Refugees (Jewish and Others) Coming From Germany.

27 Albert Sarraut forms a new French government after Daladier is defeated on a budget issue.

NOVEMBER

12 Nearly 90 percent of German voters approve Hitler's decision to withdraw from the Disarmament Conference and the League. Nazi Party candidates win 87.8 percent of the votes in the Reichstag elections.

13 The Saar Basin Governing Commission prohibits Germans from moving into the Saar.

16 The United States recognizes the Soviet Union in an exchange of notes that include the freedom of worship for American citizens in the USSR and restraints on Soviet-sponsored propaganda in the United States.

19 Spain's right-wing parties win 44 percent of the seats in the Cortes to the left's 21 percent; the Falange Española, Spain's fascist party, is founded.

25 During a visit to Rome, Avenol meets with Mussolini to discuss the Duce's objection to the voting pro-

---

After his first six months in office, Secretary-General Joseph Avenol discussed the problems of the League and the World Disarmament Conference, which he attributed in part to "selfish nationalism." (Source: *The New York Times*, December 31, 1933.)

A crisis in League affairs is shown by the fact that two members of the Council [Japan and Germany] have given notice of their intention to withdraw from the League, and a third member [Italy] has openly expressed her desire to see radical changes made in it. The very large majority of countries in the world who still believe in the League appear to be losing confidence in its ability to deal effectively with the major problems of the day.

While in an ideal world States would be regarded as equal before the law, the Covenant makes no attempt to introduce such an ideal system. It accepts the existence of Great Powers and gives them, as permanent members of the Council, adequate opportunities of exercising the authority in world affairs which belongs to great people. The Covenant does not abolish war, but it makes it as difficult as it can for a State to wage war or having once started, to wage it successfully.

The problem of disarmament is the root cause of the crisis in the League. The problem of disarmament has been reduced to one of equality of rights. This is a purely European matter, but it predominated the General Disarmament Conference in such a way that reduction of armaments had to be relegated to the background, while the problem of equality was dealt with almost entirely by the Great Powers negotiating among themselves.

The result has been that the other powers attending the conference have learned almost simultaneously of the lack of success achieved by the Great Powers in their negotiations and of the decision of Germany to withdraw from the League. How can the League secure cooperation between its members and how can it assume a responsibility distinct from that of its principal members in regard to problems with which its constitutional bodies have not been invited to deal?

cedure in the League and his belief that the major powers should have greater authority in decision-making.

27 Unable to secure legislative approval to balance the French budget, Sarraut resigns, and Camille Chautemps becomes premier.

DECEMBER

10 The French Foreign Ministry informs Secretary-General Avenol that it opposes Mussolini's proposal to change the League's "democratic character." Meeting with British leaders, Avenol expresses his belief in a "flexible League" but insists that changes must be made in conformity with the procedures established by the Covenant.

15 Secretary of State Cordell Hull presents a new American policy of non-intervention in hemispheric affairs to the Pan American Conference in Montevideo.

26 The Pan American Conference recommends that Bolivia and Paraguay accept League mediation to end the Chaco War.

29 Rumanian Prime Minister Ion Duca is assassinated by the Iron Guard; the liberal government maintains control by arresting the leaders of the fascist organization.

31 Secretary-General Avenol blames the current "crisis in League affairs" on the Disarmament Conference and its preoccupation with "equality of rights" rather than arms reduction.

1934

JANUARY

1 Germany begins manufacturing aircraft for its *Luftwaffe* in violation of the Treaty of Versailles.

1 **–19** France rejects a German proposal for arms equality, and Germany refuses a French counterproposal, as the Disarmament Conference withers.

7 Paraguay refuses to extend the truce reached in December 1933, and fighting resumes in the Chaco War.

15 **–18** Cuba's President Grau San Martín resigns under pressure, and the revolutionary junta ultimately appoints Colonel Carlos Mendieta as his successor.

24 Sean Lester succeeds Helmar Rosting as High Commissioner to Danzig.

27 The Serge Stavisky bond fraud implicates French government officials and topples the Chautemps ministry. Édouard Daladier forms a new French cabinet.

29 **–30** Great Britain proposes the limited rearmament of Germany and partial disarming by the other powers, but Hitler demands equality. Mussolini supports the expansion of Germany's army provided Hitler rejoins the League.

Édouard Daladier became premier of France on January 27, 1934.

FEBRUARY

6 **–9** The Stavisky scandal triggers rioting in Paris between right- and left-wing political factions that leaves 21 dead and 2,400 seriously injured. Gaston Doumergue forms a National Union ministry, composed of officials untouched by the scandal, to end the civil strife in France.

9 Greece, Rumania, Turkey, and Yugoslavia sign the Balkan Pact, pledging to observe their boundaries.

11 **–15** Chancellor Dollfuss outlaws the Social Democratic Party in Austria. The violence used by the government arouses the hostility of the working classes.

17 Great Britain, France, and Italy announce their support of Austrian independence.
King Albert I of Belgium dies and is succeeded by his son Leopold III.

MARCH

1 Japan installs Henry Pu-yi as emperor of Manchukuo, with the title "Kang Teh."

6 **–11** Bolivia and Paraguay reject the peace plan offered by the League's Commission of Inquiry for the Chaco War and pursue bilateral negotiations.

17 Austria, Italy, and Hungary adopt the Rome Protocols to develop closer economic and political relations. Their Danubian Bloc is intended to balance the Little Entente.

24 The American Tydings-McDuffie Act provides for the independence of the Philippine Islands in 1945.

28 Hitler rejects a Soviet overture for a joint pledge of peace to Estonia, Finland, Latvia, and Lithuania.

APRIL

4 Estonia, Latvia, and Lithuania extend their nonaggression pacts with the Soviet Union.

7 Finland renews its nonaggression pact with the Soviet Union.

10 Japan objects to British and American loans and credits to China.

13 Roosevelt signs the Johnson Act, barring loans and credits to nations that have defaulted on debts to the United States.

17 Japan advises foreign nations not to extend loans to China without Japanese approval.

19 Uruguay's President Gabriel Terra is reelected under a new constitution and continues the Liberal Party's program of social and economic reform.

26 France seeks a renewal of its alliance with Czechoslovakia.

30 The Austrian parliament ratifies a new constitution that transforms the country into a corporate state and gives Chancellor Dollfuss dictatorial power.

MAY

3 Avenol assures Japan that League aid to China is purely technical and that no loans are involved.

5 The USSR and Poland extend their nonaggression pact for ten more years.

8 Hungary submits its border dispute with Yugoslavia to the Council.

12 The Council calls for an embargo on arms shipments to Bolivia and Paraguay.

14 Brazil initiates a new peace move by the ABCP powers to end the Chaco War.

18 France and the USSR discuss an Eastern European pact of nonaggression and mutual assistance.

19 Colonel Kimon Gueorguieff leads an army coup in Bulgaria.

24 Colombia and Peru sign a peace protocol that ends the Leticia conflict and provides for agreements on customs houses, free navigation of rivers, and policing of frontiers.

25 Argentina attempts to mediate the Chaco War.

28 The United States joins the League embargo on military sales to Bolivia and Paraguay.

29 Tomáš Masaryk is elected president of Czechoslovakia for the fourth successive time.
The Disarmament Conference reopens, and Great Britain and France immediately clash over policy toward Germany. Sir John Simon urges concessions to Berlin, and Louis Barthou refuses to let Germany "impose her will" on the conference.

30 Cuba and the United States sign a treaty ending the Platt Amendment, which authorized American intervention in Cuba's domestic and foreign affairs.

31 The League agrees to act on Bolivia's call for mediation to end the Chaco War.

JUNE

9 The Little Entente powers establish formal diplomatic relations with the USSR.

11 Chairman Arthur Henderson blames France for the failure of the Disarmament Conference to reach an agreement before adjournment.

14 –15 Hitler and Mussolini meet for the first time but do not agree on any common policy.

15 Finland is the only debtor nation to pay its full obligations to the United States.

19 Roosevelt approves a Joint Resolution of Congress authorizing United States membership in the International Labour Organisation.

23 Mussolini orders a naval show of force in Albanian waters as an apparent response to French Foreign Minister Louis Barthou's visit to the Balkans and to give his assurance to Rumania that its frontiers would be preserved.

30 On the Night of the Long Knives, Hitler purges his opposition within the Nazi Party; at least seventy-seven people are killed, including Ernst Roehm, commander of the Brown Shirts, and Gregor Strasser, a former leader of the Nazi Party.

JULY

2 General Lázaro Cárdenas is elected president of Mexico and promises to "revive the revolutionary activity of the masses."

7 Admiral Keisuke Okada becomes prime minister of Japan.

12 Austria announces the death penalty for terrorists as Dollfuss continues to oppose the Nazis.

13 Great Britain supports France's proposal for an Eastern European Locarno agreement, which would be comparable to the Western European Locarno pact of 1925 and would have Germany, the USSR, Poland, and the Baltic States guaranteeing existing frontiers.

19 Great Britain announces that its Royal Air Force will be expanded by 1,000 fighter aircraft.

21 Hungary and Yugoslavia settle their border dispute after discussions in the Council.

25 Austrian Nazis assassinate Dollfuss in a coup attempt that fails.

Benito Mussolini (left) and Adolph Hitler found that they did not have any common policies when they met for the first time on June 14–15, 1934.

Mussolini orders an Italian military deployment along the Austrian frontier and announces that he will defend Austria's independence. Germany denies any connection with the incident.

30 Kurt von Schuschnigg becomes chancellor of Austria.

AUGUST

2 –19 Paul von Hindenburg dies, and Hitler assumes presidential power. By plebiscite, 88 percent of German voters approve Hitler's uniting the powers of the president and the chancellor, and accept his wish to be known as the Fuehrer. All army and naval personnel take a personal oath to him.

21 Schuschnigg and Mussolini agree on the retention of Austria's independence.
    The Boycott Commission of the World Jewish Conference calls for increased economic pressure against Germany to restore the rights of German Jews but acknowledges that "fear of German reprisals" hampers support in the Jewish community. The American Jewish Congress recommends a cautious policy.

SEPTEMBER

1 Secretary-General Avenol stresses the need for an independent League effort to settle the Chaco War and criticizes his predecessor's willingness to let non-League groups assume responsibility in the crisis.

10 Germany rejects France's proposal for an Eastern European Locarno agreement.

12 The Baltic States sign a treaty of cooperation and pledge their support to the League.

14 The Little Entente supports an Eastern European Locarno agreement and the admission of the USSR into the League.

18 Faced with the threat of Hitler's Germany and an expansionist Japan, the USSR retracts its previous denunciation of the League and enters the world body.

25 The League announces that twenty-eight nations are cooperating to bar arms trade with Bolivia and Paraguay.

27 France, Great Britain, and Italy declare their support for Austrian independence.
    Despite its continued hostility toward Great Britain, Afghanistan is influenced by the USSR's example and joins the League.

27 –28 The Assembly appoints a Committee of Twenty-Two to settle the Chaco War, but the committee fails to devise a formula for the talks between Bolivia and Paraguay.

28 Influenced by the League's role in the Leticia dispute, Ecuador enters the world body to protect its claims to territory in the Amazon Basin.

29 Italy and Ethiopia renew their 1928 treaty of friendship.
    Secretary-General Avenol admits that the League "has lost in popularity and prestige" but insists that the alternative to the League is "complete anarchy."

OCTOBER

5 The socialists, communists, and anarcho-syndicalists call for a general strike in Spain to protest the conservative government of Alejandro Lerroux. The government suppresses rioting in Madrid, an independence movement in Catalonia, and a communist regime in Austurias.

9 King Alexander I of Yugoslavia and Foreign Minister Barthou of France are assassinated in Marseilles by a Macedonian revolutionary.

24 –November 5 Great Britain and the United States insist that a proposed oil monopoly by Manchukuo would violate both open-door policy and the Nine Power Treaty. Japan denies all responsibility for Manchukuo's actions and recommends that London and Washington communicate directly with that government.

NOVEMBER

2 League intervention settles the conflict between Peru and Colombia over Leticia.

22 Yugoslavia charges Hungary with complicity in the death of King Alexander I, and both countries request a League investigation.

DECEMBER

1 The assassination of Stalin's close collaborator, Serge Kirov, signals a purge of many of the prominent members of the Soviet Communist Party.

Hitler climbs stairs in Nuremberg to speak to 160,000 Brown Shirts.

1935

JANUARY

1 Ethiopia requests League intervention in its dispute with Italy.

4 –8 In negotiations with Mussolini in Rome, French Foreign Minister Pierre Laval offers concessions in Africa that the Duce interprets to include a "free hand" in Ethiopia.

13 In a League-conducted plebiscite, 90 percent of Saar voters favor reunion with Germany.

14 –16 Since Bolivia has accepted the League peace plan while Paraguay has rejected it, the League Advisory Committee on the Chaco War recommends lifting the arms embargo against Bolivia but retaining it against Paraguay.

17 Gregory Zinoviev, Leo Kamenev, and other Old Bolsheviks are imprisoned in the Soviet Union for treason, conspiracy against Stalin, and the murder of Kirov.

29 The U.S. Senate rejects participation in the PCIJ.

31 United States–Soviet Union negotiations concerning American claims dating back to the Bolshevik Revolution break down.

FEBRUARY

3 The United States announces that it will withhold most-favored-nation treatment from all countries that discriminate against American goods.

11 Italy mobilizes two divisions for service in Italian Somaliland.

14 Germany rejects an Anglo-French invitation to participate in the negotiations for the Eastern European Locarno agreement.

5 Italian and Ethiopian troops clash at the Wal Wal oasis, near the border of Ethiopia and Italian Somaliland.

10 The Council's investigation of the death of King Alexander I of Yugoslavia concludes that some Hungarian officials were delinquent in their duty to prevent acts of terrorism. Hungary agrees to undertake a further study of the matter and to report to the Council.

10 –18 Bolivia accepts the League peace plan to end the Chaco War, but Paraguay rejects it.

16 Italy refuses mediation by the League in the Italo-Ethiopian crisis.

22 An international military force sent by the League arrives in the Saar to insure an orderly plebiscite.

29 Japan renounces the 1930 London Naval Treaty after Great Britain and the United States refuse the Empire parity.

30 Mussolini orders his military command to plan for war against Ethiopia.

Saarlanders mark their ballots as part of the League-sponsored plebiscite on January 13, 1935 that decided the fate of the Saar.

23 Paraguay withdraws from the League because of the arms embargo.

MARCH

1 The Saar is officially reunited with Germany.

9 Germany announces the existence of its air force despite its prohibition by the Treaty of Versailles.

15 **–22** France extends the term of service to two years for all conscripts called until 1939.

16 In another direct violation of Versailles, Hitler announces German rearmament and the institution of compulsory military service.

21 Persia is renamed Iran.

23 The USSR agrees to turn over the Chinese Eastern Railway to Manchukuo.

27 **–28** Secretary-General Avenol expresses regret at the official termination of Japan's membership in the League and pledges to do nothing

that will injure the relations between Japan and the world body. China protests Avenol's failure to refer to the League's condemnation of Japan's seizure of Manchuria.

APRIL

1 Austria begins military conscription in violation of the Treaty of St. Germain-En-Laye.

3 Ethiopia again asks the League to intervene in its dispute with Italy.

7 The Danzig Nazis win only forty-three of the seventy-two seats in the senate, which is less than the two-thirds necessary to revise the constitution.

9 France takes the issue of German rearmament to the League.

10 **–11** Manchukuo implements an oil monopoly, and Japan again informs the United States that it holds no responsibility for the actions of Manchukuo.

11 **–14** France, Great Britain, and Italy meet in Stresa to formulate a joint policy concerning German rearmament and Eastern European security.

15 **–17** The Council condemns Germany's violation of the disarmament clauses of the Treaty of Versailles.

MAY

2 France and the Soviet Union sign a five-year mutual assistance treaty.

16 Czechoslovakia and the Soviet Union sign a mutual assistance pact. The Soviet obligation to aid Prague is contingent upon France's fulfillment of its prior military commitment to Czechoslovakia.

19 The Sudeten German Party wins forty-four seats in the Czech elections and becomes the second-strongest single party in the Chamber of Deputies.

20 The Assembly entrusts the responsibility for ending the Chaco War to the Buenos Aires Mediatory Conference, composed of Argentina, Brazil, Chile, Peru, the United States, and Uruguay.

20 **–25** The Council adopts a resolution calling on Italy and Ethiopia to resolve their dispute through arbitration, as required by their treaty of 1928.

29 Austrian Chancellor Schuschnigg rejects union with Germany.

JUNE

7 After two governments fall in one week, Laval becomes France's new premier.

Stanley Baldwin succeeds MacDonald as British prime minister, with Sir Samuel Hoare becoming foreign secretary. Anthony Eden is named British minister for League of Nations affairs.

12 The Buenos Aires Mediatory Conference arranges a cease-fire between Bolivia and Paraguay, and the Chaco War ends on June 14.

18 An Anglo-German naval agreement allows Germany a surface fleet that is 35 percent of the British strength, another violation of the Treaty of Versailles.

Hitler reviews troops as Germany reoccupies the Saar on March 1, 1935.

19 Ethiopia insists that Italy's build-up in Eritrea and Somaliland points to war and asks the League to send neutral observers to the frontier to prevent any incidents.

23 Mussolini rejects Eden's plan to settle the Ethiopian crisis.

25 Ethiopia and Italy begin arbitration talks at The Hague.

27 A League of Nations Union ballot in Great Britain indicates strong popular support for the League.

JULY

5 Before adjournment, the Canadian parliament enacts a broad program of social and economic legislation to combat the Depression.

11 The United States informs Italy that its Ethiopian actions seem to violate the Kellogg-Briand Pact.

12 In a British radio address, Secretary-General Avenol asserts that the League provides the only "sane and safe way of international adjustment" and expresses confidence that Great Britain will continue to support it.

12 –13 The secretary-general is identified as the source of a proposal that Ethiopia surrender unspecified territory and grant more economic control to Italy in order to resolve the conflict between the two countries. Avenol hopes to avoid League intervention, which would alienate Italy.

25 Great Britain prohibits the sale of arms and munitions to Italy and Ethiopia.

25 –28 In a sudden reversal of policy, the Seventh World Congress of the Comintern approves communist participation in Popular Front governments with leftist and moderate parties to combat fascism.

31 –August 3 Despite Secretary-General Avenol's efforts to postpone its meeting, the Council convenes. However, it takes no action because Great Britain, France, and Italy announce on August 1 that as signatories of the 1906 Tripartite Pact on Ethiopia, they will seek a solution to the crisis.

AUGUST

2 Great Britain approves the Government of India Bill, which creates an All-India Federation with some autonomy, but since defense, foreign affairs, and other vital powers are reserved for the viceroy, many Indians denounce the new constitution as a "sham."

12 Ethiopia asks the League to lift the embargo on its purchase of arms and munitions.

16 –18 Mussolini rejects an Anglo-French proposal to obtain some concessions for Italy from Ethiopia.

18 Roosevelt appeals to Mussolini to preserve the peace.

20 José M. Velasco Ibarra is deposed as president of Ecuador by a military junta.

26 Italy warns the League against the application of sanctions.

31 The United States passes neutrality legislation that bars the export of arms and munitions to belligerent nations and travel by American citizens on belligerent vessels.

SEPTEMBER

3 The Ethiopian Arbitration Commission exonerates both Italy and Ethiopia from responsibility in the Wal Wal incident.

6 The League appoints a Committee of Five to seek a settlement of the Ethiopian crisis.

9 The Assembly elects Rumania, Poland, and Ecuador to the Council.

10 –16 During the Nazi Party Congress in Nuremberg, Goering announces the National Citizenship Law, which divides Germans into two classes—citizens with rights and members whose rights are not defined. Jews are designated as the latter. The Law for the Protection of German Blood and German Honor bars Jews from marrying outside their race.

11 –13 Hoare and Laval pledge the support of Great Britain and France to the League in the Ethiopian crisis.

20 In a show of force, the British Home Fleet joins the Mediterranean Fleet for maneuvers.

22 Italy rejects the Committee of Five's plan to settle the Ethiopian crisis and instead demands a full mandate over part of western Ethiopia, a partial mandate over the remainder of the nation, and partial control of the Ethiopian army. The committee finds this unacceptable.

28 Selassie orders a general mobilization of Ethiopia's forces.

OCTOBER

1 Great Britain asks for a French commitment to reinforce its Royal Navy if it is attacked by the Italian fleet in the Mediterranean.

2 Martial law is proclaimed in Bulgaria to protect King Boris III against a possible coup attempt.

Italy announces general mobilization and warns the League against the use of sanctions.

3 Without a declaration of war, Italy invades Ethiopia.

5 The United States embargoes the export of arms and munitions to Italy and Ethiopia.

Italian troops advance on Addis Ababa after Italy invades Ethiopia without a declaration of war on October 3, 1935.

7 The Council condemns Italy as an aggressor.

10 Premier Panayoti Tsaldaris' government in Greece is overthrown by monarchists led by War Minister George Kondylis.

11 The League of Nations Sanctions Committee votes an arms embargo against Italy, and member states resume the sale of military supplies to Ethiopia. On October 14, the committee approves an embargo on credits for Italy, and on October 19, it recommends the prohibition of imports from Italy. The effective date is set at November 18.

21 Germany's membership in the League is officially ended. Hitler indicates that Germany will remain neutral in the Italo-Ethiopian crisis. He continues to fortify the Rhineland in violation of the Treaty of Versailles.

23 Mackenzie King becomes prime minister of Canada when his Liberal Party wins by a landslide.

24 Secretary-General Avenol tries to arrange a meeting between Hoare, Laval, and Mussolini to settle the Ethiopian crisis before sanctions are applied.

30 Great Britain and Italy discuss a mutual reduction of military forces in the Mediterranean.

NOVEMBER

3 Léon Blum organizes a Popular Front government in France.

11 Italy protests the League's imposition of sanctions.

14 Prime Minister Baldwin's coalition wins 428 seats to the opposition's 184 seats in the British general elections.

15 The Philippine Islands receive Commonwealth status, and Manuel Quezon becomes the first president.

Canada and the United States sign a reciprocal trade agreement.

16 The League considers imposing oil, iron, and steel sanctions against Italy.

25 King George II returns to Athens after a November 3 plebiscite—which his opponents claim was rigged—favors restoration of the Greek monarchy.

DECEMBER

1 Chiang Kai-shek is elected president of China.

8 A Hoare-Laval agreement assigning Italy the virtual control of Ethiopia is revealed by the Paris *Oeuvre*.

9 France, Great Britain, Italy, Japan, and the United States convene the London Naval Conference.

12 The League postpones consideration of an oil embargo against Italy.

13 Eduard Beneš succeeds Tomáš Masaryk, who resigns at eighty-five from the presidency of Czechoslovakia.

19 Hoare resigns as British foreign secretary in the uproar that follows his attempted appeasement of Italy. He is succeeded by Anthony Eden.

22 Ethiopia accuses the Italian army of using mustard gas.

27 Uruguay charges the Soviet diplomats with subversive activity and breaks relations with the Soviet Union.

Eduard Beneš becomes president of Czechoslovakia on December 13, 1935.

1936

JANUARY

3 Ethiopia asks the League to investigate the Italian bombing of undefended villages.

11 Syrian nationalists stir political unrest against French control.

15 Japan leaves the London Naval Conference when its demand for parity with the United States and Great Britain is rejected.

18 Supported by Japan, rebels proclaim the independence of Inner Mongolia from China.

20 Ethiopia calls on the League to tighten its economic embargo against Italy.

Great Britain mourns the sudden death of George V, who is succeeded by Edward VIII.

22 Laval resigns as French premier in the wake of opposition to his proposal to sacrifice Ethiopia, and Albert Sarraut forms a new ministry.

FEBRUARY

15 The Italian army wins a major victory at Amba Aradam, the mountain that is the key to the district of Enderta.

16 **–19** The Popular Front coalition takes a majority of 265 seats to the 142 seats for the monarchists and the 66 for the center, or "neutrals," in the Spanish general elections. Manuel Azaña becomes premier, and the Popular Front proposes to nationalize land and banks, as it calls for a proletarian dictatorship.

17 Dissatisfaction among Paraguay's military leaders with the Chaco peace negotiations leads to a revolt against President Eusebio Ayala, and Rafael Franco becomes provisional president.

26 **–29** A Young Officers group of Japanese army extremists assassinates moderate and peace-oriented officials in an abortive attempt to establish military domination.

27 The French Chamber of Deputies approves the Franco-Russian mutual assistance pact.

29 Roosevelt signs a new United States neutrality law, which forbids the sale of arms and munitions plus the extension of loans and credits to belligerents.

MARCH

3 A major rearmament program begins in Great Britain when the defense budget is increased by £36 million.

7 **–9** Hitler orders German troops to reoccupy the Rhineland. British Foreign Secretary Anthony Eden criticizes the unilateral action, and France and Belgium ask the League to consider the step a violation of the Treaty of Versailles and of the Locarno Pact.

9 Koki Hirota, an expansionist, becomes Japan's prime minister in a cabinet dominated by the military. Admiral Kenkichi Takahashi advocates a greater cruising range for naval vessels so that they can reach the Dutch East Indies and New Guinea, areas of future commercial development for Japan.

14 **–24** An extraordinary session of the Council adopts resolutions that are critical of Germany's remilitarization of the Rhineland.

20 Ethiopia demands that the League respond to Italy's aggression.

21 **–23** The foreign ministers of Austria, Italy, and Hungary sign the Rome Pact, which includes a guarantee of Austrian independence.

24 The Council discusses the possibility of lifting sanctions and inviting direct negotiations between Italy and Ethiopia after a cease-fire is secured.

German troops cross the bridge at Mayence after Hitler orders the reoccupation of the Rhineland on March 7, 1936.

25 France, Great Britain, and the United States sign the London Naval Treaty, which limits the tonnage and armaments of ships but does not fix any ratio among the powers on the total tonnage allowed. The treaty also contains an "escalator clause" similar to that in the London Naval Treaty of 1930. Italy withholds its approval.

29 A German plebiscite overwhelmingly approves Hitler's action in the Rhineland by 98.7 percent.

APRIL

7 Niceto Alcalá Zamora is replaced as president of Spain when the left becomes dissatisfied with both his sympathy for the Catholic Church and his moderate republican principles. Diego Martínez Barrio is named provisional president.

8 The League agrees to investigate Italy's use of mustard gas in the Ethiopian conflict.

10 –17 Secretary-General Avenol and Council Chairman Salvador de Madariaga attempt to win Ethiopian and Italian agreement to open peace talks, but Selassie insists that Rome first state the terms of peace, a condition that Mussolini refuses.

12 –25 Twelve Arabs and eighteen Jews are killed in the continuing violence in Palestine, and the British High Commissioner orders a strong show of force to end the rioting. The Arab High Committee organizes to unite all Arabs and calls a general strike, which lasts until October 12.

15 Amendments to the constitution of Honduras enable General Tiburcio Carías to continue the dictatorial power that he assumed in 1933. He holds this power until 1949.

17 –20 The Council announces its failure to end the Ethiopian conflict but repeats its appeal to the belligerents to make peace.

28 King Faud of Egypt dies and is succeeded by his son Farouk.

MAY

2 –9 Emperor Haile Selassie flees into exile. Three days later, Italian troops occupy Addis Ababa. Marshal Pietro Badoglio is named viceroy of Ethiopia, and Victor Emmanuel III is proclaimed the new emperor.

3 In the French election, the Popular Front wins 387 seats, including 72 seats taken by the communists.

10 –13 As rioting by communists and socialists destroys churches, convents, and schools in Madrid, Azaña is elected president of the Spanish Republic and appoints Santiago Quiroga as premier.

12 Italy refuses to participate in League meetings if the Ethiopian delegation is allowed to remain.

13 Sean Lester is reappointed High Commissioner to Danzig by the Council.

14 Guatemala announces it will withdraw from the League due to the cost of membership.

17 The Bolivian army ousts President Tejada Sorzano and installs Colonel David Toro as provisional president.

JUNE

2 General Anastasio Somoza leads the Nicaraguan National Guard in a successful revolt against President Juan Bautista Sacasa. The United States announces that it will not intervene in the coup.

4 Léon Blum becomes premier of the first Popular Front government in France and launches a program of economic benefits for the working class and the nationalization of some industries.

18 Australia, Canada, and Great Britain withdraw economic sanctions against Italy.

19 All public demonstrations in Danzig are prohibited following disorders caused by local Nazis.

22 **–26** Honduras and Nicaragua resign from the League because of their budget assessments.

29 Japan announces that it will no longer observe the London Naval Treaty limitations, since Great Britain has invoked the escalator clause due to German naval construction.

30 In an emotional address to the Assembly, Haile Selassie warns that the "very existence of the League of Nations" is at stake because of its treatment of Ethiopia. He also criticizes the League's failure to fulfill its obligations to his country.

JULY

4 In a fateful admission of the failure of collective security, the League lifts its sanctions against Italy.

Léon Blum became premier of France on June 4, 1936.

18 **–19** General Emilio Mola and General Francisco Franco lead a military revolt against the Spanish Republic. Premier Quiroga resigns and is succeeded temporarily by Martínez Barrio and then by José Giral.

20 The Montreux Convention restores Turkish control over the Dardanelles and the Bosphorus, allowing fortification of these straits. The Russian Black Sea Fleet may use the straits to enter the Mediterranean in peacetime.

20 **–25** The Spanish Republic asks Blum's Popular Front government for French military aid, but after consulting with Great Britain, France declines to provide the assistance.

23 Belgium, France, and Great Britain propose a new Locarno-type pact to Germany and Italy to respect European boundaries and to keep peace.

25 Spanish rebels set up a provisional government in Burgos.

Following the conquest of his country by Italy, Emperor Haile Selassie I of Ethiopia addressed the Assembly on June 30, 1936, not only as an anguished ruler but also as a voice of conscience of the League, which he accused of betraying its Covenant.

I am here today to claim that justice that is due to my people, and the assistance promised to it eight months ago by fifty-two nations who asserted that an act of aggression had been committed in violation of international treaties. . . .

I pray Almighty God that He may spare nations the terrible sufferings that have just been inflicted on my people. . . .

It is my duty to inform the governments assembled in Geneva, responsible as they are for the lives of millions of men, women, and children, of the deadly peril which threatens them, by describing to them the fate which has been suffered by Ethiopia.

It is not only upon warriors that the Italian government has made war. It has, above all, attacked populations far removed from hostilities, in order to terrorize and exterminate them [by mustard gas]. . . .

I unhesitatingly stated that I did not want war, that it was imposed upon me, and that I should struggle for the independence and integrity of my people, and that in that struggle I was defending the cause of all small States exposed to the greed of a powerful neighbour. In October 1935 the fifty-two nations who are listening to me today gave me an assurance that the aggressor would not triumph, that the resources of the Covenant would be implemented in order to ensure the rule of law and the failure of violence. . . .

I assert that the issue before the Assembly today is a much wider one [than the fate of Ethiopia]. It is not merely a question of a settlement in the matter of Italian aggression. It is a question of collective security; of the very existence of the League; of the trust placed by States in international treaties; of the value of promises made to small States that their integrity and their independence shall be respected and assured. . . . In a word, it is international morality that is at stake. . . .

At a time when my people is threatened with extermination, when the support of the League may avert the final blow, I may be allowed to speak with complete frankness . . . such as is demanded by the rule of equality between all States Members [*sic*] of the League. Apart from the Kingdom of God, there is not on this earth any nation that is higher than any other. If a strong government finds that it can, with impunity, destroy a weak people, then the hour has struck for that weak people to appeal to the League of Nations to give its judgment in all freedom. God and history will remember your judgment.

Franco requests German aircraft to ferry troops from Spanish Morocco to the mainland.

Despite Japanese objections, Germany signs a trade treaty with China that provides for an exchange of German munitions and Chinese raw materials in times of war.

28 The Spanish Republic confiscates all religious property.

29 Fearing a new wave of violence in Palestine, where forty Arabs, thirty Jews, and six British soldiers have been killed, the British government orders the First Division to the Holy Land and appoints a Royal Commission to undertake an on-site study of the situation.

30 The crash of three Italian aircraft in French Morocco reveals covert Italian aid to Franco.

AUGUST

1 –4 France proposes an international agreement to prevent the involvement of foreign nations in the Spanish Civil War. It is supported by Great Britain.

4 With the approval of Greece's King George II, Premier John Metaxas establishes a dictatorship based on the military, but he also inaugurates a program of social and economic benefits to win popular support. Having received his military education in Potsdam, the Little Moltke brings a pro-German influence to the Greek court.

7 The United States announces that it will maintain neutrality in the Spanish Civil War.

15 France and Great Britain draft a non-intervention agreement, and most European states—including Germany and Italy—endorse it.

19 –23 Zinoviev, Kamenev, and others are retried in the USSR on treason charges for supporting Trotsky. Confessing their guilt openly, sixteen are sentenced to death.

24 Germany raises its conscript service from one to two years.

26 Great Britain and Egypt sign a twenty-year alliance; Britain ends its military occupation of Egypt everywhere but in the Suez Canal Zone.

31 Germany and Poland sign an agreement regarding fees for German railroad traffic across the Polish Corridor.

SEPTEMBER

4 President Azaña names a radical and socialist leader, Francisco Largo Caballero, as premier. Largo Caballero has asserted that the proletariat will establish a Spanish Soviet regime.

8 –14 One million Nazis who have convened in Nuremberg for the Party Conference hear Hitler attack Bolshevism and suggest Germany's expansion eastward.

9 Representatives of the twenty-five nations forming the International Committee for the Application of the Agreement for Non-Intervention in Spain agree to bar the export of military equipment to Spain.

9 –10 Secretary-General Avenol meets with Mussolini and Foreign Minister Galeazzo Ciano; the press reports that he is willing to sacrifice Ethiopia's representation in Geneva in order to retain Italy's membership.

Gregory Zinoviev was among those tried for treason in the USSR on August 19–23, 1936; his true crime was supporting Leon Trotsky.

15 Spain's Republican government charges that Germany, Italy, and Portugal are supplying military aid to Franco, a complaint that will be repeated throughout the civil war.

19 Secretary-General Avenol informs the Council that Italy will return to the League if the world body bars the Ethiopian delegation.

21 The Assembly elects Bolivia, New Zealand, and Sweden to the Council; it names China and Latvia as the two new nonpermanent members.

25 The Spanish Republic insists that the non-intervention agreement is a violation of its rights as the *de jure* government to acquire the military and nonmilitary supplies necessary for its defense.

30 Sean Lester, High Commissioner to Danzig, is named deputy secretary-general of the League.

OCTOBER

1 Franco is appointed commander of the Spanish Nationalist army and "chief of the Spanish State" by the junta in Burgos.

7 The USSR warns that it will withdraw from the non-intervention committee unless the other members cease their aid to the Spanish Nationalists.

10 The Assembly appoints a Committee of Twenty-Eight to examine proposals to reform the Covenant.

Austria's Chancellor Schuschnigg breaks the hold of Prince Ernst von Starhemberg on the *Heimwehr* by absorbing Starhemberg's 120,000 private troops into the government's Fatherland Front Militia.

11 When the leftist parties win the Peruvian elections, President Oscar Benavides nullifies the results and extends his own term for three years.

14 Belgium withdraws from its fifteen-year military alliance with France.

25 –27 During a conference at Berchtesgaden, Hitler and Italian Foreign Minister Ciano agree that Germany will recognize Italy's conquest of Ethiopia, both nations will consider recognition of Franco, and both will oppose Soviet participation if a new Locarno Pact is drafted.

29 Soviet-supplied tanks and planes support the Spanish Republicans during the bitter siege of Madrid by Franco's forces.

NOVEMBER

1 Mussolini announces the formation of the Rome-Berlin Axis and calls on Great Britain and France to isolate Bolshevik Russia and to abandon the League with its delusions of collective security.

Roosevelt is reelected president of the United States in a landslide vote, winning 524 electoral votes to Alfred Landon's 7.

6 Germany supplies aircraft and tanks to Franco's army; some 10,000 German troops will serve in the Civil War.

7 The Republican government in Spain moves from Madrid to Valencia.

11 Austria and Hungary recognize Italy's conquest of Ethiopia.

14 Germany renounces the international control of its waterways that was established by the Treaty of Versailles.

18 Germany and Italy recognize Franco's government.

25 Germany and Japan sign the Anti-Comintern Pact, which they say is not a military alliance directed against the USSR but is opposed to the international organization that incites world revolution.

27 The Spanish Republic appeals to the League for condemnation of the German and Italian aid to Franco.

DECEMBER

1 –23 The Inter-American Conference for the Maintenance of Peace, meeting in Buenos Aires, reaches agreement on a collective security pact, mediation, a Pan American highway, and cultural exchange.

5 The Soviet Union adopts a new democratic constitution that provides for universal suffrage with secret balloting and the guarantee of all civil rights. However, the Communist Party is the only political group that is permitted existence.

10 When the Baldwin ministry and the Dominion governments refuse to consent to his morganatic marriage to Wallis Warfield Simpson, an American divorcée, Edward VIII becomes the first British monarch to abdicate the throne voluntarily. He is succeeded by his brother, George VI.

12 –25 Chinese warlords kidnap Chiang Kai-shek in Sian, but Chou En-lai secures his release. Chiang agrees to join the communists in a common war effort against Japan.

23 The Non-Intervention Committee adopts a resolution to set up land and sea patrols to enforce the embargo agreement regarding the Spanish Civil War.

1937

JANUARY

1 Secretary-General Avenol calls upon the delegates from the major powers to provide leadership during this period of international crisis.

The Spanish Republic accepts the Non-Intervention Committee's plan to enforce its international agreement, but Franco's Nationalists reject it.

2 An Anglo-Italian agreement pledges mutual respect for rights in the Mediterranean and the maintenance of Spanish independence.

5 Poland and Danzig extend their agreement on the use of Danzig harbor until 1939.

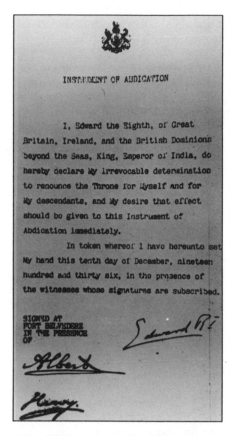

Edward VIII became the first British monarch to relinquish the throne voluntarily when he signed this Instrument of Abdication on December 10, 1936.

10 Great Britain prohibits its citizens from serving in the Spanish Civil War; France follows suit on January 15.

11 Poland recognizes Italy's conquest of Ethiopia.

France and Germany agree to maintain the territorial status quo in Spain and its possessions.

14 The United States opposes the enlistment of its citizens in the Spanish conflict.

23 –30 The purge trials of the Old Bolsheviks continue in Moscow, with thirteen condemned to death. Karl Radek, the prominent *Izvestia* journalist, is sentenced to ten years' imprisonment.

29 The Non-Intervention Committee proposes to establish an international naval patrol in Spanish waters, embargo arms shipments to both belligerents, and deploy frontier observers to prevent foreign volunteers from entering Spain. The effective date for the patrols is February 20.

30 Hitler calls for the return of Germany's colonies and renounces the "war guilt" clause of the Treaty of Versailles. He also indicates Germany's willingness to guarantee the neutrality of Belgium.

FEBRUARY

4 General Senjuro Hayashi becomes premier of Japan after the fall of the Hirota government.

When leftist parties win Venezuela's congressional elections, President Eleázar López Contreras suppresses their organizations and exiles their leaders.

8 Italian troops support the Spanish Nationalists in the capture of Málaga.

18 Carl Burckhardt succeeds Sean Lester as High Commissioner to Danzig.

The Prague government reaches an agreement with its German parties concerning concessions for minorities.

19 Marshal Rodolfo Graziani, viceroy of Ethiopia, is wounded by grenades thrown from a crowd of natives in Addis Ababa.

23 Paraguay withdraws from the League as a protest against the arms embargo imposed on it during the Chaco War.

MARCH

7 A Nazi plot in Hungary fails when Ferenc Szálasi and other leaders are arrested, but the movement appeals to the agrarian proletariat, as well as the German minority.

8 The Non-Intervention Committee adopts a resolution to consider the withdrawal of foreign volunteers from the Spanish Civil War.

12 –21 Mussolini's visit to Libya is interpreted by Great Britain and France as a bid for popularity in the Arab world.

16 Bolivia cancels the oil concessions of foreign nations and confiscates their property.

21 Pope Pius XI's encyclical *Mit brennender Sorge*, condemning Nazi violations of the concordat with the Vatican, is ordered read in all Catholic churches in Germany.

23 Mussolini refuses to discuss the withdrawal of volunteers from Spain. It is estimated that 50,000 to 75,000 Italian troops support Franco's army.

25 Italy and Yugoslavia sign the Belgrade pact guaranteeing their borders and pledging neutrality if the other party is attacked.

APRIL

1 The new Indian constitution becomes effective, but Gandhi sets conditions for the Indian National Congress's participation that the British refuse.

Aden and Burma are separated from India by the new constitution.

21 Mussolini informs Schuschnigg that he no longer will guarantee military intervention to preserve Austrian independence.

26 German aircraft serving under Franco's command destroy Guernica, the traditional capital of the Basques, and arouse worldwide condemnation. The ruthless destruction will be memorialized by a Picasso painting.

29 Mexico appropriates American-owned land.

MAY

1 A new United States neutrality act continues the arms embargo, bans loans and credits, and prohibits American travel on belligerent vessels. However, it does allow the cash-and-carry trade of noncontraband goods.

8 The Danzig Nazis win a two-thirds majority in the senate.

11 Neville Henderson becomes the new British ambassador to Germany and is expected to improve the relations with Hitler.

17 Juan Negrín succeeds Largo Caballero as premier of the Spanish Republic; he announces that he will make the war effort his first priority and will delay the social revolution.

24 The Italian naval vessel *Barletta* is attacked in Palma by Spanish Republican aircraft.

26 Egypt joins the League as the last new member to enter the world body.

28 Stanley Baldwin is succeeded as British prime minister by Neville Chamberlain, who hopes to preserve the peace with Germany and Italy through concessions, a policy that becomes known as appeasement.

The Spanish Republic presents a protest to the Council concerning the Italian troops aiding Franco.

29 The League condemns air attacks on open cities in Spain.

29 –31 Spanish Republican aircraft bomb the German battleship *Deutschland*, which was serving with the Non-Intervention Committee's naval patrol. Germany refuses to continue to participate in patrols or meetings of the committee until a guarantee against future attacks on naval vessels is obtained. Italy takes similar action. Units of the German navy shell the Republican-held port of Almería in retaliation for the attack on the *Deutschland*.

JUNE

1 The German ambassador to the Vatican is recalled pending an apology for an anti-Nazi speech delivered by George Cardinal Mundelein, the archbishop of Chicago.

3 Prince Fumimaro Konoye forms a National Union cabinet in Japan

The cooperation between Hitler (left) and Franco brought such consequences as the ruthless destruction of the Spanish city of Guernica by German aircraft on April 26, 1937.

JULY

2 Soviet and Chinese officials agree to withdraw their forces after clashing over the Soviet occupation of the islands in the Amur River.

7 The British Royal Commission recommends partitioning Palestine between the Jews and the Arabs, with the British occupying a corridor from Jaffa to Jerusalem. Parliament withholds its endorsement of the plan, and both Arab and Jewish spokesmen denounce it.

Chinese and Japanese troops clash near Peking, beginning an undeclared war.

13 Army leaders remove Bolivia's President David Toro, and Colonel Germán Busch becomes provisional president.

14 The British government presents new proposals to the Non-Intervention Committee concerning the supervision of Spanish ports, withdrawal of foreign volunteers, and granting of belligerent status to both sides once the withdrawal of foreign personnel is confirmed.

16 China claims that the Japanese attack near Peking is a violation of the Nine Power Treaty.

21 The United States offers to mediate the Sino-Japanese dispute.

25 The Cuban government embarks on a three-year program of state economic planning for the sugar and mining industries.

26 El Salvador gives its notice of withdrawal from the League. Although it indicates economic reasons, its decision appears to be related to its closer ties with Germany and Italy.

27 Chamberlain sends a personal message of friendship to Mussolini in response to a note from the Duce.

27 **–29** France, Great Britain, and the United States appeal to China and Japan to end the fighting in

when he becomes prime minister after the general elections.

11 Marshal Mikhail Tukhachevsky and seven other general officers are executed in the USSR after confessing to treason. As the purge continues throughout the army command, military analysts question the ability of the Soviet Union to fight a major war.

13 The Paraguayan army opposes the efforts of its government to fulfill the terms of the Chaco peace.

16 **–23** Germany and Italy agree to resume their participation in the Non-Intervention Committee's naval patrol, but on June 18, the German

cruiser *Leipzig* reports an attack by a Republican submarine, and the two Axis powers again withdraw from the committee's operations.

21 Temporarily deserted by the communists, who want aid for the Spanish Republic, and unable to secure Senate approval for dictatorial power over the economy, Léon Blum resigns as French premier and is succeeded by Camille Chautemps.

25 Chamberlain's first speech to the British Parliament is seen as an overture for improved relations with Germany.

northern China. Japan rejects this foreign interference.

28 Japan acknowledges the Italian sovereignty over Ethiopia.

31 Japanese troops capture Peking.

AUGUST

9 The Asian fighting spreads to Shanghai when Japanese naval personnel are shot by a Chinese guard.

13 An unidentified submarine attacks a French merchant vessel in the Mediterranean. Similar attacks by "pirate" units harass ships carrying supplies to the Spanish Republic.

15 Paraguay's dictator, Rafael Franco, is ousted after his economic policies arouse domestic and foreign opposition. A conservative leader, Felix Paiva, becomes provisional president.

21 The Spanish Republic accuses Italy of being responsible for the "pirate" attacks against ships and appeals to the League and European nations for assistance.
China and the USSR sign a five-year nonaggression pact.

25 Poland protests the compulsory attendance of Polish children in Danzig German schools.

31 The British destroyer HMS *Havock* reports an attack by an unidentified submarine.

SEPTEMBER

5 Roosevelt warns American citizens in China that they are staying there at their own risk.
Japan completes a naval blockade of China except in Tsingtao and Kwangchowan, both of which Tokyo indicates are being left open in consideration of the foreign interests there.
Roberto Ortiz succeeds Agustín Justo as Argentina's president.

6 **–14** France and Great Britain call for a conference of European powers in Nyon to deal with the piracy in the Mediterranean. Germany and Italy turn down their invitations. The powers that do attend agree to establish a naval patrol to counter the attacks on merchant vessels. The USSR protests the Italian sinking of its merchant vessels carrying supplies to the Spanish Republic.

7 Hitler demands *lebensraum* ("living space") for Germany.

12 China asks for League action against Japan, and the Council refers the matter to the Far East Advisory Committee.

13 The Assembly elects Belgium, Iran, and Peru to the Council.

14 The United States forbids government-owned ships from transporting arms or munitions to China or Japan. It advises the owners of private vessels that they will carry such goods at their own risk.
Great Britain informs the Council that it is appointing another commission to develop proposals regarding Palestine.

17 The Nyon Conference agrees to suppress piratical aircraft as well as naval units.

19 **–25** The United States and several European powers protest Japan's repeated air attacks against Nanking and Canton.

23 Germany refuses to join the discussions of the Far East Advisory Committee on the Sino-Japanese dispute.

25 Japan insists that its dispute with China should be resolved through bilateral negotiations.

25 **–29** Mussolini visits Hitler, and both leaders deliver speeches emphasizing their desire for peace.

27 **–28** The Far East Advisory Committee unanimously passes a resolution condemning Japanese bombing of Chinese cities. The Assembly adopts the resolution, and the United States supports it.

30 Italy joins the Nyon Conference.

OCTOBER

5 Roosevelt calls for "quarantining the aggressors" of the world.

5 **–6** The Assembly charges Japan with violating the Nine Power Treaty and resolves to recommend that countries give aid to China on an individual basis. The United States announces its support of the Assembly's actions.

8 Japan rejects the League's charge that it has violated the Nine Power Treaty.

12 Roosevelt states that the only objective of the Nine Power Conference, called for by the League, would be mediation of the Sino-Japanese dispute.

14 Nicaragua presents charges to the League that Honduras has mistreated Nicaraguan nationals.

Dr. Wellington Koo, Chinese representative to the League, urged the condemnation of Japan's aggression against his country in a speech he made to the Assembly on September 15, 1937.

Addressing the Assembly on September 15, 1937, China's representative, Dr. Wellington Koo, urged members to condemn Japan's aggression against his country or face the breakdown of international law and the League Covenant.

The effect of continued Japanese aggression, however, is not limited to the menace to the territorial integrity and political independence of China, nor to the injury of the material interests of a few foreign powers. The moral and spiritual aspect of the situation is equally, if not more, significant. . . .

It may be claimed that times are difficult and that there are preoccupations in Europe to-day where the situation is anything but reassuring. But the situation in Europe to-day is not really unconnected with the situation in the Far East. It is a natural consequence, in our view, of the failure to enforce the obligations of the Covenant at the time when the Manchurian crisis was before the League. Peace is indivisible; and its maintenance is of common interest to us all. . . . If the problem of the Far East created by the repeated Japanese aggression is satisfactorily solved by the application of the principles of the Covenant, it is bound to have a most salutory effect upon Europe and will pave the way for an equally satisfactory solution of its own problem.

The League of Nations embodies an ideal and represents an order of international life which must be made to prevail if nations are to feel a sense of security and the world is to be a livable place for all. It is the only priceless issue of the great ordeal of the world which took place twenty years ago. . . .

The principle of collective security, which underlies the Covenant and which we have all accepted, is beyond question the only logical and sound basis for any system of organized peace in the world. It is the same principle which has enabled every modern State to evolve peace and maintain order within its borders. International life, if it is to be blessed with peace and order, no less depends upon the full application of this principle.

I hope it will be generally realized that self-interest in the maintenance of peace, as well as considerations of justice and the conscience of mankind, dictate that we should cooperate fully and sincerely to devise ways and means to check armed aggression and reduce lawlessness wherever they arise in the world. It is in the loyal and joint discharge of our obligations under the Covenant and other treaties to which we are parties that lies the hope of extinguishing the conflagration in the Far East and reinforcing the peace of the Pacific and Europe.

15 The Dominican Republic and Haiti agree to an international investigation of the alleged murder of Haitian immigrants in the Dominican Republic.

18 Konrad Henlein, leader of the Sudeten Germans, calls for the immediate autonomy of those areas of Czechoslovakia where Germans are a majority.

21 Chamberlain refuses to consider the use of sanctions against Japan.

22 Costa Rica, the United States, and Venezuela offer to mediate the Nicaraguan-Honduran boundary dispute.

23 –31 Anti-Jewish riots break out in Nazi-dominated Danzig, and the World Jewish Congress protests the persecution.

27 Japan refuses an invitation to attend the Brussels Conference to discuss its dispute with China.

28 British Foreign Secretary Eden criticizes Mussolini for supporting Hitler's demand for the restoration of Germany's colonies.

NOVEMBER

5 Hitler informs German leaders that his plans for expansion begin with Austria and Czechoslovakia, and extend to the Ukraine.

6 Italy joins the Anti-Comintern Pact.

10 Brazil's President Getulio Vargas proclaims a new constitution that makes him president for six more years and grants him dictatorial powers.

12 Japan captures Shanghai after heavy casualties are suffered by both armies and by the civilian population.

13 –16 China petitions the League to move against Japan; the Brussels Conference charges Japan with aggression. Japan warns that it will regard both sanctions against Japan and aid to China as unfriendly acts.

16 The International Conference on Repression of Terrorism issues two conventions to prevent and punish such acts.

17 –21 Lord Halifax (Edward Wood) visits Hitler to seek a peaceful solution to the Sudeten problem.

24 The Brussels Conference reaffirms the principles of the Nine Power Treaty but concedes that it cannot restore peace in the Far East. It adjourns after calling on China and Japan to stop fighting.

28 Franco announces that the Nationalists have established a blockade of the entire Spanish coast.

29 Italy extends diplomatic recognition to Manchukuo.

DECEMBER

1 Japan establishes diplomatic relations with Franco's government, and the Spanish Nationalists recognize Manchukuo.

5 The Spanish Republican army opens a major counteroffensive against Teruel, which falls on December 19, but the government forces lack the men and logistical support for sustained operations.

11 Mussolini withdraws Italy from the League, referring to both the sanctions the League imposed and its failure to offer "reparation"—the recognition of Italian sovereignty over Ethiopia.

12 Germany states that its withdrawal from the League is permanent.

12 –24 Japanese aircraft sink the USS *Panay* in the Yangtze River, killing two Americans and wounding thirty. Hiroshi Saito, the Japanese ambassador to the United States, publicly apologizes for the incident, and the United States accepts the Japanese settlement.

13 A League study shows that world expenditures for armaments in 1937 will reach nearly $12 billion.
Japanese troops shoot hundreds of Chinese civilians and prisoners of war, as several days of atrocities begin the Rape of Nanking. The total death toll is estimated at 20,000.

17 –26 The Dominican Republic now requests bilateral talks with Haiti, rather than an international investigation of the Haitian deaths in the Dominican Republic.

28 Prime Minister Octavian Goga sponsors legislation that deprives Rumanian Jews naturalized after 1920 of their citizenship, prohibits all Jews from holding land, and closes the professions to Jews.

Rescue workers aid victims from the USS *Panay*, sunk by Japanese aircraft on December 12, 1937. In all, two Americans were killed and thirty were wounded.

1938

JANUARY

2 Chiang Kai-shek rejects the Japanese peace offer, which includes as its terms the recognition of Manchukuo, payment of the costs of the war, acceptance of Japanese advisers, and economic collaboration with Japan.

4 Great Britain names a new commission under Sir John Woodhead to study the effects that partition would have on the Palestine mandate.
Chancellor Schuschnigg reaffirms Austria's determination to maintain its independence.

9 Great Britain informs France and the United States that it opposes Japan's efforts to gain control of the International Settlement in Shanghai.

10 Japanese troops occupy the port of Tsingtao and advance south along the Hankow Railroad.

12 Austria and Hungary recognize Franco's government.

14 A political crisis shakes the Popular Front government in France after the General Staff charges that the communists had planned a coup on November 16, 1937. The communists and socialists withdraw their support from Camille Chautemps, but when they are unable to form their own ministry, the socialists commit themselves to returning Chautemps to power.

16 –21 Japan announces that there will be no further negotiations with Chiang Kai-shek. The Japanese puppet government in China sets up a tariff program favoring Japan.

20 The British Labour Council petitions the League to impose sanctions against Japan.

25 The American Federation of Labor continues its boycott of Japanese goods, adopted on October 13, 1937.

28 Roosevelt announces that the United States will begin a rearmament program.

31 The Anglo-French naval patrol in the Mediterranean adopts a "shoot on sight" order after an unidentified submarine sinks a British merchant vessel.

The Dominican Republic pays an indemnity of $750,000 to Haiti in settlement of the dispute over the killing of Haitians in the Dominican Republic.

FEBRUARY

2 The Council calls on League members to aid China, as provided by the Assembly resolution of October 6, 1937.

4 Hitler appoints Joachim von Ribbentrop to succeed Konstantin von Neurath as foreign minister.

10 King Carol suspends Rumania's constitution and proclaims martial law. During the next few months, he attacks the Fascist Iron Guard for plotting against the Crown. Iron Guard leader Corneliu Codreanu and his associates are killed while in police custody.

12 In response to complaints from the U.S. State Department, Japan promises to safeguard American personnel and property in China's war zones.

12 –16 Hitler threatens to invade Austria unless concessions are made for the Austrian Nazis. Schuschnigg grants amnesty to imprisoned Nazis and appoints Nazi Artur Seyss-Inquart as minister of the interior.

17 –18 British Foreign Secretary Eden recommends that Great Britain invoke the Stresa agreement of 1934 with France and Italy to deter German action against Austria, but Mussolini refuses to act.

20 Eden resigns in protest against Chamberlain's conciliatory policy toward Italy and is succeeded by Lord Halifax.

Hitler asserts the right of self-determination for the Germans in Austria and Czechoslovakia, and pledges to protect German minorities everywhere.

Germany recognizes Manchukuo.

21 Chamberlain advises the smaller nations not to rely on the League to protect them by collective security.

The Austrian government prohibits all political demonstrations except by the Fatherland Front.

21 –24 Italy and Germany agree to withdraw their volunteers from Spain.

22 The United States presents an indemnity claim of $2,214,007 to Japan for the loss of the USS *Panay*.

24 Schuschnigg again asserts Austria's desire to remain free, but the local Nazis carry out disruptions and rioting.

25 –27 France pledges support to Czechoslovakia and the USSR.

MARCH

2 The USSR agrees with reservations to remove its volunteers from Spain. Chamberlain states that Great Britain

Anthony Eden resigned as British foreign secretary on February 20, 1938, in protest against Prime Minister Neville Chamberlain's conciliatory policies toward Italy and Germany.

Lord Halifax (Edward Wood) succeeded Anthony Eden as British foreign secretary on February 20, 1938.

is not committed to defending Czechoslovakia.

2 –15 Stalin's purge trials now claim as victims Nikoli Bukharin, Alexei Rykov, Genrich Yagoda, and other Bolsheviks accused of advocating a retreat from pure communism.

3 Sir Harold MacMichael replaces Sir Arthur Wauchope as High Commissioner in Palestine, with indications that the British government will begin a more intensive campaign to maintain order.

4 Czechoslovakia declares that it will resist outside interference and rejects Hitler's call for self-determination by the Sudeten Germans.

6 The Japanese army advances to the Yellow River.

9 –12 Schuschnigg calls for a plebiscite to decide the issue of Austria's independence, but Hitler orders the German army to prepare an invasion to prevent the referendum. Faced with the threat of war, Schuschnigg cancels the plebiscite and resigns. His successor, the Austrian Nazi Seyss-Inquart, requests the entry of German troops to maintain order. The Stresa Front collapses, as France and Great Britain protest Germany's action, but Italy declines to object.

12 France again assures Czechoslovakia that it will observe its treaty obligations.

13 Hitler announces the *Anschluss* ("union") of Germany and Austria, and calls for plebiscites to confirm the action.

15 –16 Italy and Hungary recognize the annexation of Austria by Germany.

16 Great Britain opposes a French proposal to terminate the Non-Intervention Agreement and to take joint steps to support the Spanish Republic and prevent Franco's victory.

Great Britain informs France that it is not committed to aiding Czechoslovakia and, on March 24, refuses to assure France of British support if France goes to war on behalf of Prague.

17 The Soviet Union suggests a meeting between itself and France, Great Britain, and the United States to discuss the international situation, but on March 24, Chamberlain rejects the overture.

18 Continuing a policy of expropriation adopted in November 1936, President Lázaro Cárdenas orders seizure of the Mexican holdings of American and British oil companies, valued at a total of $400 million.

Franco states that he will not cede any Spanish territory to a foreign power.

19 Great Britain recognizes Germany's annexation of Austria.

Lithuania establishes diplomatic relations with Poland.

21 Hitler informs the League that Austria is no longer a member.

23 Pope Pius XI asks Franco's government to end the bombing of Spanish civilian populations and cities.

24 The United States invites twenty-nine nations to plan assistance for the political refugees from Germany and Austria.

27 Italy warns France that its involvement in the Spanish Civil War will provoke a general European war.

28 Japan sets up a puppet Chinese regime in Nanking—the Reformed Government of the Republic of China.

31 France, Great Britain, and the United States invoke the escalator clause of the London Naval Treaty of 1936 against Japan.

APRIL

2 Chiang Kai-shek is given dictatorial powers for the duration of the war against Japan.

6 Great Britain asks the Council to resolve the issue of recognition of Italian sovereignty over Ethiopia, since some nations have acknowledged Rome's action and others have not.

France and Great Britain reject the requests of the Spanish Republic to end the Non-Intervention Committee arms embargo against it.

10 The Austrian plebiscite overwhelmingly approves of union with Germany by 99.73 percent.

The French senate rejects Blum's request for dictatorial power for the Popular Front, and in the midst of demonstrations in Paris by some 10,000 socialists, Minister of Defense Édouard Daladier becomes premier.

15 Franco's forces take Viñaroz and cut the Loyalist-held territory in two. Heavy fighting along the Ebro River continues through the summer.

16 An Anglo-Italian agreement trades the British recognition of Italy's conquest of Ethiopia for the withdrawal of Italian forces from Spain.

21 The German army completes its plan for the invasion of Czechoslovakia.

24 –25 The Sudeten Germans present their Eight-Point Carlsbad Program to the Prague government, which immediately rejects it.

25 Great Britain and Eire agree to remove their tariff barriers, and London returns three naval bases to Irish control.

25 –28 Secretary-General Avenol, British Prime Minister Chamberlain, and French Foreign Minister Georges Bonnet agree on procedures for the Council session in May, when the issue of recognizing Italy's conquest of Ethiopia will be considered.

27 –29 France and Great Britain ask Czechoslovakia to make concessions to the Sudeten Germans, but when German army units deploy on the border, Prague mobilizes 400,000 troops.

28 Gandhi rejects the demand of Ali Jinnah and the Moslem League that this group alone represent India's Moslems.

28 –29 Press reports that Daladier and Chamberlain are forging "an unwritten military alliance" are discounted when a vague communiqué refers to their "close community of interests."

MAY

3 –10 Military and cultural events dominate public attention during Hitler's visit with Mussolini in Rome. No agreements are revealed, but the Fuehrer pledges "to consider inviolable for all time the frontier of the Alps."

10 –11 Czechoslovakia's Hungarian and Polish minorities present demands similar to those made by the Sudeten Germans.

12 Poland and Rumania inform France that they will not permit Soviet troops to cross their nations to aid Czechoslovakia.

The Council decides to allow member states to use their own judgment in recognizing Italian sovereignty over Ethiopia.

The United States declines to participate in the international conference proposed by the Soviet Union.

Portugal recognizes Franco's government.

13 The League rejects the Spanish Republic's request that it review the issue of foreign intervention in the Civil War.

14 The Council sets up an autonomous office to assist refugees.

The Council acknowledges Switzerland's decision not to be bound by the sanctions article of the Covenant.

Japan's use of poisonous gas in China is condemned by the League. The Council renews its recommendation that member states aid China.

Czechoslovakia agrees to negotiate with its German and other minorities.

16 The Vatican recognizes Franco's regime.

20 Czechoslovakia begins partial mobilization, as clashes erupt between the Sudeten Germans and the police.

21 Great Britain warns Germany that it might be drawn into war if France comes to the aid of Czechoslovakia against Germany.

Germany recalls its military advisers from China.

25 The USSR announces that it will support Czechoslovakia's resistance to aggression.

The withdrawal of Guatemala from the League becomes official.

28 U.S. Secretary of State Hull asks Germany and Czechoslovakia to observe the Kellogg-Briand Pact and to seek a peaceful solution to the Sudeten crisis.

JUNE

1 China appeals to League members and other nations to help end the Japanese bombing of its cities.

Great Britain offers to mediate the Spanish Civil War, but Franco rejects the overture.

2 Chile announces its withdrawal from the League after rejection of its proposal to seek suggestions from nonmembers—including Japan, Germany, and Italy—on reform of the Covenant.

3 Great Britain recommends the establishment of an international commission to ascertain responsibility for the bombing of Spanish cities and civilian populations.

11 The U.S. State Department urges American manufacturers to stop selling aircraft and equipment to nations responsible for bombing civilian targets.

13 An American member of the Advisory Committee on Opium and Other Dangerous Drugs accuses Japan of spreading drug use in China.

20 Japan advises foreign governments to evacuate their nationals from the war zones in China.

Italy ties the withdrawal of its troops from Spain to a French pledge to bar aid to the Republican government.

Germany requires foreign-born Jews living in Germany to register their property.

23 –27 Germany conscripts all civilians into a mandatory labor system and announces that it will regulate wages and working conditions.

24 Japan advises foreign nations that in areas of China under its control, Japanese rather than Chinese law will apply.

27 Great Britain and France protest Japan's occupation of Hainan Island.

29 British authorities in Palestine are encountering Jewish terrorism by militant Revisionists, in addition to Arab terrorism. By August 15, the toll from bombings and riots reaches 155 Arabs killed and 278 wounded, with 72 Jews killed and 217 wounded. Iraq calls for a *jihad* ("holy war") against the Jews and British in Palestine.

JULY

4 –7 France occupies the Paracel Islands on the grounds that they are part of Annam, Indochina. Japan insists that the occupation violates China's title to the islands.

5 France, Germany, Great Britain, and Italy accept a plan for the withdrawal of foreign volunteers from Spain.

6 –11 The Evian Conference on Refugees convenes to seek new homelands for Jews fleeing from Germany and Austria; an Intergovernmental Committee on Political Refugees is created.

11 –August 11 Soviet and Japanese troops clash along the Manchukuo border.

12 France reaffirms its alliance responsibility to Czechoslovakia.

Venezuela withdraws from the League.

13 The Spanish Republic accepts the Non-Intervention Committee's plan for the withdrawal of foreign volunteers.

19 –21 King George VI and Queen Elizabeth visit France in a demonstration of Anglo-French entente.

21 Mexico rejects a proposal by the United States to arbitrate the claims for the land expropriated by the Cárdenas government.

26 Chamberlain names Lord Runciman (Walter Runciman) as mediator in the Sudeten crisis with the approval of France, Czechoslovakia, and Germany.

27 Great Britain announces that it will provide economic aid to China and maintain its interests in that nation.

AUGUST

3 Italy establishes anti-Semitic laws affecting marriage, education, and residence.

10 The Spanish Republic again appeals to the League to end the Nationalist bombing of its cities.

21 Franco refuses to accept the Non-Intervention Committee's plan to withdraw foreign volunteers.

26 The Sudeten German Party adopts a "self-defense" manifesto.

27 Sir John Simon, chancellor of the Exchequer, states that Great Britain would not be able to avoid involvement if a Central European war broke out.

SEPTEMBER

1 Italy revokes citizenship acquired by Jews after January 1, 1919. Jews who settled in Italy after that date must leave the country within six months.

A British commission concludes that the bombing of Republican-held cities by Franco's forces was deliberate.

3 Hitler schedules the invasion of Czechoslovakia for September 27.

4 –5 French Foreign Minister Bonnet again pledges his country's commitment to Czechoslovakia. France cancels all army leaves and mobilizes some reserves, bringing about 1 million men to active duty.

5 –7 The Czech government and Lord Runciman agree on a plan to resolve the Sudeten Germans' demands, but the Sudeten Germans break off the talks and renew their demonstrations.

10 –11 The United States denies that it will support France and Great Britain on the Czech issue. However, the USSR assures France that it will assist Czechoslovakia, and Chamberlain speaks of the "probability" of Britain backing France in the crisis.

11 The Council responds to China's appeal for action by inviting Japan to attend a conference. If Japan refuses, says the Council, more drastic steps could follow.

13 In a Nuremberg speech, Hitler insists that the oppression of the Sudeten Germans must end or Germany will come to their aid.

Czechoslovakia declares martial law in eight border districts as a result of clashes between Czechs and Germans.

The Netherlands and Sweden inform Secretary-General Avenol that they will not be automatically bound by the sanctions clause if it should be invoked.

14 The British fleet is ordered to "alert" status.

15 In a conference at Berchtesgaden, Hitler tells Chamberlain that he is determined to annex those areas of the Sudetenland desiring union with Germany and says that he is prepared to go to war to achieve that objective.

15 –16 Henlein calls for the union of Sudetenland with Germany, and when the Czech government charges him with treason, he flees to Germany.

18 France and Great Britain recommend that Czechoslovakia accept Hitler's demands regarding the cession of territory.

19 Czechoslovakia asks if France will support it if it rejects the Sudetenland cession. Moscow informs Prague that its aid is contingent on France's fulfillment of its alliance with Czechoslovakia.

20 Hitler encourages Hungary and Poland to seek the transfer of territories with their minorities from Czechoslovakia.

20 –21 Czechoslovakia informs France and Great Britain that it prefers arbitration under the German-Czech Treaty of 1925, rather than acceptance of the Berchtesgaden terms. When France and Great Britain warn Czechoslovakia that Germany may attack if it refuses to make the cessions, the Czech government accepts the German demands. The USSR criticizes the Anglo-French policy and asks for League action against Germany.

21 The Spanish Republic states that it will withdraw all foreign volunteers from service and invites confirmation by an international commission.

22 During a meeting in Godesberg, Germany, Hitler informs Chamberlain that the initial Czech concessions are inadequate. He now demands the immediate surrender of all areas with German majorities and plebiscites in areas with large German minorities by November 25. Chamberlain describes the new terms as "unreasonable." Czechoslovakia orders full mobilization of its armed forces.

Japan rejects League intervention in its conflict with China and establishes a United Council for China in Peiping, indicating its intention to establish a protectorate.

23 –24 Rumania announces that it will permit Soviet troops to cross its territory if war breaks out in Central Europe, and France and Great Britain are involved.

24 –25 Czechoslovakia rejects the Godesberg demands, and Paris pledges to fulfill its treaty obligations to Prague.

26 Hitler publicly states that he will invade Czechoslovakia by October 1 if his demands are not met.

Chamberlain offers England's first public assurance of support to France if France is called upon to aid Czechoslovakia.

27 Roosevelt appeals for direct talks between Hitler and Beneš to resolve the Czechoslovakian crisis.

Poland demands that Czechoslovakia transfer to it the 400-square-mile Teschen region, an area with about a 40-percent-Polish population.

28 The League authorizes its members to impose sanctions against Japan.

After receiving requests from Chamberlain and Roosevelt, Mussolini asks Hitler to convoke a conference of France, Germany, Great Britain, and Italy to deal with the Sudetenland issue.

29 –30 Chamberlain, Daladier, Hitler, and Mussolini meet in Munich and agree to transfer the Sudetenland to Germany in return for a guarantee concerning the remaining frontiers of Czechoslovakia. The Czech government submits to the terms.

OCTOBER

1 Germany occupies the 10,000-square-mile Sudetenland, the 3,500,000 inhabitants of which include 700,000 Czechs.

The League separates the Treaty of Versailles from the Covenant.

3 Japan warns that it will retaliate against nations that impose sanctions on it.

4 –6 The French Chamber of Deputies gives Daladier a vote of confidence on the Munich negotiations, and the House of Commons provides Chamberlain with an over two-to-one endorsement.

6 The United States wants the open-door policy observed in China and Manchukuo.

The Italian government bars marriage between Jews and non-Jews without the special permission of the Minister of the Interior. It also places other restrictions on Jews.

8 Italian troops who have eighteen months of continuous service in Spain will be withdrawn.

Czechoslovakia grants autonomy to Slovakia and Ruthenia.

10 An arbitration award by the heads of state of Argentina, Brazil, Chile, Peru, the United States, and Uruguay ends the long-standing Chaco conflict between Bolivia and Paraguay.

21 Japan takes Canton, the last seaport held by the Chinese, and also captures Hankow, which gives it control of the Yangtze River from that city to the coast.

28 Tokyo warns France to halt the flow of supplies through Indochina to China.

Germany arrests thousands of Jews of Polish descent and deports them to Poland.

NOVEMBER

2 Hungary acquires from Czechoslovakia a total of 5,000 square miles of southern Slovakia and southern Ruthenia, with a combined population of 1,000,000.

Japan leaves the specialized agencies of the League.

3 –4 Japan announces the creation of a "new order" in eastern Asia and states that the Nine Power Treaty no longer applies in China.

4 Manchukuo reports new clashes with Soviet troops along the frontier.

7 France, Great Britain, and the United States protest Japan's restriction of Yangtze River traffic to Japanese nationals.

Jews are banned from the Italian Fascist Party.

7 –14 Ernst von Rath, a German diplomat, is assassinated in Paris by Herschel Grynszpan in a personal retaliation for the deportation of his Polish-Jewish parents by Germany. The assassination sparks *Kristallnacht* ("Crystal Night") in Germany—a night of state-inspired attacks against Jewish people and the destruction of Jewish property. Afterwards, Hitler imposes a fine of one million marks on the country's Jewish population. Roosevelt recalls Ambassador Hugh Wilson in protest against the persecution.

9 The report of Sir John Woodhead's commission describes the partition of Palestine as "impracticable," and the British government calls for a Round Table Conference of Arabs and Jews in London to seek another solution.

16 –19 France and Great Britain recognize Italy's sovereignty over Ethiopia.

18 The United States grants a six-month extension of visitors' visas to 15,000 Austrian and German refugees.

Guards stand watch over Jewish shops in Vienna damaged during state-inspired vandalism in October 1938.

Hitler is greeted upon his entry into Salzburg in October 1938.

The American Federation of Labor calls for a boycott of German goods and services to protest the treatment of Jews.

19 Japan ignores the American protests and restricts the open-door policy in the Chinese territory under its control.

23 Danzig adopts the Nuremberg racial laws.

23 –24 France and Great Britain agree that they will not return any German colonies.

24 France and Great Britain refuse "belligerent" status to Franco until all foreign nationals are withdrawn from the Spanish Civil War.

26 The USSR and Poland renew their nonaggression agreement in an effort to bar Germany's eastward expansion.

29 Belgium, the Netherlands, and Sweden resign from the Non-Intervention Committee.

DECEMBER

3 –5 The Jews in Berlin are told that they may not possess motor cars and are banned from specific areas of the city. Jews throughout Germany are ordered to liquidate their holdings in industrial property and real estate.

5 Fascist demonstrators demand the surrender of Corsica and Tunisia to Italy, but Daladier states that France will not give up any territory.

6 France and Germany sign a friendship agreement guaranteeing their existing borders.

8 The USSR and Japan clash over Siberian fisheries and payment for the Chinese Eastern Railway.

9 The Spanish Republic asks France and Great Britain to undertake talks in Berlin and Rome to end the use of Axis aircraft for bombing cities.

14 –17 Germany offers a plan for the emigration of Jews in return for credits and trade concessions. The proposal is rejected, but George Rublee,

head of the Intergovernmental Committee on Political Refugees, continues the talks in Berlin.

15 –19 The United States announces a loan of $25,000,000 to China, while Great Britain lends it £500,000.

19 The Pan American Conference rejects a Cuban proposal to offer mediation in the Spanish Civil War.

21 The United States announces that it will provide 500,000 bushels of wheat at reduced cost to the American Red Cross for distribution to both sides in the Spanish Civil War.

23 Franco opens a major offensive in Catalonia.

24 The Pan American Conference adopts the Declaration of Solidarity; twenty-one nations pledge their mutual assistance to any member state threatened by aggression.

31 The United States objects to Japan's unilateral attempt to establish a "new order" in eastern Asia.

1939

JANUARY

5 Kiichiro Hiranuma, the civilian leader of Japan's military-fascist front, replaces Prince Konoye as premier.
Hitler calls for the union of Danzig with Germany.

10 Chamberlain visits Mussolini hoping to develop closer relations between their two countries and to weaken the Rome-Berlin Axis, but the effort fails.

12 Roosevelt requests a $552 million addition to the defense budget to purchase 3,000 aircraft and other military equipment and to modernize American bases in the Atlantic and Pacific.

15 British Foreign Secretary Lord Halifax urges France to offer territorial concessions to Italy in Africa.

20 The League again invites its member states to aid China, but it does not impose sanctions on Japan.

25 Poland refuses Germany's invitation to join the Anti-Comintern Pact.

26 Franco's forces, aided by Italian troops, capture Barcelona. The Civil War enters its final period as 200,000 Loyalists cross into France and are interned.

FEBRUARY

7 Ribbentrop declares that Germany's hostility toward the USSR is permanent.

10 Warsaw refuses to consider granting Germany transit rights across the Polish Corridor.

23 Anglo-French naval maneuvers in the Mediterranean are interpreted as a warning to Mussolini.

27 France and Great Britain recognize Franco.
   Germany notifies Great Britain and France that it cannot guarantee the borders of Czechoslovakia.

28 President Azaña of the Spanish Republic resigns, but Premier Negrín, with Radical support, tries to continue the war.

MARCH

6 A military junta, led by General José Miaja, takes control of the Spanish Republic from Negrín and seeks peace with Franco.

10 Stalin criticizes both Western democracies and fascist nations. He says that the Soviet Union will follow a cautious policy in the coming "Second Imperialistic War."

10 –16 President Emil Hácha dismisses Premier Joseph Tiso for promoting Slovakia's independence from Czechoslovakia; but Hitler encourages Tiso, and on March 14, Slovakia declares its independence. German troops

Franco reviews his troops during a victory parade in Madrid at the end of the Spanish Civil War in February 1939.

then occupy Bohemia, Moravia, and Slovakia, and Hitler announces that these territories are protectorates of Germany. On March 16, with Hitler's approval, Hungary annexes Ruthenia, completing the destruction of Czechoslovakia.

14 Chamberlain says that the Anglo-French guarantee to Czechoslovakia applies only to unprovoked aggression and is not applicable in the present situation.
   Pope Pius XII's encyclical "On the Condition of the Catholic Church in the German Reich" criticizes Nazism.

17 The Round Table Conference on Palestine meeting in London since February fails to reconcile the Jewish and Arab differences.
   Roosevelt calls for revision of the neutrality act of 1937 so that the United States can aid the victims of aggression.

18 France, Great Britain, and the USSR protest Germany's annexation of Bohemia and Moldavia, but they do not take any action.

20 The United States closes the American legation in Prague and ends its trade treaty with Czechoslovakia, which will subject future imports from the German-dominated state to higher tariffs.

21 –26 Hitler proposes that Poland take Slovakia in exchange for Danzig and grant Germany transit rights across the Polish Corridor. Warsaw rejects the plan and states that it will view any attempted change in the status of Danzig as an act of war.

23 Germany secures the right to develop Rumanian resources.
   Hitler annexes Memel from Lithuania but offers a guarantee of Lithuanian independence.

When British Prime Minister Neville Chamberlain assured the House of Commons that the Munich Agreement of September 1938 opened the path to peace, Clement Attlee, leader of the Labour Party, warned that the surrender of Czechoslovakia's Sudetenland to Germany had been "a victory for brute force."

> We have seen today, a gallant, civilized and democratic people betrayed and handed over to a ruthless despotism. . . . Herr Hitler has successfully asserted the law of the jungle. He has claimed to do what he will by force and in doing so has struck at the roots of civilized peoples. In doing this to one nation he threatens all, and if he does this, and he has with impunity, there is no longer any peace in the world even though there may be a pause in actual warfare. The whole of Europe is now under the constant menace of armed force. That is why many people cannot feel very happy about the present situation. They feel that there has been an immense victory for force and wrong. Ever since the last War people have realized that if peace is to be preserved there must be something above the will of the individual ruler of an armed state. That is the whole basis of the League of Nations and many people are surprised today to be under this menace. . . .
>
> When [Britain's] National Government overthrew the whole policy of collective security and abandoned it and the League, we told this House over and over again that we were entering on a very dangerous course. . . . The real pity of it is that, having decided to leave the League system which we practiced and in which we believed, and to embark on a policy of alliances and power politics, instead of strengthening the people whose natural interests were with ours, we have had nothing but constant flirtations with this and that dictator. The Prime Minister has been the dupe of the dictators, and I say that today we are in a dangerous position. . . .
>
> We are left with two promises, one from Signor Mussolini and one from Herr Hitler. That is really all that we have got. We have to walk by faith—the faith of the Prime Minister in Signor Mussolini and his faith in Herr Hitler. The Prime Minister has said how difficult it was for Herr Hitler to recede from a statement he had once made. I have five pages of statements made by Herr Hitler, from every one of which he has receded. . . . [B]ut the Prime Minister says against all experience that he has faith in Herr Hitler's promise, grounded on two or three interviews—a pretty flimsy support for this country.
>
> . . . What reason have we to think that Herr Hitler will stop now?

25 Hitler orders the German General Staff to develop plans for war against Poland.

28 Madrid formally surrenders to Franco, ending the Civil War, which has killed 700,000 in battle and 15,000 in air raids, and created 30,000 other victims.

29 France refuses to offer any territorial concessions to Italy in Africa.

31 France and Great Britain offer Poland a defensive alliance.

APRIL

1 The United States establishes diplomatic relations with Franco.
Germany launches the *Tirpitz*, the world's largest battleship.

3 German war plans set September 1 for the attack against Poland.

7 Italian troops occupy Albania in a sudden attack, and Mussolini announces that country's annexation.
Franco formally joins Germany, Italy, and Japan in the Anti-Comintern Pact.

11 Hungary withdraws from the League under pressure from Germany.

13 Secretary-General Avenol reviews the possibility of the League's leaving Geneva in the event of war.
France and Great Britain offer Greece and Rumania the same guarantee of aid against aggression that they gave to Poland on March 31.
The USSR rejects a French and British overture to join in protecting Poland and Rumania against attack.

14 Roosevelt asks Hitler and Mussolini to give assurances to thirty-one nations that Germany and Italy will not attack them. The Axis leaders ridicule the president's request.

17 The Soviet Union proposes a defensive alliance with France and Great Britain.

19 Great Britain pledges to defend the Netherlands, Denmark, and Switzerland.

24 Germán Busch establishes a dictatorship in Bolivia. However, he dies four months later and is succeeded by General Carlos Quintamilla.

27 Germany terminates its 1935 naval agreement with Great Britain.
Great Britain announces conscription for men aged twenty or twenty-one.

28 Hitler terminates the German nonaggression pact with Poland.

30 José Félix Estigarribia, a military hero of the Chaco War, is elected president of Paraguay.

MAY

3 Vyacheslav Molotov replaces Maxim Litvinov as Soviet foreign minister, indicating a possible shift in Soviet policy.
Hungary announces that it will expel all Jews.

Hitler visits Memel after annexing it from Lithuania on March 23, 1939.

7 Poland rejects an alliance overture from the Soviet Union.

12 Local Nazi demonstrations in Danzig call for union with Germany.

17 A British White Paper on Palestine proposes the creation, in ten years, of an independent state governed by Arabs and Jews. Jewish immigration during the next five years would be restricted to 75,000, with further immigration dependent on Arab approval. Some 5,000 Jews, calling the plan a betrayal, battle the police in Jerusalem, while Arab extremists demand an immediate end to all Jewish immigration.

17 –19 Finland, Norway, and Sweden all reject nonaggression treaties with Germany, but Denmark, Latvia, and Estonia accept them.

19 Franco-Polish military conversations commit France to attacking Germany if Poland is invaded.

22 Germany and Italy sign a ten-year military alliance—the Pact of Steel.

30 –June 2 The USSR suggests that the defensive alliance sought by France and Great Britain be expanded to include protection of the Baltic States, Belgium, Greece, Poland, Rumania, and Turkey.

JUNE

8 –11 King George VI and Queen Elizabeth become the first reigning British monarchs to visit Canada and the United States.

JULY

22 The USSR opens economic talks with Germany following the lack of progress in the negotiations with France and Great Britain.

26 The United States gives the six-month notice required for the termination of the 1911 Commercial Treaty with Japan.

27 French and British military missions are sent to the USSR in response to Molotov's request.

31 The German-dominated Danzig senate calls for the withdrawal of Polish customs officers from the Free City.

AUGUST

2 Albert Einstein informs Roosevelt that an atomic bomb can be developed.

10 Poland denies Germany's right to intervene in Danzig's affairs.

12 British, French, and Soviet officers hold their first conversations on the same day that the USSR makes a bid for negotiations with Germany.

12 –13 Ciano advises Hitler that Italy will not be ready for war until 1941.

14 Germany indicates its readiness for an accord with the USSR.

15 France and Great Britain warn Germany that they will aid Poland if it is attacked.
Molotov proposes a nonaggression pact to Germany and ends the military conversations with France and Great Britain.

20 –25 The USSR inflicts a major defeat on the Japanese army during clashes in Outer Mongolia.

23 Molotov and Ribbentrop sign the Russo-German Nonaggression Pact, which has secret clauses assigning spheres of influence in western Poland and Lithuania to Germany and in eastern Poland, Finland, Latvia, Estonia, and Bessarabia to the USSR.

24 Roosevelt appeals to Germany, Italy, and Poland to resolve their problems by peaceful means.

25 Great Britain signs a five-year mutual-assistance pact with Poland.

Soviet Commissar of Foreign Affairs Vyacheslav M. Molotov (seated) signs the Russo-German Nonaggression Pact on August 23, 1939, while German Foreign Minister Joachim von Ribbentrop (standing, second from left) and Soviet Premier Joseph Stalin (standing, second from right) look on.

25 –28 Japan denounces the Russo-German Nonaggression Pact as a violation of the Anti-Comintern Pact. General Nobuyuki Abe becomes premier of Japan, as the shock of the Nazi-Soviet agreement topples the Hiranuma cabinet.

26 Great Britain suggests that Poland seek Vatican mediation in its dispute with Germany.

30 –31 Germany charges that Poland's refusal to send a delegation to Berlin represents a rejection of the German demands.

SEPTEMBER

1 Germany invades Poland, and World War II begins. Italy announces its nonbelligerency. Great Britain and France order full mobilization and warn Germany to cease the hostilities.

3 France and Great Britain—joined by Australia, India, and New Zealand—declare war against Germany. A British blockade of Germany begins, and a German submarine sinks the British liner *Athenia*, causing the loss of 118 lives. On September 7, Hitler orders his navy to avoid attacks against passenger liners and French naval and merchant ships.

8 The United States declares a "limited national emergency."

11 Germany announces a counter-blockade of Great Britain. The British Cabinet suspends the bombing of Germany by the Royal Air Force.

15 The USSR ends its fighting with Japan along the Manchukuo border.

17 The USSR attacks Poland to secure the eastern region allotted by the Russo-German Nonaggression Pact.

20 France and Great Britain reject peace offers from Hitler.

21 Roosevelt convenes a special session of Congress to revise the arms-embargo provision of the neutrality law.

23 Germany announces that all organized resistance by Poland has ended.

28 The Soviet Union and Germany sign a formal treaty giving 73,000 square miles of Poland to Germany and 78,000 square miles to the USSR.

30 General Wladyslaw Sikorski establishes a Polish Provisional Government in Exile in Paris.

OCTOBER

2 The Congress of American Republics establishes a neutrality zone—from 300 to 1,000 miles offshore—

Finnish troops appear hopeful during Russian invasion of their country on November 30–December 1, 1939.

around the Western Hemisphere south of Canada.

12 Chamberlain rejects a new peace initiative by Hitler.
Hitler orders the deportation of Austrian and Czech Jews to Poland.

16 German naval orders permit attack of enemy merchant ships without warning and of passenger liners in a convoy after giving a warning.

NOVEMBER

4 The new American neutrality law permits the sale of arms and munitions to belligerents on a cash-and-carry basis but bars American merchant vessels from entering war zones.

8 An assassination attempt against Hitler in Munich fails.

28 –December 8 Great Britain declares that all German exports are to be treated as contraband of war, but the United States objects.

30 –December 1 The USSR invades Finland and establishes the "puppet" Democratic Republic of Finland.

DECEMBER

5 –12 Secretary-General Avenol notifies the USSR of Finland's appeal to the Council, but the Soviet Union refuses to attend the League session or to end the war against Finland.

14 The League condemns the USSR's aggression against Finland and, for the first and only time in its history, expels a member state.

1940

JANUARY

26 The United States allows its commercial treaty with Japan to lapse, opening the door to a possible trade embargo.

MARCH

12 Finland surrenders to the USSR and hands over the Karelian Isthmus and Lake Ladoga, along with other territory.

APRIL

9 Germany invades Denmark and Norway.

MAY

10 Germany attacks Belgium, the Netherlands, and Luxemburg.
Winston Churchill succeeds Neville Chamberlain as prime minister of Great Britain.

26 **–June 4** The British evacuate more than 338,000 troops from Dunkirk.

28 King Leopold III and the Belgian army surrender to Germany.

JUNE

10 Italy attacks France and declares war on Great Britain.

15 Soviet troops occupy Lithuania, Latvia, and Estonia.

17 France seeks an armistice with Germany, but Great Britain announces that it will fight alone if necessary.

21 Hitler orders the French surrender to be signed in Compiègne, the site where Marshal Ferdinand Foch received Germany's capitulation in November 1918.

JULY

5 The United States announces a limited embargo on trade with Japan.

25 Joseph Avenol resigns as secretary-general of the League of Nations, effective August 31.

AUGUST

15 Germany begins the Battle of Britain, its offensive to destroy British air power and enable the German army and navy to invade England.

30 The Vichy government of France agrees to the Japanese control of ports, airfields, and railroads in Indochina.

SEPTEMBER

3 Great Britain and the United States announce a "deal" to exchange fifty American destroyers for the long-term lease of British bases in the Western Hemisphere.
Sean Lester becomes acting secretary-general of the League of Nations.

25 U.S. Army Intelligence breaks the secret Japanese diplomatic code, or "Magic" intercepts.

27 Germany, Italy, and Japan sign the Tripartite Pact, an agreement intended to intimidate the United States.

OCTOBER

28 Italy invades Greece.

30 President Roosevelt pledges that the United States will not enter the war.

NOVEMBER

5 Roosevelt is elected to an unprecedented third term as president.

DECEMBER

8 After suffering humiliating defeats by the Greek army, Italy asks Germany for aid in the war.

1941

JANUARY

6 Roosevelt's annual message to Congress describes the Four Freedoms for which the United States stands—freedom of speech, freedom of worship, freedom from want, and freedom from fear.

10 Since Great Britain can no longer pay cash for American supplies, the Roosevelt administration supports House Resolution 1776, which authorizes the lease of equipment to countries whose defense is considered vital to the United States.
Germany signs a new trade pact with the Soviet Union.

MARCH

1 Bulgaria joins the Tripartite Pact, as Germany extends its influence in the Balkans.

11 Roosevelt signs the Lend-Lease Act.

25 **–27** Under pressure from Hitler, Yugoslavia joins the Tripartite Pact, but opponents of the union overthrow the Yugoslav government.

30 Led by General Erwin Rommel, the German Africa Corps begins an offensive that drives the British army from Libya.

APRIL

6 **–May 1** Germany invades and conquers Yugoslavia and Greece.

11 Japan and the USSR sign a nonaggression pact.

MAY

2 **–31** The British army suppresses a pro-German movement in Iraq and reinstates the pro-British regent Emir Abdul Illa.

10 –11 Rudolf Hess, deputy fuehrer and leader of the Nazi Party, flies to Scotland in a personal effort to arrange peace talks between Germany and Great Britain.

20 In the first large-scale airborne invasion in history, German paratroopers land in Crete.

27 After sinking the British Royal Navy's HMS *Hood* on May 24, the German battleship *Bismarck* is sunk by extensive British air and surface attacks.

JUNE

8 British and Free French forces invade Syria and Lebanon.

22 Germany invades the Soviet Union.

AUGUST

14 At Placentia Bay, Newfoundland, President Roosevelt and Prime Minister Churchill issue the Atlantic Charter, a declaration of common principles.

25 British and Soviet troops occupy Iran to end Germany's influence over the government of Riza Shah Pahlevi. The action guarantees Allied access to Iran's oil and opens a supply line to the USSR.

SEPTEMBER

11 Roosevelt warns Hitler and Mussolini that vessels of war will enter American defensive waters "at their own peril." He also announces that the U.S. Navy will begin convoying merchant ships "of any flag."

19 The German army occupies Kiev.

OCTOBER

18 Following the resignation of Prince Fumimaro Konoye, General Hideki Tojo becomes premier, war minister, and home minister of Japan.

NOVEMBER

18 A British offensive in Libya fails to gain a decisive victory over Rommel.

26 Responding to a Japanese proposal of November 20 that asked for a free hand in China, U.S. Secretary of State Cordell Hull calls on Japan to withdraw its troops from China and Indochina.

DECEMBER

1 Premier Tojo tells the Imperial Conference that Japan has no option but war against the United States.

7 The Japanese navy successfully carries out a surprise attack against Pearl Harbor, which cripples the American Pacific Fleet.

8 Describing December 7 as "a date which will live in infamy," President Roosevelt asks Congress to declare war against Japan.

10 –11 Germany and Italy declare war against the United States.

22 At the First Washington Conference, Roosevelt and Churchill affirm that the defeat of Germany and Italy is their first priority.

25 The British garrison in Hong Kong surrenders after a Japanese siege of seventeen days.

1942

JANUARY

1 Twenty-six nations at war with the Axis powers sign the United Nations Declaration, which incorporates the principles of the Atlantic Charter.

21 A German counteroffensive in North Africa forces the British to retreat 300 miles across Libya.

FEBRUARY

15 The Japanese capture the British naval base in Singapore, called the Gibraltar of the Pacific, and its garrison of over 55,000.

MARCH

7 The British evacuate Rangoon as Japanese forces drive into Burma.

9 Japan completes the conquest of the Netherlands East Indies.

17 Ordered by Roosevelt to leave the Philippine Islands, General Douglas MacArthur reaches Australia and pledges, "I shall return."

APRIL

9 American and Filipino troops on Bataan peninsula, Luzon, surrender to the Japanese.

18 Flying from the aircraft carrier USS *Hornet*, sixteen B-25 bombers under the command of Lieutenant Colonel James H. Doolittle attack Tokyo, Kobe, Nagoya, and Yokohama.

MAY

4 –9 The Battle of the Coral Sea, the first naval engagement dominated by carrier aircraft, checks Japan's advance in the South Pacific.

6 American resistance in the Philippine Islands ends with the fall of Corregidor, Manila Bay.

26 Great Britain and the Soviet Union sign a treaty of alliance.

30 –31 A Royal Air Force "thousand-plane raid" strikes Cologne, marking the beginning of massive nighttime bombing of Germany.

JUNE

4 American planes sink four Japanese aircraft carriers during the Battle of

Midway Island, a turning point in the Pacific war.

21 **–27** At the Second Washington Conference, Churchill and Roosevelt discuss invasion of North Africa and development of an atomic bomb.

AUGUST

7 U.S. marines invade Guadalcanal, Solomon Islands.

12 In Moscow, Churchill informs Stalin that American and British forces cannot open a "second front" in 1942.

OCTOBER

23 General Bernard Montgomery opens a British offensive in El Alamein that drives the Axis forces from Egypt.

NOVEMBER

8 American and British troops invade French North Africa.

1943

JANUARY

14 **–24** At the Casablanca Conference in French Morocco, Churchill and Roosevelt agree to invade Sicily after the Axis forces surrender in North Africa, to launch an invasion of France in 1944, and to begin round-the-clock bombing of Germany.

FEBRUARY

2 Field Marshal Friedrich Paulus and 12,000 German troops surrender in Stalingrad. They are the survivors of the 300,000 troops of the Sixth Army, which has been fighting in Stalingrad since August 22, 1942.

MAY

11 **–27** At the Third Washington conference, Churchill seeks Roosevelt's assent for the invasion of Italy.

JULY

5 **–9** Soviet forces defeat a German offensive in Kursk in the greatest tank battle of the war.

9 Anglo-American forces invade Sicily and capture the island after thirty-eight days of fighting.

25 The Fascist Grand Council ousts Mussolini from office, and Marshal Pietro Badoglio forms a new cabinet.

AUGUST

17 **–24** At the First Quebec Conference, Roosevelt and Churchill agree that the target date for the invasion of France will be May 1, 1944.

SEPTEMBER

8 **–10** Italy surrenders unconditionally after the U.S. Fifth Army lands in Salerno. German troops occupy Rome and develop strong defensive positions, forcing the Allies into a long and costly campaign.

15 Mussolini is rescued by German paratroopers from his internment in Abruzzi. He establishes the Fascist Republic in northern Italy.

OCTOBER

13 The Italian government of King Victor Emmanuel III declares war against Germany.

19 **–November 1** At the Moscow Conference of Foreign Ministers, U.S. Secretary of State Cordell Hull, British Foreign Secretary Anthony Eden, and Soviet Commissar of Foreign Affairs Vyacheslav Molotov set a target date for

the invasion of France and agree to establish a postwar organization to preserve peace.

NOVEMBER

22 **–26** At the First Cairo Conference, Churchill, Roosevelt, and Chiang Kai-shek agree that Manchuria should be returned to China and that Korea should be freed from Japanese rule.

28 **–December 1** Churchill, Roosevelt, and Stalin hold their first joint meeting, in Teheran, Iran, and discuss the future of Germany, Poland, and the Baltic states; the role of France in postwar Europe; and the new international organization. Stalin agrees to enter the war against Japan after Germany is defeated.

1944

JANUARY

22 Allied troops land in Anzio, south of Rome. However, they fail to break out of their beachhead and are trapped there for four months.

JUNE

4 Rome is occupied by American and British troops.

6 The greatest armada in history, under the command of General Dwight D. Eisenhower, invades France along a sixty-mile line.

13 The *Vergultungswaffe*, or V-1, which is the first German flying bomb, strikes London.

15 American forces invade Saipan in the Marianas. On July 18, Hideki Tojo resigns as premier, war minister, and home minister of Japan.

JULY

1 –15 Representatives of forty-four nations meet in Bretton Woods, New Hampshire, for the International Monetary Conference to create the International Monetary Fund and the International Bank for Reconstruction and Development.

20 Hitler survives an assassination attempt. Among the officers implicated in the plot is Field Marshal Erwin Rommel, who commits suicide rather than face public trial.

AUGUST

15 Allied forces invade France's Mediterranean coast.

21 –October 7 At the Dumbarton Oaks Conference in Washington, D.C., delegations from China, the Soviet Union, the United Kingdom, and the United States agree on a new international organization to replace the League of Nations.

SEPTEMBER

8 The first German V-2, a rocket that cannot be destroyed in flight, explodes in London.

11 –16 At the Second Quebec Conference, Roosevelt and Churchill agree to a proposal by U.S. Secretary of the Treasury Henry Morgenthau, Jr., to dismantle Germany's industry and convert Germany into an agricultural nation.

OCTOBER

9 Concerned over the Soviet advance into the Balkans, Churchill meets with Stalin and suggests a division of political influence in the region.

21 –22 The U.S. Navy wins the Battle of Leyte Gulf, considered the greatest sea engagement in history. The U.S. Army invades Leyte, and General Douglas MacArthur announces, "I have returned."

DECEMBER

16 The German army launches a surprise counteroffensive in the Ardennes, but after driving some sixty-five miles into Allied lines, German forces are defeated in the Battle of the Bulge.

1945

FEBRUARY

4 –12 Churchill, Roosevelt, and Stalin meet in Yalta, the Crimea, to discuss policies toward Germany, Poland, and liberated Europe; the new international organization; and the Soviet entry into the war against Japan.

19 U.S. marines land on Iwo Jima, some 750 miles from Tokyo.

APRIL

1 American forces invade Okinawa, located about 362 miles south of Kyushu, which is one of the major home islands of Japan. Japanese suicide pilots, called *kamikazes* ("Divine Wind"), inflict heavy losses on the U.S. Navy.

12 President Roosevelt dies and is succeeded by Vice President Harry S. Truman.

25 –June 26 The San Francisco Conference drafts the United Nations Charter.

28 Mussolini is executed by Italian partisans during an attempt to enter Switzerland.

30 Hitler commits suicide in his bunker at the Reich Chancellery in Berlin.

MAY

7 The German provisional government under Grand Admiral Karl Doenitz surrenders unconditionally.

JULY

16 The first atomic bomb is successfully tested in Alamogordo, New Mexico.

17 –August 2 The last Big Three meeting of the war is held in Potsdam, Germany. Truman informs Stalin that the United States has successfully tested a weapon of unprecedented power, and the Potsdam Declaration calls on Japan to surrender or face "utter destruction."

AUGUST

6 Flying from a base on Tinian, Marianas, the *Enola Gay*, a B-29 commanded by Colonel Paul Tibbets, drops the first atomic bomb; it destroys Hiroshima, Japan's eighth largest city.

8 The Soviet Union declares war against Japan and invades Manchuria and Korea.

9 Nagasaki is destroyed in a second atomic bomb attack.

14 Emperor Hirohito announces Japan's surrender, with the understanding that he will retain his position, although subject to the authority of the Supreme Commander of the Allied Powers.

SEPTEMBER

2 Japanese representatives sign the formal articles of surrender aboard the U.S.S. *Missouri* in Tokyo Bay.

1946

APRIL

18 The General Assembly of the League of Nations holds its last formal meeting. A resolution is passed officially making Sean Lester the third and final secretary-general of the League.

Appendix

The Covenant of the League of Nations[1]

THE HIGH CONTRACTING PARTIES,

In order to promote international co-operation and to achieve international peace and security

by the acceptance of obligations not to resort to war,

by the prescription of open, just and honourable relations between nations,

by the firm establishment of the understandings of international law as the actual rule of conduct among Governments, and

by the maintenance of justice and a scrupulous respect for all treaty obligations in the dealings of organised peoples with one another,

Agree to this Covenant of the League of Nations.

ARTICLE 1.
MEMBERSHIP AND WITHDRAWAL

1. The original Members of the League of Nations shall be those of the Signatories which are named in the Annex to this Covenant and also such of those other States named in the Annex as shall accede without reservation to this Covenant. Such accessions shall be effected by a declaration deposited with the Secretariat within two months of the coming into force of the Covenant. Notice thereof shall be sent to all other Members of the League.

2. Any fully self-governing State, Dominion or Colony not named in the Annex may become a Member of the League if its admission is agreed to by two-thirds of the Assembly, provided that it shall give effective guarantees of its sincere intention to observe its international obligations, and shall accept such regulations as may be prescribed by the League in regard to its military, naval and air forces and armaments.

3. Any Member of the League may, after two years' notice of its intention so to do, withdraw from the League, provided that all its international obligations and all its obligations under this Covenant shall have been fulfilled at the time of its withdrawal.

---

[1] Entered into force on January 10, 1920. Subsequent amendments to the Covenant are indicated by italics and footnotes.

ARTICLE 2.
EXECUTIVE ORGANS

The action of the League under this Covenant shall be effected through the instrumentality of an Assembly and of a Council, with a permanent Secretariat.

ARTICLE 3.
ASSEMBLY

1. The Assembly shall consist of representatives of the Members of the League.

2. The Assembly shall meet at stated intervals and from time to time, as occasion may require, at the Seat of the League or at such other place as may be decided upon.

3. The Assembly may deal at its meetings with any matter within the sphere of action of the League or affecting the peace of the world.

4. At meetings of the Assembly each Member of the League shall have one vote and may have not more than three Representatives.

ARTICLE 4.
COUNCIL

1. The Council shall consist of representatives of the Principal Allied and Associated Powers [United States of America, British Empire, France, Italy and Japan], together with Representatives of four other Members of the League. These four Members of the League shall be selected by the Assembly from time to time in its discretion. Until the appointment of the Representatives of the four Members of the League first selected by the Assembly, Representatives of Belgium, Brazil, Greece and Spain shall be Members of the Council.

2. With the approval of the majority of the Assembly, the Council may name additional Members of the League, whose Representatives shall always be Members of the Council; the Council with like approval may increase the number of Members of the League to be selected by the Assembly for representation on the Council.

2. *bis. The Assembly shall fix by a two-thirds' majority the rules dealing with the election of the non-permanent members of the Council, and particularly such regulations as relate to their term of office and the conditions of re-eligibility.*[2]

3. The Council shall meet from time to time as occasion may require, and at least once a year, at the Seat of the League, or at such other place as may be decided upon.

4. The Council may deal at its meetings with any matter within the sphere of action of the League or affecting the peace of the world.

5. Any Member of the League not represented on the Council shall be invited to send a Representative to sit as a Member at any meeting of the Council during the consideration of matters specially affecting the interests of that Member of the League.

6. At meetings of the Council, each Member of the League represented on the Council shall have one vote, and may have not more than one Representative.

ARTICLE 5.
VOTING AND PROCEDURE

1. Except where otherwise expressly provided in this Covenant or by the terms of the present Treaty, decisions at any meeting of the Assembly or of the Council shall require the agreement of all the Members of the League represented at the meeting.

2. All matters of procedure at meetings of the Assembly or of the Council, including the appointment of Committees to investigate particular matters, shall be regulated by the Assembly or by the Council and may be decided by a majority of the Members of the League represented at the meeting.

3. The first meeting of the Assembly and the first meeting of the Council shall be summoned by the President of the United States of America.

2 As amended, it went into force July 29, 1926.

ARTICLE 6.
SECRETARIAT AND EXPENSES

1. The permanent Secretariat shall be established at the Seat of the League. The Secretariat shall comprise a Secretary-General and such secretaries and staff as may be required.

2. The first Secretary-General shall be the person named in the Annex; thereafter the Secretary-General shall be appointed by the Council with the approval of the majority of the Assembly.

3. The secretaries and the staff of the Secretariat shall be appointed by the Secretary-General with the approval of the Council.

4. The Secretary-General shall act in that capacity at all meetings of the Assembly and of the Council.

5. *The expenses of the League shall be borne by the Members of the League in the proportion decided by the Assembly.*[3]

ARTICLE 7.
SEAT, QUALIFICATIONS OF OFFICIALS, IMMUNITIES

1. The Seat of the League is established at Geneva.

2. The Council may at any time decide that the Seat of the League shall be established elsewhere.

3. All positions under or in connection with the League, including the Secretariat, shall be open equally to men and women.

4. Representatives of the Members of the League and officials of the League when engaged on the business of the League shall enjoy diplomatic privileges and immunities.

5. The buildings and other property occupied by the League or its officials or by Representatives attending its meetings shall be inviolable.

ARTICLE 8.
REDUCTION OF ARMAMENTS

1. The Members of the League recognize that the maintenance of peace requires the reduction of national armaments to the lowest point consistent with national safety and the enforcement by common action of international obligations.

2. The Council, taking account of the geographical situation and circumstances of each State, shall formulate plans for such reduction for the consideration and action of the several Governments.

3. Such plans shall be subject to reconsideration and revision at least every 10 years.

4. After these plans shall have been adopted by the several Governments, the limits of armaments therein fixed shall not be exceeded without the concurrence of the Council.

5. The Members of the League agree that the manufacture by private enterprise of munitions and implements of war is open to grave objections. The Council shall advise how the evil effects attendant upon such manufacture can be prevented, due regard being had to the necessities of those Members of the League which are not able to manufacture the munitions and implements of war necessary for their safety.

6. The Members of the League undertake to interchange full and frank information as to the scale of their armaments, their military, naval and air programmes and the condition of such of their industries as are adaptable to warlike purposes.

ARTICLE 9.
PERMANENT MILITARY, NAVAL AND AIR COMMISSION

A Permanent Commission shall be constituted to advise the Council on the execution of the provisions of Articles 1 and 8 and on military, naval and air questions generally.

[3] As amended, it went into force August 13, 1924.

ARTICLE 10.
GUARANTEES AGAINST AGGRESSION

The Members of the League undertake to respect and preserve as against external aggression the territorial integrity and existing political independence of all Members of the League. In case of any such aggression or in case of any threat or danger of such aggression the Council shall advise upon the means by which this obligation shall be fulfilled.

ARTICLE 11.
ACTION IN CASE OF WAR OR THREAT OF WAR

1. Any war or threat of war, whether immediately affecting any of the Members of the League or not, is hereby declared a matter of concern to the whole League, and the League shall take any action that may be deemed wise and effectual to safeguard the peace of nations. In case any such emergency should arise the Secretary-General shall on the request of any Member of the League forthwith summon a meeting of the Council.

2. It is also declared to be the friendly right of each Member of the League to bring to the attention of the Assembly or of the Council any circumstance whatever affecting international relations which threatens to disturb international peace or the good understanding between nations upon which peace depends.

ARTICLE 12.
DISPUTES TO BE SUBMITTED FOR SETTLEMENT

1. The Members of the League agree that, if there should arise between them any dispute likely to lead to a rupture, they will submit the matter either to arbitration *or judicial settlement* or to inquiry by the Council, and they agree in no case to resort to war until three months after the award by the arbitrators *or the judicial decision*, or the report by the Council.

2. In any case under this Article the award of the arbitrators *or the judicial decision* shall be made within a reasonable time, and the report of the Council shall be made within six months after the submission of the dispute.[4]

ARTICLE 13.
ARBITRATION OR JUDICIAL SETTLEMENT

1. The Members of the League agree that, whenever any dispute shall arise between them which they recognize to be suitable for submission to arbitration *or judicial settlement*, and which cannot be satisfactorily settled by diplomacy, they will submit the whole subject-matter to arbitration *or judicial settlement*.

2. Disputes as to the interpretation of a treaty, as to any question of international law, as to the existence of any fact which, if established, would constitute a breach of any international obligation, or as to the extent and nature of the reparation to be made for any such breach, are declared to be among those which are generally suitable for submission to arbitration *or judicial settlement*.

3. *For the consideration of any such dispute, the court to which the case is referred shall be the Permanent Court of International Justice, established in accordance with Article 14, or any tribunal agreed on by the parties to the dispute or stipulated in any convention existing between them.*[5]

4. The Members of the League agree that they will carry out in full good faith any award *or decision* that may be rendered, and that they will not resort to war against a Member of the League which complies therewith. In the event of any failure to carry out such an award *or decision*, the Council shall propose what steps should be taken to give effect thereto.

ARTICLE 14.
PERMANENT COURT OF INTERNATIONAL JUSTICE

The Council shall formulate and submit to the Members of the League for adoption plans for the establishment of a Permanent Court of International Justice. The Court shall be competent to hear and determine any dispute of an international character which the parties thereto submit to it. The Court may also give an advisory opinion upon any dispute or question referred to it by the Council or by the Assembly.

---

[4] As amended, it went into force September 26, 1924.
[5] As amended, it went into force September 26, 1924.

ARTICLE 15.
DISPUTES NOT SUBMITTED TO ARBITRATION OR JUDICIAL SETTLEMENT

1. If there should arise between Members of the League any dispute likely to lead to a rupture, which is not submitted to arbitration *or judicial settlement* in accordance with Article 13, the Members of the League agree that they will submit the matter to the Council. Any party to the dispute may effect such submission by giving notice of the existence of the dispute to the Secretary-General, who will make all necessary arrangements for a full investigation and consideration thereof.[6]

2. For this purpose the parties to the dispute will communicate to the Secretary-General, as promptly as possible, statements of their case with all the relevant facts and papers, and the Council may forthwith direct the publication thereof.

3. The Council shall endeavour to effect a settlement of the dispute, and, if such efforts are successful, a statement shall be made public giving such facts and explanations regarding the dispute and the terms of settlement thereof as the Council may deem appropriate.

4. If the dispute is not thus settled, the Council either unanimously or by a majority vote shall make and publish a report containing a statement of the facts of the dispute and the recommendations which are deemed just and proper in regard thereto.

5. Any member of the League represented on the Council may make public a statement of the facts of the dispute and of its conclusions regarding the same.

6. If a report by the Council is unanimously agreed to by the Members thereof other than the Representatives of one or more of the parties to the dispute, the Members of the League agree that they will not go to war with any party to the dispute which complies with the recommendations of the report.

7. If the Council fails to reach a report which is unanimously agreed to by the Members thereof, other than the Representatives of one or more of the parties to the dispute, the Members of the League reserve to themselves the right to take such action as they shall consider necessary for the maintenance of right and justice.

8. If the dispute between the parties is claimed by one of them, and is found by the Council, to arise out of a matter which by international law is solely within the domestic jurisdiction of that party, the Council shall so report, and shall make no recommendation as to its settlement.

9. The Council may in any case under this Article refer the dispute to the Assembly. The dispute shall be so referred at the request of either party to the dispute, provided that such request be made within 14 days after the submission of the dispute to the Council.

10. In any case referred to the Assembly, all the provisions of this Article and of Article 12 relating to the action and powers of the Council shall apply to the action and powers of the Assembly, provided that a report made by the Assembly, if concurred in by the Representatives of those Members of the League represented on the Council and of a majority of the other Members of the League, exclusive in each case of the Representatives of the parties to the dispute, shall have the same force as a report by the Council concurred in by all the members thereof other than the Representatives of one or more of the parties to the dispute.

ARTICLE 16.
SANCTIONS OF PACIFIC SETTLEMENT

1. Should any Member of the League resort to war in disregard of its covenants under Articles 12, 13, or 15, it shall *ipso facto* be deemed to have committed an act of war against all other Members of the League, which hereby undertake immediately to subject it to the severance of all trade or financial relations, the prohibition of all intercourse between their nationals and the nationals of the covenant-breaking State, and the prevention of all financial, commercial or personal intercourse between the nationals of the covenant-breaking State and the nationals of any other State, whether a Member of the League or not.

2. It shall be the duty of the Council in such case to recommend to the several Governments concerned what effective military, naval or air force the Members of the League shall severally contribute to the armed forces to be used to protect the covenants of the League.

3. The Members of the League agree, further, that they will mutually support one another in the financial and economic measures which are taken under this Article, in order to minimize the loss and inconvenience resulting from the above measures, and that they will mutually support one another in resisting any special measures aimed at one of their number by the covenant-breaking State, and that they will take the necessary steps to afford passage through their terri-

---

[6] As amended, it went into force September 26, 1924.

tory to the forces of any of the Members of the League which are co-operating to protect the covenants of the League.

4. Any Member of the League which has violated any covenant of the League may be declared to be no longer a Member of the League by a vote of the Council concurred in by the Representatives of all the other Members of the League represented thereon.

ARTICLE 17.
DISPUTES INVOLVING NON-MEMBERS

1. In the event of a dispute between a Member of the League and a State which is not a Member of the League, or between States not Members of the League, the State or States not Members of the League shall be invited to accept the obligations of membership in the League for the purposes of such dispute, upon such conditions as the Council may deem just. If such invitation is accepted, the provisions of Articles 12 to 16, inclusive, shall be applied with such modifications as may be deemed necessary by the Council.

2. Upon such invitation being given, the Council shall immediately institute an inquiry into the circumstances of the dispute and recommend such action as may seem best and most effectual in the circumstances.

3. If a State so invited shall refuse to accept the obligations of membership in the League for the purposes of such dispute, and shall resort to war against a Member of the League, the provisions of Article 16 shall be applicable as against the State taking such action.

4. If both parties to the dispute when so invited refuse to accept the obligations of Membership in the League for the purposes of such dispute, the Council may take such measures and make such recommendations as will prevent hostilities and will result in the settlement of the dispute.

ARTICLE 18.
REGISTRATION AND PUBLICATION OF TREATIES

Every treaty or international engagement entered into hereafter by any Member of the League shall be forthwith registered with the Secretariat and shall as soon as possible be published by it. No such treaty or international engagement shall be binding until so registered.

ARTICLE 19.
REVIEW OF TREATIES

The Assembly may from time to time advise the reconsideration by Members of the League of treaties which have become inapplicable, and the consideration of international conditions whose continuance might endanger the peace of the world.

ARTICLE 20.
ABROGATION OF INCONSISTENT OBLIGATIONS

1. The Members of the League severally agree that this Covenant is accepted as abrogating all obligations or understandings *inter se* which are inconsistent with the terms thereof, and solemnly undertake that they will not hereafter enter into any engagements inconsistent with the terms thereof.

2. In case any Member of the League shall, before becoming a Member of the League, have undertaken any obligations inconsistent with the terms of this Covenant, it shall be the duty of such Member to take immediate steps to procure its release from such obligations.

ARTICLE 21.
ENGAGEMENTS THAT REMAIN VALID

Nothing in this Covenant shall be deemed to affect the validity of international engagements, such as treaties of arbitration or regional understandings like the Monroe Doctrine, for securing the maintenance of peace.

ARTICLE 22.
MANDATORY SYSTEM

1. To those colonies and territories which as a consequence of the late war have ceased to be under the sovereignty of the States which formerly governed them and which are inhabited by peoples not yet able to stand by themselves under the strenuous conditions of the modern world, there should be applied the principle that the well-being and development of such peoples form a sacred trust of civilization and that securities for the performance of this trust should be embodied in this Covenant.

2. The best method of giving practical effect to this principle is that the tutelage of such peoples should be entrusted to advanced nations who by reason of their resources, their experience or their geographical position can best undertake this responsibility, and who are willing to accept it, and that this tutelage should be exercised by them as Mandatories on behalf of the League.

3. The character of the mandate must differ according to the stage of the development of the people, the geographical situation of the territory, its economic conditions and other similar circumstances.

4. Certain communities formerly belonging to the Turkish Empire have reached a stage of development where their existence as independent nations can be provisionally recognised subject to the rendering of administrative advice and assistance by a Mandatory until such time as they are able to stand alone. The wishes of these communities must be a principal consideration in the selection of the Mandatory.

5. Other peoples, especially those of Central Africa, are at such a stage that the Mandatory must be responsible for the administration of the territory under conditions which will guarantee freedom of conscience and religion, subject only to the maintenance of public order and morals, the prohibition of abuses such as the slave trade, the arms traffic and the liquor traffic, and the prevention of the establishment of fortifications or military and naval bases and of military training of the natives for other than police purposes and the defence of territory, and will also secure equal opportunities for the trade and commerce of other Members of the League.

6. There are territories, such as Southwest Africa and certain of the South Pacific islands, which, owing to the sparseness of their population, or their small size, or their remoteness from the centres of civilization, or their geographical contiguity to the territory of the Mandatory, and other circumstances, can be best administered under the laws of the Mandatory as integral portions of its territory, subject to the safeguards above mentioned in the interests of the indigenous population.

7. In every case of mandate, the Mandatory shall render to the Council an annual report in reference to the territory committed to its charge.

8. The degree of authority, control or administration to be exercised by the Mandatory shall, if not previously agreed upon by the Members of the League, be explicitly defined in each case by the Council.

9. A permanent Commission shall be constituted to receive and examine the annual reports of the Mandatories and to advise the Council on all matters relating to the observance of the mandates.

ARTICLE 23.
SOCIAL AND OTHER ACTIVITIES

Subject to and in accordance with the provisions of international conventions existing or hereafter to be agreed upon, the Members of the League:

(a) will endeavour to secure and maintain fair and humane conditions of labour for men, women and children, both in their own countries and in all countries to which their commercial and industrial relations extend, and for that purpose will establish and maintain the necessary international organisations;

(b) undertake to secure just treatment of the native inhabitants of territories under their control;

(c) will intrust the League with the general supervision over the execution of agreements with regard to traffic in women and children, and the traffic in opium and other dangerous drugs;

(d) will entrust the League with the general supervision of the trade in arms and ammunition with the countries in which the control of this traffic is necessary in the common interest;

(e) will make provision to secure and maintain freedom of communications and of transit and equitable treatment for the commerce of all Members of the League. In this connection, the special necessities of the regions devastated during the war of 1914–1918 shall be borne in mind;

(f) will endeavour to take steps in matters of international concern for the prevention and control of disease.

ARTICLE 24.
INTERNATIONAL BUREAUS

1. There shall be placed under the direction of the League all international bureaus already established by general treaties if the parties to such treaties consent. All such international bureaus and all commissions for the regulation of matters of international interest hereafter constituted shall be placed under the direction of the League.

2. In all matters of international interest which are regulated by general conventions but which are not placed under the control of international bureaus or commissions, the Secretariat of the League shall, subject to the consent of the Council and if desired by the parties, collect and distribute all relevant information and shall render any other assistance which may be necessary or desirable.

3. The Council may include as part of the expenses of the Secretariat the expenses of any bureau or commission which is placed under the direction of the League.

ARTICLE 25.
PROMOTION OF RED CROSS AND HEALTH

The Members of the League agree to encourage and promote the establishment and co-operation of duly authorised voluntary national Red Cross organisations having as purposes the improvement of health, the prevention of disease and the mitigation of suffering throughout the world.

ARTICLE 26.
AMENDMENTS

1. Amendments to this Covenant will take effect when ratified by the Members of the League whose Representatives compose the Council and by a majority of the Members of the League whose Representatives compose the Assembly.

2. No such amendment shall bind any Member of the League which signifies its dissent therefrom, but in that case it shall cease to be a Member of the League.

Bibliography

In writing this volume, I drew upon the research of many scholars, but I am especially indebted to James Barros for his excellent study of Joseph Avenol's career in *Betrayal From Within: Joseph Avenol, Secretary-General of the League of Nations, 1933–1940* (New Haven, Connecticut: Yale University Press, 1969). Two valuable assessments of Avenol's tenure are in *The First Fifty Years: The Secretary-General in World Politics, 1920–1970,* by Arthur W. Rovine (Leiden, the Netherlands: A. W. Sijthoff, 1970), and *The League and the United Nations After Fifty Years: The Six Secretaries-General,* by Raymond B. Fosdick (Newton, Connecticut: By the author, 1972). I have also relied on Rovine's study of Sean Lester, the third and last secretary-general of the League, in *The First Fifty Years.* Stephen M. Schwebel's interviews with Avenol in *The Secretary-General of the United Nations: His Political Powers and Practice* (Cambridge, Massachusetts: Harvard University Press, 1952) expand our understanding of the motives surrounding the secretary-general's resignation in 1940.

For the League of Nations, the comprehensive work of former Deputy Secretary-General Frank P. Walters, *A History of the League of Nations,* two volumes (London: Oxford University Press, 1952), is indispensable. Also helpful are F. S. Northedge, who argues that the older balance-of-power politics overcame the ideal of collective security in *The League of Nations: Its Life and Times, 1920–1946* (New York: Holmes and Meier, 1986), and Elmer Bendiner, who provides a journalist's witty and critical perspective in *A Time for Angels: The Tragicomic History of the League of Nations* (New York: Alfred A. Knopf, 1975). George Scott utilizes the interwar British Cabinet papers, now open for research, in *The Rise and Fall of the League of Nations* (London: Hutchinson Publishing Group, Ltd., 1973).

The standard research aid for League documents is the *Guide to League of Nations Publications: A Bibliographical Survey of the Work of the League, 1920–1947,* by Hans Aufricht (New York: Columbia University Press, 1951). For those using the microfilm-edition "League of Nations Documents and Serial Publications, 1919–1946" (New Haven, Connecticut: Research Publications, n.d.), the guide is *League of Nations Documents, 1919–1946: A Descriptive Guide and Key to the Microfilm Collection,* three volumes, edited by Edward A. Reno, Jr. (New Haven, Connecticut: Research Publications, 1973–1975). Research guides that arrange periodical literature chronologically and by country are the *League of Nations and United Nations Monthly List of Selected Articles, 1920–1970, Political Questions,* three volumes, edited by Norman S. Field (Dobbs Ferry, New York: Oceana Publications, 1971); *League of Nations and United Nations Monthly List of Selected Articles, 1920–1970, Legal Questions,* two volumes, edited by Norman S. Field (Dobbs Ferry, New York: Oceana Publications, 1972); and *League of Nations and United Nations Monthly List of Selected Articles, 1920–1970, Economic Questions,* five volumes, edited by Norman S. Field and the Readers' Services and Documentation Section of the United Nations Library in Geneva (Dobbs Ferry, New York: Oceana Publications, 1973–1974).

The *Official Journal* of the League of Nations provides basic documentation for the proceedings of the Assembly and the Council. There are also excellent selections of political documents in the annual volumes (1929–1940) of the *Documents on International Affairs,* edited by John W. Wheeler-Bennett et al. (London: Oxford University Press, 1930–1954). The impressive companion narrative texts are *Survey of International Affairs,* edited by Arnold J. Toynbee et al. (London: Oxford University Press, 1930–1954). The published records of the major powers include:

Documents Diplomatique Français, 1932–1939, First Series (1932–1935), Second Series (1936–1939) (Paris: Imprimerie Nationale, 1963–).

Documents on British Foreign Policy, 1919–1939, Second Series

(1930–1937), Third Series (1938–1939) (London: H. M. Stationery Office, 1947–1961).

Documents on German Foreign Policy, 1918–1945, Series C (1933–1937), Series D (1937–1941) (Washington, D.C.: U.S. Government Printing Office, 1949–1983).

I Documenti Diplomatici Italiani, 7ª Serie (1922–1935), 8ª Serie (1935–1939), 9ª Serie (1939–1943) (Rome: La Liberia della Stato, 1953–   ).

USSR, Ministry for Foreign Affairs, *Soviet Peace Efforts on the Eve of World War II*, two volumes (Moscow: Novosti Press, 1973).

Foreign Relations of the United States, 1929–1940 (Washington, D.C.: U.S. Government Printing Office, 1943–1961).

See also *Soviet Documents on Foreign Policy*, three volumes, edited by Jane Degras (New York: Oxford University Press, 1951–1953).

The principal sources for the Chronology are the annual volumes of the *Survey of International Affairs* (New York: Oxford University Press, 1930–1954) and of *The United States in World Affairs* (New York: Harper & Brothers, 1932–1940); *An Encyclopedia of World History*, fifth edition revised, compiled and edited by William L. Langer (Boston: Houghton Mifflin Company, 1972); and *The Chronology of World History*, by G.S.P. Freeman Greville (London: R. Collings, 1975). *The New York Times* and *Time* magazine provided additional information for the general entries in the standard reference works.

Books and Articles

Álvarez del Vayo, Julio. *Freedom's Battle*. Translated by Eileen E. Brooke. New York: Alfred A. Knopf, 1940. The foreign minister of the Spanish Republic presents the Loyalist criticism of the policies of the major powers during the Spanish Civil War.

Armstrong, Hamilton Fish. "France and the Hoover Plan." *Foreign Affairs* 10 (October 1931): 23–33. French criticism of Herbert Hoover's moratorium on war debts and reparations.

Avenol, Joseph. *L'Europe silencieuse*. Neuchâtel, Switzerland: Éditions de la Baconnière, 1944. The former secretary-general's proposals for the postwar political and economic organization of Europe.

Baer, George W. *The Coming of the Italian-Ethiopian War*. Cambridge, Massachusetts: Harvard University Press, 1967. An excellent exposition on Italy's preparation for war and the reaction of the League.

———. *Test Case: Italy, Ethiopia and the League of Nations*. Stanford, California: Hoover Institution Press, 1976. A fine study of the League's failure to deter Italy's aggression.

Baldwin, Arthur W. *My Father: The True Story*. London: George Allen & Unwin, 1955. An effort to revise George M. Young's authorized biography of Prime Minister Stanley Baldwin.

Barros, James. *Britain, Greece and the Politics of Sanctions: Ethiopia, 1935–1936*. Royal Historical Society Studies in History Series, no. 33. Atlantic Highland, New Jersey: Humanities, 1983.

———. *Office Without Power: Secretary-General Sir Eric Drummond, 1919–1933*. Oxford, England: Clarendon Press, 1979. A balanced and overall positive account of Drummond's service.

Bassett, Reginald. *Nineteen Thirty-One: Political Crisis*. New York: St. Martin's Press, 1958. A detailed study of the formation of Great Britain's National Government of 1931 under James Ramsay MacDonald and the repudiation of the prime minister by his own Labour Party.

Beneš, Eduard. "The League of Nations: Successes and Failures." *Foreign Affairs* 11 (October 1932): 66–80. A generally favorable account; it defends the League's handling of the Manchurian crisis.

———. "Ten Years of the League." *Foreign Affairs* 9 (January 1930): 212–224. A positive assessment of the League's first decade and an optimistic prediction for its future.

———. *Memoirs: From Munich to New War and New Victory*. Translated by Godfrey Lias. Boston: Houghton Mifflin Company, n.d. The first chapter describes the events leading to the Munich Conference, but the conference itself is not discussed. France and Great Britain are criticized for not aiding Czechoslovakia.

Bennett, Edward W. *Germany and the Diplomacy of the Financial Crisis, 1931*. Cambridge, Massachusetts: Harvard University Press, 1962. A very good study of the policies of France, Germany, Great Britain, and the United States.

Birkenhead, Earl of. *The Life of Lord Halifax*. London: Hamish Hamilton, 1965. Presents Lord Halifax's "blindness" to Adolph Hitler's nature and intentions.

Birn, Donald S. *The League of Nations Union, 1918–1945*. Oxford, England: Clarendon Press, 1981. A thorough study of the most important British society supporting the League.

Bonn, M. J. "How Sanctions Failed." *Foreign Affairs* 15 (January 1937): 350–361. A good analysis of the League's inability to coerce Italy through economic sanctions.

Bracher, Karl D. *The German Dictatorship*. Translated by Jean Steinberg. New York: Frederick A. Praeger, 1970. One of the best works on Nazi Germany.

Bullock, Alan. *Hitler: A Study in Tyranny*. New York: Harper & Row, 1964. Among the best biographies of Hitler.

Carlton, David. *MacDonald Versus Henderson: The Foreign Policy of the Second Labour Government*. London: Macmillan and Company, 1969. Discusses the reparations and disarmament issues in the context of the poor relationship between the prime minister and the foreign secretary, the latter of whom then became president of the World Disarmament Conference.

Carter, Gwendolen M. *The British Commonwealth and International Security*. Westport, Connecticut: Greenwood Press, 1971. Describes the policies of the British Dominions toward the League of Nations.

Ciano, Galeazzo. *Ciano's Hidden Diary, 1937–1938*. Translated by Andreas Mayor. New York: E. P. Dutton & Company, 1953.

Colton, Joel. *Léon Blum: Humanist in Politics*. New York: Alfred A. Knopf, 1966. An authoritative study; sympathetic to the policies of the 1930s.

Colvin, Ian G. *None So Blind: A British Diplomatic View of the Origins of World War II*. New York: Harcourt, Brace & World, 1965. The critical reflections of Sir Robert Vansittart, permanent undersecretary of state and head of the British Foreign Office from 1930 to 1938.

Cooper, Alfred Duff. *Old Men Forget: The Autobiography of Duff Cooper, Viscount Norwich.* New York: E. P. Dutton & Company, 1954. Memoirs of the First Lord of the Admiralty from 1937 to 1938, who resigned in protest over Chamberlain's policy in Munich.

Craig, Gordon A., and Felix Gilbert, eds. *The Diplomats, 1919–1939.* 2 vols. New York: Atheneum, 1963. The second volume, *The Thirties,* contains essays on Arthur Henderson, Maxim Litvinov, and other important participants in the diplomacy of the interwar period.

Dalby, Louise E. *Léon Blum: Evolution of a Socialist.* New York: Thomas Yoseloff, 1963. A good study of Blum's literary and political careers.

Davis, Harriet. *Pioneers in World Order: An American Appraisal of the League of Nations.* New York: Columbia University Press, 1944. A collection of generally favorable essays by Americans who were associated with the League in some capacity.

Davis, Joseph S. *The World Between the Wars, 1919–1939: An Economist's View.* Baltimore, Maryland: Johns Hopkins University Press, 1975.

Del Boca, Angelo. *The Ethiopian War, 1935–1941.* Translated by P. D. Cummins. Chicago: University of Chicago Press, 1969. Incorporates the Ethiopian view of the war.

Dennett, Tyler. "Japan Defies the World." *Current History* 38 (April 1933): 9–17. Reviews Japan's plea of self-defense in the Manchurian crisis and the League's rejection of that argument.

———. "The Verdict of the Lytton Commission." *Current History* 37 (November 1932): 239–256. Praises the report of the commission as a blueprint for peace, if Japan cooperates.

Donnelly, J. B. "Prentiss Bailey Gilbert and the League of Nations: The Diplomacy of an Observer." In *U.S. Diplomats in Europe, 1919–1941.* Edited by Kenneth Paul Jones. Santa Barbara, California: ABC-Clio, 1981. A description of the brief but highly publicized appearance of Gilbert at the League Council during the Manchurian crisis.

Dorpalen, Andreas. *Hindenburg and the Weimar Republic.* Princeton, New Jersey: Princeton University Press, 1964. An objective assessment; a very good treatment of the last years of the Republic.

Drummond, Ian M. *British Economic Policy and the Empire, 1919–1939.* London: George Allen & Unwin, 1972. A good chapter on the Ottawa Conference; the second half of the book is a collection of documents.

Dubin, Martin David. "Transgovernmental Processes in the League of Nations." *International Organization* 37 (1983): 469–493. Discusses the efforts to inspire loyalty to the League among its officials and to reduce the influence of their home governments upon them.

Dugan, James, and Lawrence Lafore. *Days of Emperor and Clown: The Italo-Ethiopian War, 1935–1936.* Garden City, New York: Doubleday & Company, 1973.

Dunn, David. "Maksim Litvinov: Commissar of Contradiction." *Journal of Contemporary History* 23 (April 1988): 221–243.

Eden, Anthony, Earl of Avon. *Facing the Dictators: The Memoirs of Anthony Eden.* London: Cassell & Company, 1962. Reflections of the British minister for League of Nations affairs and then foreign secretary, who resigned because of Neville Chamberlain's policy toward Benito Mussolini.

Emmerson, James T. *The Rhineland Crisis, 7 March 1936: A Study in Multilateral Diplomacy.* Ames: Iowa State University Press, 1977. Describes the military and political weaknesses of France and Great Britain.

Farley, Miriam S. "Russia Warms to the League." *Current History* 40 (July 1934): 402–409. Warns that Russia may try to use the League as a military alliance without commitment to the ideals of the Covenant.

Feingold, Henry L. *The Politics of Rescue: The Roosevelt Administration and the Holocaust, 1938–1945.* New Brunswick, New Jersey: Rutgers University Press, 1970. A critical examination of the gulf between the expressed good intentions of the administration and the implementation of policy.

Ferrell, Robert H. *Peace in Their Time: The Origins of the Kellogg-Briand Pact.* New Haven, Connecticut: Yale University Press, 1952.

Fest, Joachim C. *Hitler.* Translated by Richard and Clara Winston. New York: Harcourt, Brace, Jovanovich, 1974. An excellent biography.

Fosdick, Raymond B. "The International Implications of the Business Depression." *International Conciliation* 267 (February 1931): 64–78. Criticism of American tariff policy.

Furnia, Arthur H. *The Diplomacy of Appeasement: Anglo-French Relations and the Prelude to World War II, 1931–1938.* Washington, D.C.: University Press of Washington, D.C., 1960. Critical of Neville Chamberlain but supportive of Édouard Daladier.

Garner, William R. *The Chaco Dispute: A Study of Prestige Diplomacy.* Washington, D.C.: Public Affairs Press, 1966. An examination of the "prestige factor," which affected not only the belligerents but also the peacemakers, producing a costly "diplomatic fiasco."

Gatzke, Hans, ed. *European Diplomacy Between Two Wars, 1919–1939.* Chicago: Quadrangle, 1972. An interesting collection of essays, which includes H. B. Braddick's "Hoare-Laval Plan."

Gehl, Jurgen. *Austria, Germany and Anschluss, 1931–1938.* New York: Oxford University Press, 1963.

Geneva Institute of International Relations. *Problems of Peace.* Freeport, New York: Books for Libraries Press, 1969. Under the general topic of "War Is Not Inevitable," diplomats, academics, and journalists assess the international situation on the eve of World War II.

Geraud, André. "The London Naval Conference: A French View." *Foreign Affairs* 8 (July 1930): 519–533. Explains France's desire for greater security commitments from Great Britain and the United States because it did not believe that the treaty provided security.

Gerig, Benjamin. "An Appraisal of the League of Nations." *International Conciliation* 369 (April 1941): 303–316. A good summary of the major problems that weakened the League. However, the author insists that much was accomplished.

Gilbert, Martin. *The Roots of Appeasement.* London: Weidenfeld and Nicolson, 1966. It defends the policy of appeasement, although it also concedes that Chamberlain's assessment of Hitler was unrealistic.

———. *Winston S. Churchill.* Vol. 5: *The Prophet of Truth.* Boston: Houghton Mifflin Company, 1977. An excellent study of Churchill's career during the 1920s and 1930s.

Greene, Nathanael. *Crisis and Decline: The French Socialist Party in the Popular Front Era.* Ithaca, New York: Cornell University Press,

1969. Discusses the struggle between Léon Blum, head of the party, and Paul Faure, party general secretary, over resistance to fascism.

Haigh, R. H., D. S. Morris, and A. R. Peters. *Soviet Foreign Policy, the League of Nations and Europe, 1917–1939.* Aldershot, Hampshire, England: Gower Publishing Company, 1986. Examines the transition from initial Bolshevik hostility to later Soviet membership in the League.

Hambro, Carl J. *How to Win the Peace.* Philadelphia: J. B. Lippincott Company, 1942. Against the background of a broader study, the last president of the League Assembly reflects on some lessons to be drawn from the world body.

Hibbert, Christopher. *Il Duce: The Life of Benito Mussolini.* Boston: Little, Brown and Company, 1962. Includes a chapter on the foreign policy of the 1920s and 1930s.

Hill, William M. *The Economic and Financial Organizations of the League of Nations.* Washington, D.C.: Carnegie Endowment for International Peace, 1946. An objective assessment of the successes and failures of these League agencies.

Hoden, Marcel. "Europe Without the League." *Foreign Affairs* 18 (October 1939): 13–28. Attributes the League's failure to France and Great Britain, not the League Covenant.

Hoskins, Halford L. "The Suez Canal in Time of War." *Foreign Affairs* 14 (October 1935): 93–101. Suggests that the closing of the canal would deter Italian aggression against Ethiopia.

Houghton, N. D. "The Present Status of the League of Nations." *International Conciliation* 317 (February 1936): 65–108. An objective analysis of the League's strengths and weaknesses.

Hudson, Manley O. *The Permanent Court of International Justice, 1920–1942.* New York: Macmillan Company, 1943. A major history of the World Court by one of its judges.

Hyde, H. Montgomery. *Baldwin: The Unexpected Minister.* London: Hart-Davis, MacGibbon, 1973. A brief treatment of the Ethiopian crisis and British policy.

Jackson, Gabriel. *The Spanish Republic and the Civil War, 1931–1939.* Princeton, New Jersey: Princeton University Press, 1965. Presents the Spanish Civil War in the context of the previous five years of the Republic and through interviews with the people.

Jackson, Julian. *The Popular Front in France: Defending Democracy, 1934–1938.* New York: Cambridge University Press, 1988. Describes the policies of the Blum government, the tensions within the coalition, and the right-wing opposition.

James, Robert Rhodes. *Anthony Eden.* London: Weidenfeld and Nicolson, 1986. Includes a chapter on Eden's appointment as foreign secretary.

Johnson, A. E. "The League of Nations: Whither Bound?" *Literary Digest* 118 (September 29, 1934): 14. An interview with Avenol on the problems of the League.

Johnston, Verle B. *Legions of Babel: The International Brigades in the Spanish Civil War.* University Park: Pennsylvania State University Press, 1967. A brief, and not altogether satisfactory, account of the foreign volunteers who served the Spanish Republic.

Jones, Samuel Shepard. *The Scandinavian States and the League of Nations.* Princeton, New Jersey: Princeton University Press, 1939. An interesting description of the efforts of Denmark, Norway, and Sweden to serve as the "conscience" of the major powers in the League.

Joyce, J. Avery. *Broken Star: The Story of the League of Nations,* 1919–1939. Swansea, Wales: Christopher Davies, 1978. A sympathetic account by an international lawyer who was an eyewitness to League events during the 1930s.

Kimmich, Christoph M. *Germany and the League of Nations.* Chicago: University of Chicago Press, 1976. Believes Germany's foreign-policy objectives precluded success in the disarmament talks and long-term German membership in the League.

Kindleberger, Charles P. *The World in Depression, 1929–1939.* Berkeley: University of California Press, 1973. Contends that the United States failed to provide leadership during the economic crisis.

Kirkpatrick, Ivone. *Mussolini: A Study in Power.* New York: Hawthorne Books, 1964. A good portrayal of the Duce's policies during the 1920s and 1930s by a former member of the British Foreign Service.

Lacouture, Jean. *Léon Blum.* Translated by George Holoch. New York: Holmes and Meier, 1982. A favorable treatment of Blum's career.

Lamont, Thomas. "The Final Reparations Settlement." *Foreign Affairs* 8 (April 1930): 336–363.

Landy, E. A. *The Effectiveness of International Supervision: Thirty Years of I.L.O. Experience.* Dobbs Ferry, New York: Oceana Publications, 1966. A detailed study of the efforts of the International Labour Organisation to secure fulfillment of treaties.

Larmour, Peter J. *The French Radical Party in the 1930s.* Stanford, California: Stanford University Press, 1964. Portrays the changing character and the problems of the Radical Party.

Laval, Pierre. *The Diary of Pierre Laval.* New York: Charles Scribner's Sons, 1948. The first section covers the period to 1940.

Lee, Bradford A. *Britain and the Sino-Japanese War, 1937–1939.* Stanford, California: Stanford University Press, 1973. Describes the hesitancy of Great Britain to deter Japanese expansion.

Leffler, Melvyn P. *The Elusive Quest: America's Pursuit of European Stability and French Security, 1919–1939.* Chapel Hill: University of North Carolina Press, 1979. Critical assessment of the response of Herbert Hoover and Franklin Roosevelt to the international dimensions of the Depression.

Lingelbach, William. "War-Strained Italy." *Current History* 44 (April 1936): 63–65. Warns that League sanctions could drive Italy into Germany's arms.

Little, Douglas J. *Malevolent Neutrality: The United States, Great Britain, and the Origins of the Spanish Civil War.* Ithaca, New York: Cornell University Press, 1985. Contends that British and American reservations toward the Spanish Republic following its establishment in 1931 strongly influenced their policies during the Civil War.

Louis, W. Roger. *British Strategy in the Far East, 1919–1939.* Oxford, England: Clarendon Press, 1971. The final three chapters develop imperial defense concerns during the 1930s.

Loveday, Alexander. *Reflections on International Administration.* Oxford, England: Clarendon Press, 1956. The assessments and recommendations of the former director of the Economic and Financial Section of the League.

Lowell, A. Lawrence. "Alternatives Before the League." *Foreign Affairs* 15 (October 1936): 102–111. Criticizes the delay in imposing effective sanctions on Italy.

———. "Manchuria, the League, and the United States." *Foreign Affairs* 10 (April 1932): 351–368. Concedes the complexity of the Sino-Japanese issues in Manchuria but is critical of the League's response.

Maass, Walter B. *Assassination in Vienna.* New York: Charles Scribner's Sons, 1972. An interesting account of the murder of Engelbert Dollfuss.

MacQueen, Norman, "Éamon de Valéra, the Irish Free State, and the League of Nations." *Éire-Ireland* 17 (Fall 1982): 110–127.

Madariaga, Salvador de. *Morning Without Noon: Memoirs.* Farnborough, Hampshire, England: Saxon House, 1973. A former member of the Secretariat and then Spanish delegate to the League provides a good review of League activities.

Marcus, John. *French Socialism in the Crisis Years, 1933–1936.* New York: Frederick A. Praeger, 1958. Traces the response of the socialists to fascism in France and abroad.

Marquand, David. *Ramsay MacDonald.* London: Jonathan Cape, 1977. The first biography based on MacDonald's private papers.

Micaud, Charles A. *The French Right and Nazi Germany, 1933–1937: A Study of Public Opinion.* New York: Octagon Books, 1964.

Middlemas, Keith, and John Barnes. *Baldwin: A Biography.* New York: Macmillan Company, 1970. A revisionist view of Baldwin's career.

Mockler, Anthony. *Haile Selassie's War.* New York: Random House, 1984.

Mommsen, Wolfgang, and Lothar Kettenacker, eds. *The Fascist Challenge and the Policy of Appeasement.* London: George Allen & Unwin, 1983. An important collection of essays that incorporates the domestic political, economic, and social issues influencing the appeasement policy of the European powers.

Nevakivi, Jukka. *The Appeal That Was Never Made: The Allies, Scandinavia and the Finnish Winter War, 1939–1940.* Montreal: McGill-Queen's University Press, 1976. A good account of the Russo-Finnish War by a member of the Finnish Foreign Service.

Nevins, Allan. "League Acts Against Italy." *Current History* 43 (December 1935): 274–280. Predicts that League sanctions will have some impact on the Italian economy.

———. "League Gains From Russia." *Current History* 41 (November 1934): 143–148. Believes that Russia's entry will help the League control events in Eastern Europe and Asia.

Noel-Baker, Philip. *The Private Manufacture of Armaments.* New York: Oxford University Press, 1937. The personal assistant to the president of the World Disarmament Conference from 1932 to 1933 presents the "evil effects" that the private-arms industry has on international relations.

Northedge, F. S. *The Troubled Giant: Britain Among the Great Powers, 1916–1939.* New York: Frederick A. Praeger, 1966. Details the reasons for England's declining power; a good examination of Chamberlain's policy toward Germany and Italy.

Ogata, Sadakon. *Defiance in Manchuria: The Making of Japanese Foreign Policy, 1931–1932.* Berkeley: University of California Press, 1964. Presents some new information on the crisis based on access to previously unavailable Japanese military and diplomatic sources.

Ostrower, Gary B. *Collective Insecurity: The United States and the League of Nations During the Early Thirties.* Lewisburg, Pennsylvania: Bucknell University Press, 1979. A valuable addition to the study of American policy during the Manchurian crisis.

Pratt, Lawrence R. *East of Malta, West of Suez: Britain's Mediterranean Crisis, 1936–1939.* London: Cambridge University Press, 1975. Relates the Ethiopian conflict to the broader responsibilities of the Royal Navy.

Ranshofen-Wertheimer, Egon F. *The International Secretariat: A Great Experiment in International Administration.* Washington, D.C.: Carnegie Endowment for International Peace, 1945. A thorough study by a former staff member.

Renborg, Bertil A. *International Drug Control: A Study of International Administration By and Through the League of Nations.* Washington, D.C.: Carnegie Endowment for International Peace, 1947. A good account by the Swedish member of the Opium Section of the Secretariat.

Rock, William R. *Appeasement on Trial: British Foreign Policy and Its Critics, 1938–1939.* New York: Archon Books, 1966. An examination of the reaction of members of Parliament, the British press, and the general public to Chamberlain's policy.

Rout, Leslie B., Jr. *Politics of the Chaco Peace Conference, 1935–1939.* Austin: University of Texas Press, 1970. An excellent study of the complex and often competing efforts to mediate between Bolivia and Paraguay.

Rowse, A. L. *Appeasement: A Study in Political Decline, 1933–1939.* New York: W. Norton and Company, 1963. Criticism of Geoffrey Dawson of *The Times* (London), Sir John Simon, and Lord Halifax.

Schlesinger, Arthur M., Jr. *The Coming of the New Deal.* Boston: Houghton Mifflin Company, 1959. Includes a good description of the conflict among Roosevelt's advisers concerning policy for the London Economic Conference of 1933.

Schuschnigg, Kurt von. *Austrian Requiem.* Translated by Franz von Hildebrand. New York: G. P. Putnam's Sons, 1946. The Chancellor's account of the *Anschluss*.

Simpson, Sir John Hope. *The Refugee Problem: Report of a Survey.* London: Oxford University Press, 1939. The most comprehensive account of the subject based on data collected to October 1938.

Sontag, Raymond. *A Broken World, 1919–1939.* New York: Harper & Row, 1971. One of the best surveys of the interwar years.

Stimson, Henry L. *The Far Eastern Crisis: Recollections and Observations.* New York: Harper, 1936. An early assessment of the breakdown of international cooperation by the American secretary of state.

Strang, Lord William. *Home and Abroad.* London: Andre Deutsch, 1956. Interesting chapters on the Czech crisis of 1938 and the abortive British negotiations in Moscow in 1939.

Svennilson, Ingvar. *Growth and Stagnation in the European Economy.* Geneva: United Nations Economic Commission for Europe, 1954. Contains a good account of the problems of the interwar years.

Sweetser, Arthur. "The First Ten Years of the League of Nations." *International Conciliation* 256 (January 1930): 3–60. An excellent survey of the accomplishments of the League.

———. "The Non-Political Achievements of the League." *Foreign Affairs* 19 (October 1940): 179–192. A positive review of the League's work in the area of public welfare.

Taylor, Arnold H. *American Diplomacy and the Narcotics Traffic, 1900–1939.* Durham, North Carolina: Duke University Press, 1969. A good description of the alternating cooperation and obstruction by the United States in the League's drug war.

Taylor, Telford. *Munich: The Price of Peace.* Garden City, New York: Doubleday & Company, 1979. Considered to be one of the best books on the conference.

Thomas, Albert. *International Social Policy.* Translated by Monica

Curtis. Geneva: International Labour Organisation, 1948. Extracts of speeches, reports, and articles by the director of the ILO from 1920 to 1932.

Thorne, Christopher. *The Limits of Foreign Policy: The West, the League and the Far Eastern Crisis of 1931–1933*. London: Macmillan and Company, 1973. Praised as "a striking new investigation" of the Manchurian crisis.

Trotter, Ann. *Britain and East Asia, 1933–1937*. New York: Cambridge University Press, 1975. Describes British economic and imperial defense interests.

Wambaugh, Sarah. *The Saar Plebiscite*. Westport, Connecticut: Greenwood Press, 1971. A detailed history, with a collection of documents, by the technical adviser and deputy member of the Saar Plebiscite Commission.

Warner, Geoffrey. *Pierre Laval and the Eclipse of France*. New York: Macmillan Company, 1969. Much of the work deals with Vichy, France, but it also covers the 1930s.

Werth, Alexander. *The Twilight of France, 1933–1940*. New York: Howard Fertig, 1966. The decline of France as witnessed by the Paris correspondent for the *Manchester Guardian*.

Wheeler-Bennett, John W. *The Pipe Dream of Peace: The Story of the Collapse of Disarmament*. New York: Morrow, 1935. An early but still important account of the failure of the World Disarmament Conference, 1932–1934.

Wilson, Hugh R. *Diplomat Between Wars*. New York: Longmans, Green & Company, 1941. Recollections about the World Disarmament Conference, 1932–1934.

Wiskemann, Elizabeth. *The Rome-Berlin Axis*. London: Collins Publishers, 1966.

Wolfers, Arnold. *Britain and France Between Two Wars: Conflicting Strategies of Peace Since Versailles*. New York: Harcourt, Brace and Company, 1940. Contains chapters on British and French policies toward the League.

Wood, Edward, Lord Halifax. *Fullness of Days*. New York: Dodd, Mead & Company, 1957. The former British foreign secretary defends the policies of Baldwin and Chamberlain.

Woods, W. S. "Has the League Failed?" *Current History* 44 (June 1936): 71–76. Defends the League's principles and charges that France and Great Britain weakened the League's reaction to Italy and Germany.

Yoshihashi, Takehiko. *Conspiracy at Mukden: The Rise of the Japanese Military*. New Haven, Connecticut: Yale University Press, 1963. Explains the role of the Kwantung army in the crisis.

Young, George M. *Stanley Baldwin*. London: Rupert Hart-Davis, 1952. An authorized but critical biography of the prime minister.

Zimmern, Alfred, "The Testing of the League." *Foreign Affairs* 14 (April 1936): 373–386. The imposition of economic sanctions against Italy revived faith in the League.

Zook, David H., Jr. *The Conduct of the Chaco War*. New Haven, Connecticut: Bookman Associates, 1960. An objective appraisal of the military campaigns of Bolivia and Paraguay.

About the Author

George J. Gill taught American history at Fordham University for more than twenty years before his retirement in 1994. He had received his undergraduate, master's, and doctoral degrees from Fordham. His service to the university included work on committees that dealt with a wide variety of issues, from personnel searches to scholarships.

Dr. Gill was a member of several professional associations, including the American Catholic Historical Association. He specialized in American diplomatic history and published his research in numerous papers.

Dr. Gill lived with his wife, Winifred T. Serridge, in Harrington Park, New Jersey, until his death in June 1995. The publisher believes that this volume does honor to his memory. *Requiescat in pace.*

Index